Strategic Security Management

Strategic Security Management

A Risk Assessment Guide for Decision Makers

2nd Edition

Karim H. Vellani

CRC Press
Taylor & Francis Group
Boca Raton London New York

CRC Press is an imprint of the
Taylor & Francis Group, an **informa** business

CRC Press
Taylor & Francis Group
6000 Broken Sound Parkway NW, Suite 300
Boca Raton, FL 33487-2742

First issued in paperback 2020

ISBN-13: 978-1-138-58366-5 (hbk)
ISBN-13: 978-0-367-77651-0 (pbk)

Library of Congress Cataloging-in-Publication Data

LoC Data here

Visit the Taylor & Francis website at
www.taylorandfrancis.com

and the CRC Press website at
www.crcpress.com

This book is dedicated to those who protect. Whether you protect your family, your organizations, or your country, you don't always get the praise you deserve or the resources you need, but you always remain strong in the face of new threats and challenges. I hope this book makes your job a little easier.

Contents

Acknowledgements

Thank you to my two beautiful and smart daughters who put up with me as I locked myself in my office for hours on end, often late into the night, and tapped away (usually the delete key) on the keyboard.

The depth of this book would not have been possible without the help of the contributing authors who bring an extraordinary amount of knowledge and expertise to their respective chapters. Thank you.

Lastly, thank you to Tina Kristof, Mark Listewnik, Andrew Rubin and Mark Bennett who provided suggestions, editorial commentary, or the well-needed kick in the pants to finish this edition.

About the Editor

Karim H. Vellani is the President of Threat Analysis Group, LLC. Karim is a Board-Certified Protection Professional (CPP), a Board Certified Security Consultant (CSC), and has over 25 years of security management experience. He holds a master's degree in Criminal Justice Management from Sam Houston State University in Huntsville, Texas. As an independent security consultant, Karim has been retained by Fortune 500 companies, large non-profit organizations, and government agencies. He has extensive experience in conducting risk assessments in diverse environments including government, healthcare, colleges and universities, and industrial facilities. Karim is the author of previous editions of this book and *Applied Crime Analysis* and has contributed to a number of other security related books and journals.

In addition to developing unique risk assessment methodologies for several industries, Karim was integral in the development of Threat Analysis Group, LLC's *Risk Assessment Methodology for Healthcare Facilities and Hospitals* and wrote the International Association for Healthcare Security & Safety's Risk Assessment Guideline. Karim also developed a crime analysis methodology that utilizes the Federal Bureau of Investigation's Uniform Crime Report coding system and a software application called CrimeAnalysis™. Since developing the crime analysis methodology, Karim has assessed crime threats at thousands of facilities and published the methodology in *Applied Crime Analysis*. This practical experience forms the basis for the knowledge and concepts in *Strategic Security Management*.

As an Adjunct Professor at the University of Houston – Downtown, Karim taught graduate courses in Security Management and Risk Analysis for the College of Criminal Justice's Security Management Program. Karim has also trained Police and Security Officers in weapons, deadly force, and profiling.

Karim also provides forensic security consulting services to insurance companies and the legal profession. In this work, Karim provides litigation support to attorneys and serves as an expert witness in security related lawsuits. Karim is a member of the International Association for Healthcare Security & Safety (IAHSS), the International Association of Professional Security Consultants (IAPSC), ASIS-International, the American Society of Criminology (ASC), and the International Association of Crime Analysts (IACA). He is a Past President of the IAPSC.

Karim can be reached via email: kv@threatanalysis.com

Contributing Authors

Norman D. Bates is a nationally recognized expert in security and the law. As the President and founder of Liability Consultants, Inc., he provides security management consulting services to private industry, as well as court-certified expert witness services nationwide to both plaintiff and defense firms in civil cases regarding inadequate security, negligent hiring or training, and workplace violence. A frequent media spokesman, Mr. Bates has been interviewed and has commented on current news stories regarding crime and liability for ABC's *20-20*, *CBS News*, *NBC Nightly News*, *The Tonight Show*, *The Wall Street Journal*, *New York Times*, *U.S. News and World Report*, *USA Today*, and *Security* magazine. In standards development, Mr. Bates' work includes his contribution as a past member of the Commission on Guidelines for ASIS International that published the ASIS General Security Risk Assessment Guideline in 2003. Mr. Bates regularly presents seminars on civil liability issues and has authored numerous articles and books on the subject. Actively involved with the drafting of various legislation, Mr. Bates authored a bill on criminal stalking in Massachusetts that was passed into law in 2000. Formerly, Mr. Bates was an Assistant Professor of Criminal Justice at Northeastern University in Boston and Director of Security and Legal Counsel to the Saunders Hotel Corporation. He received his Juris Doctor degree from Suffolk University and a Bachelor of Science degree in Criminal Justice from Northeastern University. He is a member of the Massachusetts Bar, the International Association of Professional Security Consultants, the National Crime Victim Bar Association, and ASIS International.

Dr. Robert J. Emery is Vice President for Safety, Health, Environment and Risk Management for The University of Texas Health Science Center at Houston and Professor of Occupational Health at the University of Texas School of Public Health. Bob has over 30 years of experience in health and safety and possesses master's degrees in health physics and environmental sciences, and a doctorate in occupational health. Bob has the unique distinction of holding national board certification in seven main areas of health and safety. While managing a comprehensive safety program, Bob has authored over 70 peer-reviewed scientific journal articles and book chapters on health and safety issues and has provided media interviews to major media outlets such as *The Wall Street Journal, LA Times, New York Times*, ABC, CNN, FOX, MSNBC, the BBC, and NPR. He is a frequent presenter at the local, state, national, and international level.

Jack Leonard Follis, Ph.D., is a biostatistician/data scientist and an Associate Professor in the Department of Mathematics, Statistics and Computer Science at the University of St. Thomas in Houston, Texas. In addition to his doctorate in Biostatistics from the University of Texas Health Science Center at Houston School of Public Health, he has a Master of Science degree in Mathematics from Texas Tech University, and a Master of Liberal Arts degree with a concentration in History and a Bachelor of Arts degree in Mathematics and Philosophy from the University of St. Thomas. Over the years he has provided statistical consulting for projects in a variety of disciplines, including public health, education, and sports. Articles based on projects he has worked on have appeared in academic journals such as *Diabetes Care, American Journal of Epidemiology*, and *American Journal of Clinical Nutrition*.

Steve Kaufer, CPP has served the security industry for more than forty-two years. Since 1989 he has provided security management consulting services to a variety of medium to large private sector and government organizations. He specializes in security for healthcare facilities. In 1992 he co-founded the Workplace Violence Research Institute and has trained more than 10,000 employees, managers, and supervisors in the prevention of occupational violence. In addition, he has spoken dozens of times on security topics to both professional and lay groups. He is active as a member of ASIS International and serves on the Healthcare Council. He is also a member of the Association of Threat Assessment Professionals and International Association for Healthcare Security and Safety.

Andrew Rubin has managed projects for twenty-five years in the electronics manufacturing, petroleum, financial technology, and security industries. He holds master's and bachelor's degrees in Engineering, and is certified as a Project Management Professional (PMP) by the Project Management Institute. His projects have included many process and technology implementations, corporate mergers and divestitures, and security risk assessments. He has also established and managed Project Management Offices in multiple Fortune 1000 companies.

Michael A. Silva is an independent security consultant who has been practicing in the Greater Seattle area since 1985. As an independent consultant, Michael does not sell security products or services, but instead provides expert security advice to clients for a consulting fee. This allows him to provide unbiased advice based on the client's best interests, rather than the desire to sell any specific type of security solution. During the more than thirty years he has been a consultant, Michael has provided consulting services to Fortune 500 companies; city, state and local government agencies; hospitals; and schools and other educational institutions. Michael is board-certified as a Certified Protection Professional (CPP) by ASIS International and is a member of the International Association of Professional Security Consultants (IAPSC). Michael is author of the book *Becoming an Independent Security Consultant: A Practical Guide to Starting and Running a Successful Security Consulting Practice* (2016), and regularly serves as a mentor to people who wish to enter the security consulting profession.

Ken Wheatley, MA, CPP, is the Founder and Principal Advisor of Royal Security Group LLC, an international security and litigation support consulting practice based in San Diego, California. He served for twenty-four years with Sony Electronics as the Senior Vice President and Chief Security Officer for their global operations. He was the president of the Challenged Athletes Foundation and also served as an FBI Special Agent in a variety of investigative and undercover operations involving kidnapping, espionage, drugs, fugitives, and violent criminal apprehensions. He is a national board member, serving on the Executive Committee with the Forensic Expert Witness

Association and also serves as the president of the San Diego Chapter. He's a former president of the International Security Management Association, the global association of leading chief security officers, and has also served on the board of directors for the International Association of Professional Security Consultants. He earned his undergraduate degree from Florida International University, and graduated summa cum laude (4.0) with his master's degree from Webster University. He's completed Senior Executive Education Programs at the Harvard JFK School of Government, the University of Michigan Business School, and Kellogg School of Management. He has been Board Certified in Business and Organizational Security Management since 1997 and is a licensed investigator in the State of California.

Introduction

If you picked this book up, you're probably looking for more than the beginner's guide to security. *Strategic Security Management* is unique in that it fills the need for a definitive text on the concept of security, introduces the notion of analysis for security decision making, and discusses advanced threat, vulnerability, and risk assessment techniques that you can apply to your organization's security program. You'll learn how to enhance a security program using security metrics to gain a true understanding of the problem instead of relying upon gut instinct or anecdotal evidence. This book will also teach you how to use security metrics to select and implement countermeasures and fine tune the program to ensure constant improvement and continual effectiveness.

The primary reason I wrote this book is simple: After searching many online and offline bookstores, I couldn't find a book that went beyond the security basics in a practical manner. No doubt, you've read plenty of great books written by security practitioners and others written by visionaries and theorists, but there wasn't that one book which brought it all together. Thus, the goal of *Strategic Security Management* is to bridge the gap between theory and reality, so to speak, on data-driven security and evidence-based security decision making.

As was the case with the first edition of this book, research on the efficacy of many security measures in use today has not been done and the research that has been conducted has produced mixed results. There remains a scarcity of peer-reviewed research regarding the efficacy of many types of security measures. For example, literature reviews conducted by the International Association of Professional Security Consultants in 2010 and 2017 produced few research studies that addressed the effectiveness of Security Officers in preventing crime in general and no studies regarding their effectiveness in preventing violent crime specifically. Research into other security measures has often produced mixed results with effectiveness correlated to the criminal and their mindset. Criminals engaged in disorder crimes (e.g. vandalism) and property crimes (e.g. theft) are more likely to be deterred via common security measures, while those engaged in violent crimes (e.g. robbery) are less likely to be deterred. Not all crime can be prevented. Violent crime is more difficult to prevent.

Further confounding the crime prevention issue is that some places are easier to secure than others. For example, a single-tenant building is easier to secure than a building with multiple tenants. A company owned data center is easier to secure than a garden style apartment complex. In a hospital, protecting the morgue is easier than protecting the intensive care unit (ICU). The intensive care unit is easier to protect than the emergency department.

What is it about places that can inhibit or mitigate crime? One factor is access. Who has it? In the hospital example, morgue access is limited to hospital employees, making it easier to secure. Access to an ICU is often limited to hospital employees, ICU patients, and the patient's visitors. As such, the ICU is less secure than the morgue, but still relatively easy to secure given the narrow group of people needing access. The emergency department, on the other hand, is open to anyone. The challenge is that many types of place cannot have limited access without an adverse impact on the operations or business of the place. Imagine a gas station surrounded by a fence and a vehicular gate.

Additionally, security metrics are woefully lacking in our industry today, but are commonly used tools in other industries, including our cousins in the information technology security industry. With the goal of bridging that gap, *Strategic Security Management* is written for three groups of people: Security professionals; other professionals who are responsible for making security decisions; and security management and criminal justice students.

For security professionals, those that carry the titles of Chief Security Officer, Vice President of Security, Security Manager, or Security Consultant, *Strategic Security Management* expands upon the collective body of knowledge in our industry and provides you with a fresh perspective on the risk assessment process. It will also give you some food for thought on the more controversial and complex issues of our business.

Other readers who will benefit from this book are those professionals that do not hold a traditional security title, such as security director or loss prevention manager, but are nonetheless charged with protecting their organization's assets. Your title may be facility director or property manager. As long as you make the security decisions for your company, *Strategic Security Management* makes the decision making process easier.

Security management and criminal justice students will find that *Strategic Security Management* provides some insight into the diverse business that is security. You'll read many security books that will teach you the basics needed to perform entry level responsibilities in this industry. Conversely, this book provides you with the foundation needed to climb the next step up the corporate ladder.

For the most part, this book uses the term *security decision maker* to refer to anyone responsible for making decisions relating to security. The term, security professional, is also used when the issue under discussion is complex or a newer security concept. The structure of *Strategic Security Management* follows the standard risk assessment methodology, diagrammed in Figure I.1, and adds some unique chapters that will help you constantly improve your security program.

Chapter 1, Data Driven Security, sets the tone for the rest of the book with its discussion of a relatively new security concept, using data to drive the security program. Security professionals, only recently, have started using quantitative data to determine appropriate security levels. This chapter provides some of that food for thought mentioned above as well as a "how-to" for developing security metrics.

Chapter 2, Identifying Assets in Need of Protection, discusses the first two steps of the risk assessment process, the identification and categorization of organizational assets, and the itemization of existing security measures. Critical assets, those that are integral to the organization's mission, are the focal point of the first half of this chapter, while three types of security measures are discussed in the latter half. Also included in this chapter is a list of definitions so we're all speaking the same language as we progress through the book.

Chapter 3, Threat Assessments, should be an exciting section for most readers ... well, as exciting as it gets for professional books. The goal of this chapter is to illustrate the dynamic nature of threats that organizations deal with on a daily basis as well as the high impact threats which we face less frequently, but can have a detrimental impact on the assets and organizations we protect.

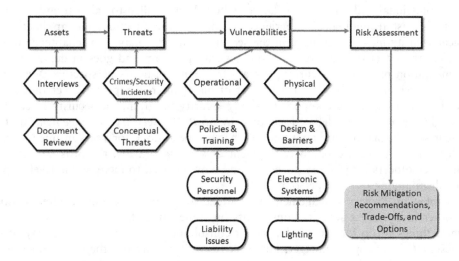

FIGURE I.1   Strategic risk assessment process. Copyright ©2019 by Threat Analysis Group, LLC. Used by permission. Additional information available from Threat Analysis Group, LLC via www.threatanalysis.com.

Chapter 4, Crime Analysis, is a component of a comprehensive threat assessment and the first major expansion on the crime analysis methodology published in *Applied Crime Analysis*. I've learned a lot since I originally outlined that book in 1999 and the security industry has advanced further toward the data driven security concepts developed during the intervening years. If you read *Applied Crime Analysis*, you'll add to that knowledge by reading this chapter. If you didn't read it, well, that's a dollar in royalties I didn't earn. Fear not, I included an overview of the original material for you before getting into the new stuff.

Chapter 5, Vulnerability Assessments, is the fourth step in the risk assessment process. Much like the rest of this book, this chapter presents material not found in any other security text. Basically, a "how-to" for conducting security surveys, this chapter also helps you put together a vulnerability assessment team and write effective vulnerability assessment reports.

Chapter 6, Risk Assessments, wraps up the process of assessing your organization's risk once you have identified the existing and emerging threats and the vulnerabilities at your facilities. Both quantitative and qualitative risk models are considered.

Chapter 7, Crime Prevention Theories, serves as a primer for the major crime prevention theories in use today with the hope of enticing the reader to seek out more information from other sources. This chapter provides the theoretical discussion for security professionals to assist them in making practical and logical decisions for a sound security program by building a bridge between crime prevention theorists and security professionals.

Chapters 8 through 10 discuss the three types of security measures used in the protection of assets. Chapter 8, Governance, covers the different types of written policies, procedures, protocols, and training used to support a security program and the importance of documentation. Chapter 9, Physical Security, is written by Michael A. Silva, a true professional and a fellow consultant whom I am thrilled to call a friend. Michael utilizes his vast technological experience to identify the function and application of physical security measures utilized in the security industry today. This chapter will help you select the effective measures for your security program and goes in depth into the implementation phase of a security program from an end user's perspective. Michael is a true professional and you'll get a lot out of his chapter. Chapter 10, Personnel, discusses the most expensive component of any security program, the security force. This just might be the most debated chapter in *Strategic Security Management* in that I present some ideas that are contrary to what has been done for years in our business. You'll learn about metric based deployment of security officers, the pros and cons of using police officers for security purposes, and why we need to increase the level of professionalism among our line personnel.

Chapter 11, Project Management, was added to the book's topic list after working with other independent security consultants on some rather large projects. One of the toughest things to do for most independent consultants is to get out of the way of the guy designated as project manager. However, consultants are not the only audience for this chapter. It is written for any security decision maker charged with implementing a new security project or upgrading an existing one.

Chapter 12, Gaining Support for Security, was written by Robert J. Emery, and provides an overview of methods for making a compelling case for obtaining resource from those that hold the purse-strings.

Chapter 13, Forensic Security Consultants and Security Liability, is written by my good friend Noman Bates. In his chapter, Norm draws on his extensive experience and past research studies to provide you with a comprehensive treatise on negligent security liability. The objective of this chapter is to help us understand the liability risks we face every day as security decision makers.

Chapter 14, Workplace Violence Prevention, was written by Steve Kaufer. Workplace violence is a growing concern and has expanded well beyond the common definition of worker-on-worker assaults. Today, workplace violence includes all types of violence and assaults against workers, no matter who the perpetrator. Like other crimes, understanding the exact nature of workplace violence incidents is critical to effective prevention. This chapter explains the process for developing an effective workplace violence prevention program.

Chapter 15, Security Risk Modeling, was written by Jack Follis. Jack's chapter teaches us how to think of a statistical analysis as a story. Every story has a theme, characters, and a plot that ties everything together. For a statistical analysis project, the goal of the project is the theme, the data being used are the characters in the story, and the analysis is the plot. For a story, understanding the characters in a story can help clear up the plot, and one of the keys to a sound statistical analysis is understanding the data. Data, as you will see in this book, is key to successful security outcomes.

Chapter 16, Security Program Leadership is written by Ken Wheatley. Ken's chapter wraps up many of the concepts outlined in the book. As a Chief Security Officer at a global organization, Ken brings unparalleled experience to put the bow on this book. As Ken states in his chapter, *Protecting everything, is not possible, practical, or even business savvy. And one of your jobs as the security leader, or the person tasked with security as part of your responsibilities, is to help the organization determine where along that spectrum the organization should fall.*

So that's the overview, sixteen chapters of new concepts, food for thought on older security principles, and advanced techniques that I am confident will assist you in your job as a protector. One last thought before we dive into the first chapter ... while researching this book, I sought out the wisdom of others and came across a quote by William O. Douglas which I think captures the essence of *Strategic Security Management*: "Security can only be achieved through constant change, through discarding old ideas that have outlived their usefulness and adapting others to current facts." I think that pretty well sums up the intent of this book. Grab a cup of coffee and read on ...

CHAPTER 1

Data-Driven Security

Karim H. Vellani

CONTENTS

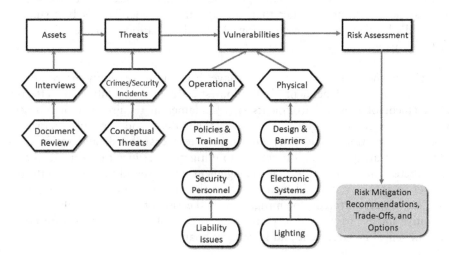

FIGURE 1.1 Strategic Risk Assessment Process, Copyright ©2019 by Threat Analysis Group, LLC. Used by permission. Additional information available from Threat Analysis Group, LLC via www.threatanalysis.com.

DATA-DRIVEN SECURITY

What cannot be measured cannot be managed. This is a commonly accepted business paradigm, yet its acceptance within the security industry is not as far reaching as in other industries. Simply put, data-driven security refers to using measurable factors to drive a security program. While not all elements of a security program lend themselves to measurement, many components can be measured effectively. For example, physical protection systems are measured via penetration times, and barriers are measured using delay and defeat times. Other security components can be measured, though not mathematically, including the morale of protection forces.

Some would argue that the security is more of an art than a science. While they are correct, the business of security is not an art. The security department is a business unit, not unlike other business units within a company that must justify their existence. The higher security moves up the corporate ladder, the more challenges the security director will face and the more business acumen will be required. Given the security industry's growth out of public law enforcement, it is no surprise that it has taken the industry significant time to develop into a full-fledged corporate entity. With this growth comes the need to depart from the police mentality. Thirty years ago, most security directors were retired law enforcement agents who made the jump to private security as a way to supplement their retirement income. This has proven to slow the growth of security within the corporate hierarchy, but was probably a necessary step in the history of the industry. This is not to say that retired law enforcement personnel do not have a place in the security industry. To the contrary, many have proven to be exemplary business leaders who have made significant leaps for the security departments in their companies.

As the security industry grows to not only include physical security but also information/cyber security, it is incumbent upon today's security directors to focus more on the business side of security rather than the operational side. This is best summarized by the world's leading security association, ASIS – International, in their Chief Security Officer Guideline:

> Today's business risk environments have become increasingly more severe, complex, and interdependent, both domestically and globally. The effective management of these environments is a fundamental requirement of business. Boards of Directors, shareholders, key stakeholders, and the public correctly expect organizations to identify and anticipate areas of risk and set in place a cohesive strategy across all functions to mitigate or reduce those risks. In addition, there is an expectation that management will respond in a highly effective manner to those events and incidents that threaten the assets of the organization. A proactive strategy for mitigation of the risk of loss ultimately provides a positive impact to profitability and is an organizational governance responsibility of senior management and governing boards.

The guideline goes on to discuss the role of the Chief Security Officer (CSO) as a business leader, a problem solver, as well as an expert in security for their company. Interestingly, the guideline also suggests that the CSO's background includes business, not law enforcement, since their key responsibility "is to develop and implement a strategy that demonstrates the processes in understanding the nature and probability of catastrophic and significant security risk events." As the company security departments grow and begin to encompass more responsibility for the protection of people, property, and information, so too must the ability to fall back on empirical data to support our position. No longer can security professionals rely solely on gut instincts.

Too often recommendations from the security department are presented with little or no thought to why certain procedures or security equipment should be used. Often, the reason for deploying a security measure is because other companies are doing it (benchmarking). It is all too common in the security industry for there to be a propensity for using certain security measures without complete understanding of the problem or a thorough analysis of the security measures' ability to be effective given the specific situation. Data-driven security can help security directors overcome this problem by identifying key concerns, the ability for specific security measures to solve the problem, and the anticipated cost.

How can security professionals justify to senior executives a sizable and usually growing annual security budget? By now, most security directors are keenly aware that a security program's success depends on the commitment and support of senior executives. Using anecdotal evidence to justify spending on physical security measures and costly protection personnel no longer suffices. A data-driven security program helps management understand that security is more than a must-have expense; it justifies costs to management by showing the proof of success that, when presented effectively, can garner the necessary buy-in from upper management and demonstrate a convincing return on investment. Security expenditures, just like other departmental budgets, need to be justified with empirical data and supplemented with cost-benefit analyses and comparisons.

Throughout the first part of this book, various assessments used in the security industry are discussed, including threat, vulnerability, and risk assessments along with specific types of assessments like crime analysis. Common to each of these is a quantitative approach to establish a baseline from which security effectiveness can be measured. Assessments are the foundation upon which a security program is built by establishing a baseline of risks that companies face. Assessments guide the strategic planning and design of countermeasures intended to mitigate the identified security risks.

Such a logical approach brings benefits which are unattainable with only qualitative assessments which are still used throughout the public and private security sectors. While qualitative assessments cannot be abandoned, their use should be limited to those instances where quantitative ones cannot be used for lack of measurable elements. Thus, physical security is, and shall remain, more of an art than a science, though science can be infused into an otherwise abstract process.

> I don't care how skilled you are as a diplomat or how brilliant you are at leading, if you are not professional about security, you are a failure.
>
> *Former U.S. Secretary of State Madeline Albright*

SECURITY METRICS

Between September 2001 and the writing of the first edition of this book in April 2006, the United States suffered no major terrorist attacks. While this fact made for a great sound bite for political talking heads, it is not an accurate metric of the true threat faced by the United States as has been proven in the intervening years where we experienced numerous terrorist acts, primarily active shootings by lone wolves. A more appropriate metric would be the number of attacks thwarted since September 2001 or arrests made of known terrorists. When providing asset protection, accurate measurement of security effectiveness can have a profound impact on management's level of support for the security department. "Near misses" are sometimes evidence of our success in mitigating risks.

As mentioned earlier, a common paradigm in business is that an activity cannot be managed if it cannot be measured. Security is one such activity. Security metrics communicate vital information about security activities and drive decision making. Metrics for various security components, such as the protection force or access control system, can be an effective tool for security professionals to understand the effectiveness of the overall security program. Metrics, as previously discussed, may also identify risk based on failures or successes of security components, and can provide solutions to security problems. Security metrics focus on the results of security decisions such as reduction in thefts after implementation of a video surveillance system, an increase in visibility or customer service ratings after a change in security officer uniforms, or a reduction in terrorist acts as a result of terrorist cell arrests.

Security metrics help define how secure and effective we are. They assist security professionals in answering basic questions posed by management, such as:

- Are company assets protected?
- Which assets need more protection?
- Can the asset protection program be improved?
- What resources should be allocated to security?
- How does our company compare to others?
- Are we reducing our liability exposure?

The National Institute of Standards and Technology (N.I.S.T.) defines metrics as tools designed to facilitate decision making and improve performance and accountability through collection, analysis, and reporting of relevant performance-related data. Thus, security metrics assist security professionals in making asset protection decisions through the measurement of performance-based characteristics of security components. Simply stated, security metrics are tools used for measuring a company's security posture.

For the security metrics to be accurate, security professionals must have two elements in the metrics model:

- proper performance data for the specific countermeasure under evaluation; and
- an appropriate baseline from which to compare.

Baseline measurements are often difficult to obtain, especially in the business of security where companies are, out of necessity, secretive about their protection systems. In recent years, industry associations such as ASIS-International, the International Association for Professional Security Consultants, and the International Association for Healthcare Security and Safety have promulgated standards, guidelines, and best practices. Even non-security associations, such as the National Fire Protection Association, have written security guidelines. In addition to published and accepted industry standards, the courts have outlined baselines of measurement for the security industry. An example of this is a Texas Supreme Court case, Timberwalk v. Cain, which outlines the specific factors necessary for establishing foreseeability of crime in premises liability lawsuits. In Timberwalk, the court set forth five criteria for measuring the risk of crime including recency, proximity, publicity, frequency, and similarity of past crimes. An example of crime metrics legislation is the 1996 Illinois Automated Teller Machine Act. Section 20 of the Act provides procedures for evaluating the safety of ATM's regarding "the incidence of crimes of violence in the immediate neighborhood of the ATM."

Texas has a similar ATM Safety law which requires that financial institutions collect crime metrics. Some states have also required collection and reporting of workplace violence metrics in some areas such as healthcare. Thus, the professional security practitioner will stay abreast of industry standards and the law. While laws must normally be reasonably followed, security professionals may fine-tune published industry standards to meet the needs of their company.

In addition to establishing a baseline for comparing company metrics, metrics are also used to justify budgets, provide data for decision making, and improving security practices. Metrics can be used to justify budgets and provide the basis for obtaining additional resources for the security department. Security metrics may be plugged into cost-benefit analyses to identify the need for various security components. For security decision making, metrics can unveil trends and patterns in the security program's performance from which security decision makers can make decisions to modify the program. For example, once a physical protection system is alerted of an intruder, security force personnel may respond. By measuring time needed to respond from the security officer's fixed post to the breached access point, the security decision maker can determine if the response time is adequate or if another post needs to be established closer to the access point. Finally, metrics assist in the development of good security practices. An example of this may be found in the use of security personnel to provide escorts for company personnel exiting the building to the parking areas. While this is a common practice in some companies, an analysis of security incidents during peak times may indicate a sharp increase in security breaches because security personnel are distracted from their primary protection duties while escorting personnel. In this instance, the value of providing escorts must be balanced with other duties when determining the company's security practices.

S.M.A.R.T. Metrics

Good metrics are attainable when security professionals strive for S.M.A.R.T. metrics. S.M.A.R.T. stands for Specific, Measurable, Actionable, Relevant, and Timely.

Specific – a metric must measure a specific variable.

Measurable – a metric measure that is measurable. Not all components of a security program are measurable. For example, morale among security forces or employee "fear of crime" are often "measured" but not in a quantitative manner.

Actionable – a metric should not measure variables which cannot be acted upon. If a security decision maker cannot remedy a problem, there is not much sense in wasting time on that variable.

Relevant – a metric that fails to provide any information to improve the security program should be avoided. If the metric cannot tell us where we can improve, it is not relevant.

Timely – metrics have expiration dates. Historical data is an excellent indicator of the future; however, the older the data, the less important it may be. A metric system incapable of assessing the latest data is useless. Placing more weight on more recent data is a common practice.

An example of useful security metrics in the healthcare industry may include the following:

- Number of workplace violence incidents per 1,000 employees
- Security and workplace violence incidents per adjusted patient day (or similar)

- Security and workplace violence incidents de-escalated as a percent of total incidents
- Security call volume by call type
- Security response time by call type
- Number of disruptive/combative codes per month
- Behavioral health evaluations as a percent of census per adjusted patient day (or similar)
- Time patient sitters and/or security officers spend on 1:1 patient observation
- Time between medical clearance and transfer to a behavioral health facility
- Patients requiring restraints (physical or chemical) per adjusted patient day (or similar)
- Security and workplace violence prevention program cost as a percent of revenue
- Average security and workplace violence prevention program cost as a percent of total incidents
- Percent of security or workplace violence incidents resulting in regulatory or legal consequences
- Ratio of security officers to total hospital employees
- Staff fear/anxiety of workplace violence (qualitative surveys).

As discussed in the introduction to security metrics, the number of attacks against the country or the number of crimes at a location may not be the best indicator of an effective security program. While luck does play a part in the protection of assets, there are other factors which can be measured in answering the question of how secure we are. To develop a security metrics system, security professionals can adapt the Six Sigma methodology used to eliminate defects. The author has successfully implemented a variation of this methodology for use with protective forces within the federal government. The methodology involves seven steps which are easily modified for our use in security metrics:

1. Define the metrics system goals.
2. Decide what metrics to generate.
3. Develop strategies for generating the metrics.
4. Establish benchmarks.
5. Develop a metrics reporting system.
6. Develop and implement an action plan.
7. Create a formal system review cycle.

Going through each step should enable security professionals to adapt the methodology to their needs.

> The only security is the constant practice of critical thinking. The only security is the constant practice of critical thinking.
>
> *William Graham Sumner*

Step 1: Define the metrics system goals

Critical in today's business environment is the need to set performance-based goals. Setting high, yet reasonable, goals during the development of a security metrics system is a necessary step. The goals should be well defined and based on the needs of the security department, though continued refinement of the goals while moving through the seven steps is acceptable. Each goal should clearly state the desired result to which all metrics collection and analysis efforts are directed. An example of a metric goal within the personnel department of a security program is, "The response time metric shall clearly communicate to supervisors the average time needed for a security officer to patrol and secure the fifth floor office space."

Step 2: Decide what metrics to generate

Deciding what to measure is crucial to an effective metrics system. As referenced above, during the almost four year period covered since the September 11, 2001 attack and the writing of this book, the United States suffered no major terrorist attacks. While this is obviously good news, it is not a true measure of our vulnerability. Thus, step 2 is to identify the specific security components or practices which have kept us free from terrorism. One example of this is the number of arrests within US borders of known terrorists. Another example may be the number of attacks thwarted due to intelligence efforts.

Step 3: Develop strategies for generating the metrics

Collecting the data for metrics can be a daunting task. The security professional's strategy for data collection should identify the source of information and the frequency at which that raw data is collected by the source. It is not uncommon for a security decision maker to require data from other departments. Successful identification of the sources is key to a sound metrics program. An example of this can be found in crime analysis. Security decision makers often use traffic levels at a facility to calculate the crime rate at that facility. While the security department typically has no way to determine themselves how many people pass through a facility in a given day, month, or year, other departments do normally have this data. It is incumbent upon the security professional to seek out that source and ensure the data meets the quality control requirements of the metrics system.

Step 4: Establish benchmarks

As discussed above, there are industry benchmarks and also internal benchmarks from which to compare. Benchmarking may be defined as the process of identifying and adapting outstanding security practices from organizations within the industry for the purpose of improving company security practices. In the crime analysis field, the author has had the opportunity to evaluate both internal and external crime reporting systems at many companies. With this information, the author has been able to improve the reporting systems at one client based on the system at another company.

Step 5: Develop a metrics reporting system

The collection and analysis of metrics is not enough to improve the security program. The system must also include a reporting component whereby those who carry out the line function can work to improve their work. Effective communication is vital to the metrics system. The frequency, content, and method of dissemination of reports should also be established at this step. Continuing the example used in step 1, collecting and analyzing response times does not in itself correct the problem. The security department must communicate the results to line personnel supervisors so that corrective action can be taken.

Step 6: Develop and implement an action plan

A security metrics action plan guides the users toward the end result. The plan identifies and defines all tasks required for the metrics system to be effective, as well as a time-line of events leading up to the reporting of metric results. The plan should be written and available to everyone involved in the program.

Step 7: Create a formal system review cycle

Similar to the business environment, security is dynamic and must be adjusted to the needs of the day. A formal system review at regular intervals ensures that the security department is measuring what it should be measuring. As time moves on, things change and more security components may be added to a security program which require metrics generation, while other components are removed and no longer require metrics.

Developing a security metrics system is time consuming, but can prove to be a panacea for a security department. The methodology outlined above makes the process easier and should be adapted to meet the security department's needs. The incentive for this project is that the resulting security program will not only be effective within the company but may also be regarded as the benchmark by other organizations.

DATA-DRIVEN ASSESSMENTS

The purpose of this section is to briefly introduce the reader to the various definitions and tools used throughout the remainder of this book. Each topic presented below will be discussed in depth in later chapters. Among the more commonly used terms are threats, vulnerabilities, and risks. While various definitions are used in the industry and many people use these terms interchangeably, this book will attempt to clarify the differences among definitions. Generally speaking, threats are things that can go wrong or that attack the system, that is, what we're protecting against. Examples include natural disasters and intentional acts. Vulnerabilities are those things that make the facility more prone to attack by the threats or provide the opportunity for bad things to happen. Vulnerabilities are exploited by threats. For example, lack of access control may be a vulnerability that can be exploited by a person to gain access to a target or asset. Risk is a function of threats and vulnerabilities, that is, risk exists at the intersection of assets, threats, and vulnerabilities. Countermeasures are things that reduce or block opportunity for threats to exploit vulnerabilities. Countermeasures are preventive in nature. An access control system is a countermeasure that can deter or delay access to a target by a threat.

For security assessments, whether they be vulnerability, threat, or risk assessments, the primary goal should be to make the process as objective as possible. There are two types of assessments: quantitative and qualitative. Both types of assessment can and should be utilized depending on the scenario (Figure 1.2).

Qualitative assessments are normally used when the assets in need of protection are of lower value or when data is not available. The results of qualitative assessments

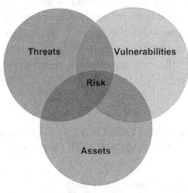

Security Risk Formula

FIGURE 1.2   Security risk formula process. Copyright ©2019 by Threat Analysis Group, LLC. Used by permission. Additional information available from Threat Analysis Group, LLC via www.threatanalysis.com.

depend on the assessment skills of the people involved in the assessment. Risk levels are normally given in abstract values such as high, medium, or low, or color coded like the Homeland Security Advisory System.

Quantitative assessments, on the other hand, are metric based and assign numeric values to the risk level. Overall risk levels are derived from all available security metrics. In a physical protection system, for example, the metrics used in determining the risk level include the threat level, probability of detection, delay times, and response force times. Quantitative assessments are commonly used for the protection of business critical or high value assets.

Threat assessments, as already discussed, identify things that can go wrong or that attack the system. When focused on the people threat, threat assessments ask who the bad guys are and what their capabilities are. When focused on the general threat, crime analysis, as discussed in depth in a later chapter, is a type of threat assessment that focuses on crimes at specific properties.

Vulnerability assessments identify weaknesses in a security program without regard to the threats after taking into consideration existing security measures. Vulnerability assessments are common in business continuity planning where loss of assets is considered. The US Military has a number of declassified documents which outline vulnerability assessments. One such document is the United States Army Training and Doctrine Command Regulation 525–13 for Force Protection Programs (FPP). Vulnerability assessments may also be quantitative or qualitative; however, quantitative assessments are fairly easy to accomplish since the emphasis is on assets whose values are typically known.

Finally, risk assessments are comprehensive and logical reviews that look at assets, threats, and vulnerabilities (Figure 1.2). Risk assessments can be both quantitative, qualitative, or a hybrid. This type of assessment thoroughly evaluates the overall risk including asset identification, threat analysis, and vulnerabilities in the day-to-day facility operations at the facility or in the company. Assets include people, property, and information. Qualitative assessments are based on the data available and the skills of the assessment team, while quantitative assessments utilize numeric data to evaluate risk. Risk assessments are typically a staged process whereby critical assets are identified, current countermeasures are enumerated, threat and vulnerabilities are defined, and prioritized recommendations are made to protect critical assets based on probabilities of attack. The first two steps of the risk assessment methodology, asset identification and security inventory, are discussed in Chapter 2.

GENERAL CHARACTERISTICS OF A COMPREHENSIVE RISK ASSESSMENT METHODOLOGY

Designed for a specific organization or industry.
Complies with regulations and is guided by industry best practices.
Designed for information technology security, physical security, or a combination of both.
Categorizes assets based on criticality to the organization's mission.
Identifies existing security measures used to protect assets.
Determines threats using multiple sources.
Uses tools and techniques to identify vulnerabilities.
Analyzes risk to assets based on threats and vulnerabilities.
Recommends multiple strategies for reducing risk.

CHAPTER 2

Identifying Assets in Need of Protection

Karim H. Vellani

CONTENTS

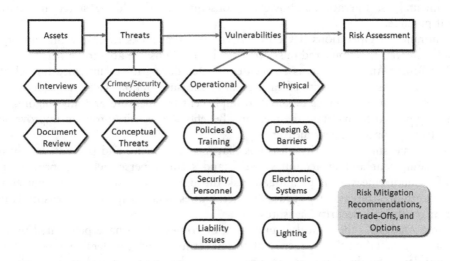

FIGURE 2.1 Strategic Risk Assessment Process, Copyright ©2019 by Threat Analysis Group, LLC. Used by permission. Additional information available from Threat Analysis Group, LLC via www.threatanalysis.com.

All security programs, regardless of their complexity or industry application, are designed to protect assets and, generally speaking, assets are anything of value. This chapter introduces the concepts of asset identification, determination of criticality, and consequence analysis. Also discussed is how assets are selected by adversaries, those that seek to damage, destroy, or obtain assets. Properly determining what needs protection is a necessary first step in the risk management process, for without asset identification, security measures are often haphazardly selected and deployed. This chapter also serves as a launching off point for more complex concepts discussed in the remainder of the book. Thus, the first part of this chapter contains a list of terms and their definitions used throughout the book to ensure a commonality in understanding.

DEFINITIONS

Adversary – An individual or group that is motivated and capable of stealing, damaging, or destroying critical assets. Adversaries are threats. Adversaries can include insiders, outsiders, or a combination of insiders and outsiders.

Asset – People, property, and information. People may include employees and customers along with other invited persons such as contractors or guests. Property assets consist of both tangible and intangible items that can be assigned a value. Intangible assets include reputation and proprietary information. Information may include databases, software code, critical company records, and many other intangible items.

Capability – The ability of an adversary to obtain, damage, or destroy an asset.

Consequence – The extent of loss that can be anticipated from a successful adversarial attack against an asset. The impact of loss may be human, economic, political, environmental, or operational; however, consequences should be stated in financial terms if possible.

Continuity of Operations (COOP) – A concept that seeks to ensure that an organization's essential functions and mission critical operations are able to be performed.

Cost-Benefit Analysis – An assessment conducted during the countermeasure selection phase of the costs and benefits of each security measure option. Costs typically include the money and time resources required to implement the measure and any ongoing time and money needed to maintain the measure. Benefits are security program improvements derived from planned security measures.

Countermeasures – Security measures that include policies and procedures, physical security equipment and protection systems, and security personnel. The primary purpose of a countermeasure is to mitigate risk through a prevention process that eliminates or neutralizes threats and reduces vulnerabilities. The term countermeasure is used interchangeably with security measures.

Crime Analysis – the logical examination of crimes which have penetrated preventive measures, including the frequency of specific crimes, each incident's temporal details (time and day), and the risk posed to a property's inhabitants, as well as the application of revised security standards and preventive measures that, if adhered to and monitored, can be the panacea for a given crime dilemma. Crime analysis, as defined by the International Association of Crime Analysts (2014), is a profession and process in which a set of quantitative and qualitative techniques are used to analyze data valuable to police agencies and their communities. It includes the analysis of crime and criminals, crime victims, disorder, quality of life issues, traffic issues, and internal police operations, and its results support criminal investigation and prosecution, patrol activities, crime prevention and reduction strategies, problem solving, and the evaluation of police efforts.

Crime prevention – the anticipation, the recognition, and the appraisal of a crime risk and the initiation of action to remove or reduce it.

Criticality – The operational impact on the organization's mission due to the loss, damage, or destruction of an asset.

Delay – A security strategy designed to slow the progression of adversaries into or out of the facility. Barriers are an example of a delay measure.

Defeat – A security strategy designed to neutralize adversaries before an asset is lost, damaged, or destroyed. For defeat to occur, the security program must be operating at an optimum level.

Detection – A security strategy designed to assess the threat and alert security personnel to an adversary's presence. Cameras and sensors are examples of detection measures.

Deterrence – A security strategy designed to discourage adversaries by increasing the risks to the adversary, promoting a sense of security, and instilling doubt on behalf of an adversary. Deterrence posits that crime can be prevented if potential offenders believe the costs of committing a crime outweigh the benefits. Three key concepts play an important role in deterrence theory: the certainty, severity, and swiftness of punishment.[1]

Emergency – any event or combination of events which have the potential to negatively impact the organization's mission or components of that mission for a period of time, and which require immediate response and action to continue normal mission operations.

Exposure – An instance of being exposed to losses from a threat. A weakness or vulnerability can cause an organization to be exposed to possible damages.

Facility – A structure or group of structures in one physical location.

Hybrid Assessment – A type of assessment which includes both qualitative and quantitative data and components. Hybrid assessments typically numerically measure that which can be measured, such as response times and assess qualitatively that which cannot.

Infrastructure – The underlying foundation of assets needed for an organization to perform its essential functions and mission critical operations.

Mitigation – The act of causing a consequence to have less adverse impact on the organization's mission.

Project Management – The planning and execution of all aspects of a security project and application of skills, knowledge, and methods to achieve the project's objectives, goals, and requirements on time, within budgetary limitations, and with a high level of quality.

Qualitative Assessment – A type of assessment which is driven primarily by the assessment subject's characteristics. Qualitative risk assessments are dependent upon the assessor's skills. Scenario-based risk assessments are typically qualitative in nature. The National Terror Alert System is an example of a Qualitative Threat Assessment.

Quantitative Assessment – A type of assessment which is metric based and assigns numeric values to the risk level. For example, quantitative assessments incorporate security response times and barrier delay times.

Risk – A function of threats and vulnerabilities. Risk is the possibility of asset loss, damage, or destruction as a result of a threat exploiting a specific vulnerability.

Risk Management – a process which seeks to identify assets and manage threats, vulnerabilities, and risks within an organization. Risk management involves assessing risk, evaluating and selecting security measures to reduce identified risks, and implementing and monitoring the selected measures to ensure that the measures are effective in reducing risk to an acceptable level.

Risk Assessment – The process to identify and prioritize risks. A quantitative, qualitative, or hybrid assessment that seeks to determine the likelihood that an adversary will successfully exploit a vulnerability and the resulting impact (degree of consequence) on an asset. A risk assessment is the foundation for prioritizing risks in order to effectively implement countermeasures.

Security Decision Maker – Anyone who has an active role within an organization for asset protection. This term, or its acronym, SDM, is used throughout this text since some organizations do not have a formal position of security manager or security director. Risk managers also fall within the Security Decision Maker definition.

Security Survey – a fact finding process whereby the assessment team gathers data that reflects the who, what, how, where, when, and why of an organization's existing operation and facility. The purpose of a security survey is to identify and measure the vulnerabilities to the facility or to specific assets by determining what opportunities exist to exploit current security policies and procedures, physical security equipment, and security personnel.

Threat – Anything that can exploit a vulnerability, intentionally or accidentally, and obtain, damage, or destroy an asset. Threats are classified as either human or natural. Threat can also be defined as an adversary's intent, motivation, and capability to attack assets.

Threat Assessment – An evaluation of human actions or natural events that can adversely affect business operations and specific assets. Historical information is a primary source for threat assessments, including past criminal and terrorist events. Crime analysis is a quantitative example of a threat assessment, while terrorism threat analysis is normally qualitative.

Vulnerability – Weaknesses or gaps in a security program that can be exploited by threats to gain unauthorized access to an asset. Vulnerabilities include structural, procedural, electronic, human, and other elements which provide opportunities to attack assets.

Vulnerability Assessment – An analysis of security weaknesses and opportunities for adversarial exploitation. A security survey is the fundamental tool for collecting information used in the vulnerability assessment. A vulnerability assessment is sometimes referred to as a security vulnerability assessment, or SVA for short.

ASSET CLASSIFICATION

What is an asset? Assets are anything of value to an organization and range from the basic to the mission critical. It is the latter which is of primary importance for protection by the security program. Generally, assets consist of people, property, and information. Critical assets are those which are needed for the organization to execute its primary missions and functions.

People

People assets may include employees and customers along with other invited persons such as contractors or guests. At a typical chemical facility, for example, the employees and contractors are the people in need of protection from various threats, including chemical leaks and explosions to natural disasters. On the other hand, at a hotel, the employees and guests are considered assets, for without the employees the hotel will not operate and without guests, the hotel does not serve its intended purpose.

Property

An organization's property assets consist of both tangible and intangible items that can be assigned a value. Tangible assets are usually simple to identify, while intangible assets are more difficult to identify and assign a value. Intangible assets include the organization's reputation and proprietary information. While all property assets have value, not all are critical to the organization's mission.

Information

Among other things and dependent upon the type of organization, information assets may include databases, software code, and company financial records. Proprietary information, such as vital records, formulas, and methods, are also assets. Vital company records normally do not exceed 2 percent of an organization's records and may include incorporation certificates, stock records, corporate meeting minutes, and some financial records.

Critical Assets

Identifying the organization's critical assets is the first step in risk management. Critical assets within industrialized nations include electrical power, gas and oil production, telecommunications, banking and finance, water supply systems, transportation, government operations, and emergency services. Business critical assets are those which are needed to perform the primary mission of the business. Assets are deemed critical based on two primary factors: The value as defined by the organization, and the short-term and long-term consequence to the business operations due to its loss, damage, or destruction. The critical assets of a business are those which are necessary for continued business operations and in need of protection. For governments, critical assets are those which sustain the economy, security, political landscape, and social services. Assets do not have equal value to the business operation. Whatever the critical assets of any organization, a value must be assessed for each, and each asset must be prioritized based on the consequence of its loss due to human actions. For example, in the oil industry, pipelines are considered a critical asset as any damage to or loss of a pipeline reduces the availability for refineries to continue production. For small professional service firms, computer files containing company information and client data may be the only critical asset.

The protection of assets is the principal goal of any security program. These assets have both tangible and intangible value which can often be quantitatively assessed using the following elements:

- Criticality of the asset to business operations
- Replacement value
- Relative value of the asset.

Criticality is a function of operational impact on the organization's mission due to the loss, damage, or destruction to an asset. The more impact assets have on the business operation, the more critical they are. The criteria for assessing the level of criticality should be specific. Does an asset affect companywide operations, or would the loss, damage, or destruction impact only part of the operations? In the oil example, it was determined that pipelines are critical assets; however, pipelines vary in their value for oil and gas production. Some pipelines are more significant because of their throughput, while others are less valuable.

Assets are categorized by their level of criticality. This may be a quantitative assessment based on their actual value, or the impact on business operations from their loss, damage, or destruction. Numerically assigned criticality levels can be more difficult to ascertain but can be meaningful to the overall risk assessment. Alternatively, qualitative assessments can also be used by rank order the assets on relative scales such as high, medium, or low. Descriptive values such as catastrophic, critical, marginal, or negligible may also be used in understanding the relative value to business operations. A matrix of critical assets may be beneficial in understanding the relative nature of asset loss, damage, and destruction.

For effective business continuity planning, security decision makers should not only consider the immediate impact of asset loss but also the time and cost to replace the asset. Time to replacement can significantly impact the criticality level due to operational downtime, which in turn leads to loss of revenue. The longer the time necessary to replace a critical asset, the higher the consequence. For some critical assets, it is imperative to have a fully operational backup in place. Take, for example, a professional services firm whose primary deliverables to clients are reports and other data files. The reports and data files are generated on a computer word processing application. Should the firm's computer be destroyed, reports cannot be generated, and a substantial loss of revenue can result. Most small firms such as the one described could either have a backup personal computer, or their client files are stored on a storage device, such as a compact disc or flash drive, and a location where they can use another computer. The loss of one asset may affect other assets as well and should be considered in identifying the overall asset criticality analysis. For example, in preparing for natural disasters, medical hospitals use electrical generators to provide a backup source of power in the event of a loss of electricity to provide continued support to patients.

IDENTIFYING CRITICAL ASSETS

Asset information can come from various sources; however, critical asset information is best obtained for those who manage the day-to-day operations of the organization. This may be the asset owners themselves or their designees. Comprehensive interviews of these people should be conducted to obtain the information regarding each asset. Oftentimes, a consultant is brought in to conduct a risk assessment. Interviewing key personnel is the first step that the consultant will take, guiding the interviewee through a series of questions which will allow the consultant to fully understand the process and procedures of the organization. For example, a consultant hired by a manufacturing company would start the project with a series of interviews with site personnel, review security manuals and other documentation, and seek out other sources of information to assist in ranking assets based on their mission criticality.

Depending on the organization's mission, asset information may be available via the internet and other public sources. Property management companies, for example, often list their entire portfolios on their website. From a marketing perspective this makes sense, but this information can also be used by adversaries to help them select a target.

TARGET SELECTION

From the adversarial perspective, assets are called targets. Targets may not be of the same value to the adversary as they are to the owner. As such, asset value must be based not only its mission critical level but also on its value to the adversary. Target value must be calculated based on the best available information. For example, from a national security perspective, certainly the Pentagon and US Capitol are of higher value to the US Government than One World Trade Center in lower Manhattan. A foreign government would certainly place a high value on the Pentagon when waging a war against the United States. However, for terrorist groups, the World Trade Center presented a far more attractive target in 2001 because of its social, economic, and political value. Likewise, One World Trade Center presents the same level of attractiveness. Depending on the industry for which a risk assessment is being performed, certain factors should be considered in evaluating target values:

- Casualty and injury rates
- Asset potential for loss, damage, or destruction
- Damage to the political landscape
- Disruption to operations
- Disruption to the economy
- Media attention
- Impact on the organization's reputation
- Impact on employee morale
- Fear.

Depending on the nature of a company's business, asset value may not be obvious to security decision makers. Threat assessments can help discern which assets are susceptible to loss, damage, or destruction. In the grocery business, for example, criminals target small, high value items such as infant formula and over-the-counter medicines. For US national security purposes, particularly for terrorism prevention, political and economic assets are more likely to be targeted. With recent and realistic threat information, security professionals can make decisions based on asset attractiveness and provide for higher security levels.

CONSEQUENCE ANALYSIS

History indicates that the likelihood of crime and terrorism, as well as other threats, is inversely related to its magnitude. That is, the probability of attack decreases as consequence increases since it is easier to conduct small-scale attacks than large-scale ones. The history of Al Qaeda provides a good example of this with the number of relatively low level attacks executed prior to and since the September 11 attack.

We have to get it right every day and the terrorists only have to get it right
once. So we have to be ahead of the game.

Former TSA Spokeswoman Lauren Stover

Consequence analysis is an assessment of the effect on operations if an asset is lost,
damaged, or destroyed. Operations may include business operations or national
defense. Business continuity planning is based on consequence analysis. By estimating
the likelihood and magnitude of asset loss, security decision makers can prepare alternative methods to continue operations and restoration of primary operations capability.
Organizations need to be prepared for a wide range of attacks based on statistical probabilities of occurrence. A consequence analysis allows the assessment team to prioritize
assets in need of protection given their criticality to the organization. Consequence analysis is a fundamental step in the risk assessment process since the organization may not
be able to afford the same level of protection for all vulnerable assets, thus prioritizing
assets allows the organization to protect those which are most critical.

Consequences can be categorized in a number of ways: economic, financial, environmental, health and safety, technological, operational, and time. For example,
a process control center may be essential for the safe production of a particular product. Its loss, or inability to function properly, could result not only in a disruption of
production (with its concomitant loss of revenue and additional costs associated with
replacing the lost capability), but it might also result in the loss of life, property
damage, or environmental damage, if the process being controlled involves hazardous
materials. The loss of an asset might also reduce a company's competitive advantage,
not only because of the financial costs associated with its loss but also because of the
loss of technological advantage or loss of unique knowledge or information that would
be difficult to replace or reproduce. Individual firms, too, have to worry about loss of
reputation. The American Petroleum Institute and the National Petrochemical and
Refiners Association (API/NPRA) in their Security Vulnerability Assessment Methodology for the Petroleum and Petrochemical Industries also suggested considering the
possibility of "excessive media exposure and resulting public hysteria that may affect
people that may be far removed from the actual event location."

A criticality assessment is a process designed to systematically identify and evaluate
important assets and infrastructure in terms of various factors, such as the mission and
significance of a target. For example, nuclear power plants, key bridges, and major
computer networks might be identified as "critical" in terms of their importance to
national security, economic activity, and public safety. In addition, facilities might be
critical at certain times, but not others. For example, large sports stadiums, shopping
malls, or office towers when in use by large numbers of people may represent an
important target but are less important when they are empty. Criticality assessments are
important because they provide a basis for identifying which assets and structures are
relatively more important to protect from an attack. The assessments provide information to prioritize assets and allocate resources to special protective actions. These assessments have considered such factors as the importance of a structure to accomplish
a mission, the ability to reconstitute this capability, and the potential cost to repair or
replace the asset. Thus far, what has been discussed is a quantitative assessment of
assets using actual costs, replacement values, and operational downtime. Criticality can
be measured qualitatively also using relative terms to prioritize asset loss, damage, or
destruction. A four level scale is suggested from low to critical.

Critical – Assets which, if lost, damaged, or destroyed, can result in mission failure.

High – Serious unwanted impact which may impair normal operations in its entirety or complete loss of a portion of the operations for an extended time period.

Medium – Moderate operational impact which may only affect a portion of the business processes and for a short period of time.

Low – A manageable impact to business operations and a no likelihood of mission failure.

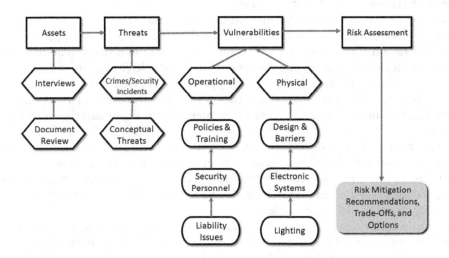

FIGURE 2.2   Strategic risk assessment process. Copyright ©2019 by Threat Analysis Group, LLC. Used by permission. Additional information available from Threat Analysis Group, LLC via www.threatanalysis.com.

SECURITY MEASURE INVENTORY

Asset identification is but the first step in the risk assessment methodology. The second step involves inventorying existing security measures designed to protect the assets at the facility. Depending on the quality of previous assessments, existing countermeasures may or may not be effective in protecting the facility and its critical assets. While time brings change to both the assets and the countermeasures, previous risk assessments and subsequent security program designs should be working to protect assets.

Existing countermeasures may include security personnel, physical measures, and policies and procedures. Security personnel include people specifically designated or indirectly working toward the protection of assets. Uniformed security officers would be the most visible and recognizable example of security personnel. Others may be involved in the protection as well who are not as easily identified, including undercover officers, security managers dressed in business attire, and common employees who are trained in how to handle security incidents. Physical security measures may include a range of low technology items such as barriers, bollards, fencing, and curbing to high tech measures such as video analytics and bio-metrics. Physical security measures may also include items not visible to the naked or untrained eye, such as pressure mats and alarm sensors. Policies and procedures are written documents and unwritten rules which relate directly to asset protection and guide the security program. Security manuals and security post orders are examples of policies and procedures.

One of the best sources of information regarding current security measures at a facility is the security officer who is trained in observation and awareness and spends much of his or her time simply observing. Other sources may include the security manager or facilities and engineering personnel who are often asked to provide input on planned security systems. Security manuals, if updated, can also provide invaluable information regarding the security program.

Controlling the capability and motivation of adversaries is a difficult proposition for security decision makers. Motivation is created by the actual asset/target and is considered the reason for security breaches. Since organizations usually require assets to operate, the removal of motivation is not always possible. Most organizations must instead turn their attention to blocking the opportunity of crime. As seen in Figure 2.3, reducing vulnerabilities for security breaches leads to a reduction in incidents. Thus, security decision maker's strategic goal of countermeasure deployment is to reduce the opportunity for security breaches to occur by reducing vulnerabilities. Opportunities relate to targets in that removing or hardening an asset will lead to a reduction or an elimination of vulnerabilities. Asset protection programs integrate a combination of policies and procedures, physical countermeasures, and security personnel to protect assets against a design-based threat. The characteristics of asset protection programs include deterrence, detection, delay, and defeat.

Typical security measures of a comprehensive security program include governance, physical security measures, and security personnel. These security measures are inventoried during the risk assessment and categorized into key areas as described below. Governance:

- Security policies and procedures
- Security management plan
- Emergency management plan

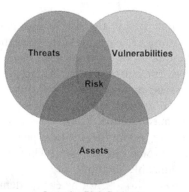

Security Risk Formula

FIGURE 2.3   Security risk formula. Copyright ©2019 by Threat Analysis Group, LLC. Used by permission. Additional information available from Threat Analysis Group, LLC via www.threatanalysis.com.

- Workplace violence prevention programs
- Crisis intervention policy
- Sensitive information protection policy
- Key control policy
- Visitor management policy
- Security escort policy
- Physical security system testing procedures
- Security force deployment practices
- Bomb threat policy and checklist
- Access control policy
- Key control policy
- Employment background investigations policies and practices
- Employee training.

Physical security measures:

- Alarm systems
- Control panels/communicators and keypads
- Door and window contacts
- Motion sensors
- Glass break detectors
- Object detectors
- Miscellaneous detectors
- Duress alarms
- Video surveillance systems
- Cameras
- Monitoring capabilities
- Recording capabilities
- Intelligent video/video analytics
- Access control systems
- Standalone devices
- System controllers
- Card readers
- Locking devices
- Delayed egress devices
- Alarmed egress devices
- Request to exit devices
- Door contacts
- Turnstiles
- Perimeter security systems
- Fencing
- Gates
- Bollards
- Lighting
- Specialized protection systems
- Metal and explosive detectors
- Ballistic resistant materials
- Metal detectors.

Security personnel:

- Proprietary security force
- Contractual security force
- Off-duty law enforcement officers
- Other personnel who serve in a protection capacity.

SECURITY ASSESSMENTS

The remaining steps of a risk assessment involve various evaluations designed to analyze threats, vulnerabilities, and overall risks, and a suggested course of remediation. Each step is a systematic approach to determining the actual risk posed to the assets, and specifically those that are mission critical. As discussed in Chapter 1, there are three types of security assessments: vulnerability, threat, and risk assessments. The final step of the risk assessment is to evaluate the costs and benefits of remedial measures, including redeployment of resources to protect higher risk areas or assets. This step often provides the greatest heartache to security decision makers since it oftentimes involves reducing security from one asset and redeploying those resources to protect more critical assets or at-risk assets. While the heartache is justified, the task is possible. It is possible. It is reasonable. It is defendable. In a nutshell, the risk assessment is designed to provide a continuous process of identifying critical assets, threats to those assets, and reducing any vulnerabilities by careful analysis and implementation of effective countermeasures to achieve an optimum level of protection.

Security assessments are very specific in nature to the type of organization or facility being assessed. Likewise, the methodology used must also be specific to the organization or industry. An assessment methodology designed for chemical facilities will not be useful for a university campus. An assessment methodology designed for healthcare facilities will not be useful for a garden style apartment complex. If an industry-specific methodology is used, it should be clear in identifying the type of facility for which it is designed and any limitations. Similarly, security assessment methodologies are designed to address certain security arenas. Currently, the division is twofold: physical security and information technology security. While the gap is closing through the process of convergence, the two fields still stand alone and require different methodologies.

Regardless of the type of organization or whether the assessment is physical security related or information technology security related, the assessment should state what critical assets require protection, what type of information is needed for each asset, and how the asset's loss, damage, or destruction would impact the mission of the organization. The assessment should also include a threat assessment, vulnerability assessment, and risk assessment that allows security decision makers to prioritize asset protection protocols. Finally, the assessment should make specific recommendation as to how to block opportunities for adversaries to attack and how to protect specific assets.

Once the risk assessment has been completed, certain assets may have a high critical rating, but a lower security level may be required for the overall facility. A typical qualitative approach to facility security levels is:

Security Level 1

Minimum Security: A system designed to impede some unauthorized external activity.

Security Level 2

Low Level Security: A system designed to impede and detect some unauthorized external activity.

Security Level 3

Medium Security: A system designed to impede, detect, and assess most unauthorized external activity and some unauthorized internal activity.

Security Level 4

High Security: A system designed to impede, detect, and assess most unauthorized activity.

Security Level 5

Maximum Security: A system designed to impede, detect, assess, and neutralize all unauthorized activity.

SUMMARY

This chapter explained how to identify the organization's assets, determine their criticality to the organization's mission, and inventory the existing security measures used to protect those assets. The next chapter describes how to conduct a threat assessment to identify human or natural acts that negatively affect the organization's assets.

NOTE

1 Focused Deterrence Strategies, Practice Profile, National Institute of Justice, accessed April 9, 2019, www.crimesolutions.gov/PracticeDetails.aspx?ID=11

REFERENCE

International Association of Crime Analysts. (2014). *Definition and types of crime analysis*. [White Paper 2014-02]. Overland Park, KS: Author.

CHAPTER 3

Threat Assessments

Karim H. Vellani

CONTENTS

Threat Formula
Threat Identification and Classification
Threat Information Sources
Assessing Threats
Emerging Threats
Threat Dynamics
Homeland Security Advisory System

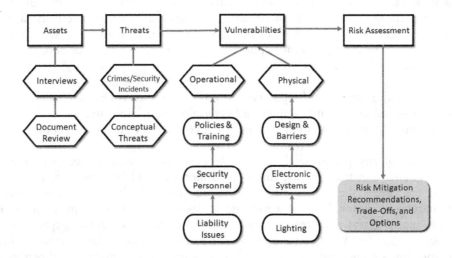

FIGURE 3.1 Strategic Risk Assessment Process, Copyright ©2019 by Threat Analysis Group, LLC. Used by permission. Additional information available from Threat Analysis Group, LLC via www.threatanalysis.com.

THREAT FORMULA

THREAT = INTENT + CAPABILITY + MOTIVATION

Following the asset identification and security inventory steps of the risk assessment process, the third step is to perform a threat assessment. As discussed previously, a threat is anything that can exploit a vulnerability, intentionally or accidentally, and obtain, damage, or destroy an asset. Threats are classified as either human or natural. Threat can also be defined as an adversary's intent, motivation, and capability to attack assets. Threat assessments, then, are evaluations of human actions or natural events that can adversely affect business operations and specific assets. Historical information is a primary source for threat assessments, including past criminal and terrorist events, while real time information is also being used with increasing frequency due to its availability in some arenas. Threat assessments can be quantitative or qualitative. Crime analysis is a quantitative example of a threat assessment, while terrorism threat analysis is normally qualitative. An important distinction is that threats are acts or conditions that can be adverse to organizational assets; adversaries are the people, groups, and organizations that are hostile to the assets. Adversaries are also characterized by their history of attacking assets, the intention to attack assets, and the capability and motivation to continue to attack assets.

Threat assessments are used to evaluate the likelihood of adverse events, such as terrorism and crime, against a given asset as well as other hazards such as natural disasters which may affect business operations. As such, the focal points of threat assessments are assets (targets) and the threats that seek to compromise those targets. Threat assessments also ask who the bad guys are by evaluating each threat on the basis of capability, intent, and impact of an attack. General threat assessments estimate the likelihood of adversarial attacks, including the type of adversary, their tactics, and their capabilities. Facility-specific threat assessments also define the number of adversaries and their method of operation or attack. With this information, security decision makers use threat assessments as a decision-making tool that helps to establish and prioritize safety and security program requirements, planning, and resource allocation. The process of threat assessment includes:

Threat identification – identify potential adversaries and their characteristics.
Asset classification – identify targets and determine their criticality.
Consequence/Criticality analysis – assesses the effect of an asset's compromise.

Whether security professionals are in the business of national security or in the commercial and industrial sectors, threat assessments should be conducted as often as necessary to meet the needs of the organization. While threat assessment is a continuous activity for the US government, businesses and other organizations should strive for annual threat assessments. Crime analysis is the most common type of threat assessment undertaken by US businesses. Crime analysis is done every year at minimum and is sometimes completed as often as once a quarter. Location-specific threat assessments at infrastructure facilities, such as ports, are carried out less frequently, but threat data is usually updated constantly. It should be noted that the biggest failing in threat assessments is a lack of specificity. For example, when the national terror alert system was first introduced, a move in the threat level required all industries and agencies, regardless of geographic location, to change their readiness level. Upon further reflection, the Department of Homeland Security adjusted the model to consider location or sector-specific information. Since this change, the United States has seen increases in threat levels to certain parts of the country or within certain sectors. For example, after the London Underground (subway) bombings, the threat level in the United States did not rise; however, US mass transit was put on alert. Likewise, the United States has seen threat increases in the Northeast while the rest of the country remained at a lower level. Similarly, it is the task of security professionals to use a targeted approach to threat assessment, whether it be targeted by geography or asset classification. Of primary concern with raising the threat level across all jurisdictions, or across all organizational operations, is the cost associated with a higher level of preparedness. Depending on the threat, security professionals can assess the likelihood and types of potential attacks if specific information is available on potential targets. Based on their assessment, specific, targeted countermeasures can be implemented.

Threat assessments evaluate the full spectrum of threats that can impact assets, including natural disasters, criminal activity, terrorism, safety-related accidents, and common security breaches such as unauthorized access. Each potential threat must be analyzed using all available information to establish the likelihood of occurrence. Gulf coast states such as Texas, Louisiana, and Mississippi, for example, have a wealth of historical data to plan for hurricanes during high risk months. Urban convenience stores also have ample evidence of their general crime threat level. Despite an awareness of general threats, security decision makers must refine their assessments to include specific scenarios in the protection of assets. A convenience store located in a high crime area that experiences an inordinately high level of crime on their premises should elevate their site-specific threat level and allocate security resources accordingly.

Asset attractiveness should also be considered in the threat assessment. Certain assets and businesses have a higher inherent threat level because of their inherent attractiveness to the criminal element. One example is jewelry stores. Despite no previous crimes at a particular jewelry store, the threat level for robberies and burglaries is still high. This is not to say that jewelry stores are inherently vulnerable, only that the threat level is higher. Another example of a business with an intrinsically elevated threat level is construction sites, which typically have a higher rate of accidents resulting in injury to workers when compared to other sites. Again, the threat exposure is there, but the vulnerability need not be. This concept will be discussed further in the vulnerability chapter.

THREAT IDENTIFICATION AND CLASSIFICATION

The best predictor of the future is the past. This same idea holds true when assessing adversaries. A thorough understanding of how adversaries operated in the past can assist security decision makers in predicting future adversarial operations. Without fear of jumping to conclusions, many security professionals knew immediately that Osama Bin Laden was responsible for the World Trade Center and Pentagon attacks on September 11, 2001 as soon as the second plane hit the World Trade Center. This accurate assessment was based on knowledge of prior attacks by a terrorist organization that the world came to know as Al Qaeda.

While the Al Qaeda example is universally understood in the security industry, the same logic can be applied to commercial and industrial targets. If security decision makers understand the adversary's perspective, effective protection measures can be efficiently allocated to reduce the threat. How do adversaries select targets? What types of assets have been targeted in the past? What are their intentions, capabilities, and motives? Bank and financial institution security professionals have made excellent use of threat information sharing to prevent certain crimes. Likewise, retailers have shared information to track baby formula thefts.

While the goal of any security decision makers should be to quantitatively identify threats, it is not always possible, and some threats must be assessed qualitatively based on assumptions and educated guesses. Crime threats can normally be quantitatively assessed based on historical crime data, while understanding a particular criminal must be qualitatively addressed. This is a key difference of crime analysis, the examination of historical crimes with little regard to the criminal him/herself, the adversary.

For this chapter, the focus will be on understanding the adversary or the qualitative perspective. In the crime analysis chapter, a data-driven, quantitative method will be discussed. So what type of information is needed to describe a threat qualitatively?

The type of adversary.
The adversary's intentions.
The adversary's motivations.
The adversary's capabilities.

Threats can be classified as either human or natural. Human threats include people working on the inside of the organization such as employers and contractors (insiders), people who attack from outside of the organization (outsiders), or a combination of the two. Natural threats are those events that are not man-made such as tornados, hurricanes, floods, fires, and other environmental events.

Human threats can be further categorized as insider, outsider, and insiders working with outsiders. Insiders may be sub-classified as criminal employees, disgruntled employees, criminal contractors, and disgruntled contractors. Threats from insiders are considerable given their security program awareness, opportunity, and unfettered access to the facility. Insider threats may be active and violent or stealthy acting as silent participants with outsiders. While workplace violence poses a high risk to other employees, insiders who are blackmailed or threatened by outsiders create a more difficult problem for security decision makers. Since the insider threat is typically the result of policies and procedures, security decision makers cannot rely on traditional security measures such as alarms, cameras, and lighting to thwart the insider threat. There are good mitigation strategies for protecting against the insider threat, though strong policies and procedures are among the most reasonable and effective. Policies should include personnel reliability programs, recurring background checks, and limitations on access to sensitive areas of the facility.

Outsiders may be sub-classified as foreign governments and militaries, gangs, criminals, extremists, and terrorists. The depth of classification should meet the security organization's needs. For example, the US Government classifies terrorists as political, religious, or environmental. Terrorist characteristics may include a willingness or desire to die or martyr themselves, inflict a high level of damage, injuries, and deaths, cause psychological pain to the citizens, and showcase their abilities to terror fund raisers. Outsiders may be motivated by ideological goals, economic gain, or personal reasons.

Insiders colluding with outsiders pose the greatest threat and may be classified as coerced or willing participants. Coerced insiders are unwilling participants in the attack forced by threat of harm to themselves or family, or by blackmail. Willing insiders may have a financial interest (bribes) or are ideologically sympathetic to the outsider's cause.

Threat assessments should consider the possibility of all three types of human threats and be based on reasonable intelligence available from multiple sources, including internal information, law enforcement data, red teams, specialists, media reports, and federal and private intelligence sources. It is rare that security decision makers will have accurate knowledge of a specific threat beforehand. Information may be incomplete or vague. As such, educated judgments must be made in defining a threat. The more complete the available threat information is, the better the assessment.

Adversary Motivation

Adversaries may be motivated by any number of factors; however, the most common motivations are economic, personal, and ideological. The most common motivation to understand is economic where the gain of valuables including money is the driving force behind a criminal attack. Economic criminals include robbers, burglars, and thieves. While this appears quite simplistic, it may not be as these criminal perpetrators may actually be driven to commit economic crimes for personal reasons. Drug addicts are a great example of this wherein the economic crime is committed purely to obtain valuables to exchange for drugs, a personal motivation. A similar example is the teenager who steals electronic music players, such as the Apple iPod, or basketball shoes, such as Air Jordan's, to raise their self-esteem and fit in with their peers.

As alluded to earlier, personal motivators are often emotionally driven, such as an angry husband who abuses his wife, or a disgruntled employee who commits acts of workplace violence. Motivation for the insider threats are often personal and driven by poor workplace management, real or perceived, resulting in an unhappy worker who bears a grudge usually against management. Personal crimes are sometimes difficult to prevent since they can be committed as a spontaneous act of rage or from a mental disorder. Andrea Yates, the Texas mother who drowned her kids in a bathtub, is an example.

Ideological motivations are linked to philosophical beliefs. Environmental criminals are those that seek to harm those they believe are damaging the environment. Take the example from California where environmental terrorists, such as the Earth Liberation Front (ELF), committed an act of arson at car dealerships that sold high fuel consumption sport utility vehicles. Other terrorist groups are ideologically motivated to protect animals and attack laboratories which experiment on animals. Of course, most of the world understands what motivates terrorist groups like Al Qaeda. The 1993 World Trade Center attack, while not indicative of Al Qaeda's capability, showed that terrorists were motivated to attack landmark buildings.

Adversary Capability

Assessing adversarial capability relies heavily on good intelligence. No better example exists than the failure of US intelligence to forecast the Japanese attack on Pearl Harbor during World War II. Without delving into the politics of this event, it is fair to say that incomplete and slow intelligence underestimated Japan's capability. Time and time again, history has shown that faulty intelligence over- and underestimates adversarial capability.

In the commercial and industrial sectors, where companies are in competition with one another, good intelligence is difficult to come by. Industry sharing of threat information is rare, but not impossible. Through informal organizations, some industries have successfully shared information about adversaries with each other in an effort to thwart a problem before every company is affected. Again, the banking industry does this with regularity and with great success.

For security decision makers, assessing the capability of an adversary includes the following factors:

Number of attackers
Skills
Knowledge of the facility's security
Types of weapons
Other equipment
Methods and tactics (deceit, force, stealth)
Means of transporting attackers, weapons, and equipment
Possible collusion with an insider.

Terrorist capabilities may include highly trained and skilled military units with shoulder fired weapons and explosives. Terrorists may also have the capability to develop unsophisticated nuclear weapons, known as dirty bombs or other improvised explosive devices. Terrorist capabilities also include the ability to fund operations, make fake identification including passports and driver's licenses. They may be trained in sabotage, hostage taking, and homicides.

Each threat should be specifically described in sufficient terms and relative to their ability to attack particular assets. This description is known as the design basis threat (DBT) because it forms the basis for the design of security programs. The design basis threat includes statements of intent, motivation, and capabilities of each threat. The description also includes the known tactics and methods, weapons, and equipment, and other details of past attacks by the adversary. Studying past security breaches is critical in forming the design basis threat.

THREAT INFORMATION SOURCES

As already discussed briefly, security decision makers should endeavor to seek out all possible sources of threat information. Threat information should come from multiple and redundant sources. Depending on the nature of the assets in need of protection, the sources of threat information may include internal information, security breach investigative reports, law enforcement data, red team penetration analysis reports, security consultants, media news reports, and both federal and private intelligence sources.

For security consultants and other security decision makers who are not intimately familiar with the facility they are assessing, the best starting point in gathering threat assessment data is through interviews and surveys of people more familiar with the site. A security consultant, for example, may begin a threat assessment by speaking with line level security personnel. This may include police working at the site, and proprietary and contractual security officers. Other line level personnel working on site make for good sources as well. Among the basic questions that should be asked of line personnel regarding each asset are:

What assets have been targeted in the past?

When were assets attacked?

Who targeted the assets?

Why was that asset targeted?

How was the asset attacked?

Were any remedial security measures implemented in response to the attack?

Many security conscious organizations also maintain internal records of security incidents, breaches, and crimes. This information should be reviewed by security decision makers on a regular basis while looking for trends and patterns that might indicate existing threats or point to a vulnerability that can be solved with remedial measures. An often overlooked source of threat information is prior threat assessments. Many organizations conduct risk assessments on a continual basis and have the associated reports filed away. For security consultants, this is among the documents requested from the organization during the initial days of a risk assessment, or even prior to setting foot on the premises.

External threat information should also be reviewed. This includes crime data from the local law enforcement where the facility is located. This is known as crime analysis and will be discussed in depth in the next chapter. Other external sources include private threat specialists. Especially useful for executive protection, there are some companies which specialize in threat assessments for other countries that go far beyond the basic information provided by the US Department of State. Other federal agencies, such as the Federal Bureau of Investigation, can share threat information. Even before September 11, the Federal Bureau of Investigation had created InfraGard, a partnership between the government and private industry to share terrorism, intelligence, criminal, and security information about critical national infrastructures.

ASSESSING THREATS

After collecting, reviewing, and summarizing threat information from all available resources, security decision makers must apply the threat to specific assets. Critical assets are the primary concern during the assessment; however, other assets may also be considered during the assessment phase. The goal of the assessment then is to estimate, quantitatively or qualitatively, the likelihood of occurrence that a threat will attack an asset.

The better the understanding of the intent, motivation, and capability of an adversary, the better the assessment. Of course, a history of attacks against a particular asset may be beneficial to satisfy the intent and motivation criteria. Capability assessment requires good intelligence about the adversary's current status. Looking back on the 1993 World Trade Center attack, it was quite apparent that Al Qaeda was motivated to destroy the World Trade Center towers, but their capabilities did not correlate with their intention. With the towers still an attractive target and assuming no intelligence that planes would be used as guided missiles, they certainly did not seem to have the current capability. Obviously any intelligence about the plane scenario before September 11, 2001 was reasonably treated as non-credible given no historical record of such an attack.

Because of a lack of quantitative data, scenario-driven, qualitative assessments are appropriate for high value assets that have suffered no prior attacks. A qualitative threat assessment is defined as a type of assessment which is driven primarily by the threat characteristics and are highly dependent upon the assessment team's skills. The

threat assessment team or individual, using a qualitative approach, considers each asset
in light of the given threat information for that asset, and develops scenarios that may
be used by adversaries to estimate the likelihood of attack. Using a qualitative rating
system, the threat assessment team assigns a linguistic value to each scenario.

An example of a qualitative rating scale is:

Level 5 – the adversary has a history of attacks as well as the intent, motivation, and
capability to launch a renewed attack.
Level 4 – the adversary has a history of attacks and the capability to execute an
attack, but may lack the intent and motivation to launch new attacks.
Level 3 – the adversary has a history of attacks and the intent and motivation to
launch new attacks, but lacks the capability to execute an attack.
Level 2 – the adversary has a history of attacks, but no longer has the intent, motivation, and capability to launch new attacks.
Level 1 – the adversary has no history of attacks and lacks the intent, motivation,
and capability to execute an attack.

As can be seen in the qualitative assessment scale, good threat intelligence is necessary to accurately assign threat levels. An example of a threat which can be assessed
qualitatively is weapons of mass destruction (WMD). WMD are made up of chemical,
biological, and nuclear weapons. Because these threats have a low likelihood of occurrence historically, there is little data to assess them quantitatively.

U.S. ARMY PHYSICAL SECURITY FIELD MANUAL/FM 3–19.30

THREATCON Levels

Specific security measures should be directly linked with THREATCON levels.
These considerations are:

THREATCON Normal. This THREATCON level exists when a general threat
of possible terrorist activity exists but warrants only a routine security posture.

THREATCON Alpha. This THREATCON applies when there is a general threat
of possible terrorist activity against personnel and facilities (the nature and extent of
which are unpredictable) and when circumstances do not justify full implementation
of THREATCON Bravo measures. It may be necessary to implement measures from
higher THREATCONs either resulting from intelligence or as a deterrent. The measures in this THREATCON must be capable of being maintained indefinitely.

THREATCON Bravo. This THREATCON applies when an increased and more
predictable threat of terrorist activity exists. The measures in this THREATCON
must be capable of being maintained for weeks without causing undue hardship,
affecting operational capability, or aggravating relations with local authorities.
While in Bravo, the installation should bring manning levels and physical protection levels to the point where the installation can instantly transition to THREAT-
CON Charlie or Delta.

THREATCON Charlie. The transition to THREATCON Charlie must be done on short notice. It is a result of an incident occurring or the receipt of intelligence indicating that some form of terrorist action against personnel and facilities is imminent. Charlie measures should primarily focus on manning adjustments and procedural changes. Security forces will usually enhance their security presence by acquiring additional manning or by adjusting the work-rest ratio (such as moving from a 3:1 to a 6:1 ratio). At Charlie, off-installation travel should be minimized.

THREATCON Delta. Since the transition to THREATCON Delta is immediate, Delta measures should primarily focus on manning adjustments and procedural changes. THREATCON Delta applies in the immediate area where a terrorist attack has occurred or when intelligence has been received that terrorist action against a specific location or person is likely. The security force's manning level is usually peaked in Charlie; therefore, Delta's additional manning will usually come from an augmentation force. Once in Delta, nonessential operations will cease in order to enhance the security and response posture. Normally, this THREATCON is declared as a localized condition.

Where a fair amount of threat data is available, a quantitative threat assessment is possible. A quantitative threat assessment is a type of assessment in which metrics are used to assign numeric values to the threat level. With vast amounts of prior incident data, a quantitative assessment can include mathematical projections to forecast future incidents. Using mathematical projections, quantitative threat assessments can achieve high levels of confidence, but the forecast range widens. Forecasting will be discussed in the next chapter since it is most commonly used with crime data. A quantitative threat assessment uses a numeric threat rating scale, normally using probability ratings. An example of such a scale is:

Level 5 – 90 percent or higher likelihood of attack because the adversary has a history of attacks as well as the intent, motivation, and capability to launch a renewed attack.

Level 4 – 70 to 89 percent likelihood of attack because the adversary has a history of attacks and the capability to execute an attack, but may lack the intent and motivation to launch new attacks.

Level 3 – 50 to 69 percent likelihood of attack because the adversary has a history of attacks and the intent and motivation to launch new attacks, but lacks the capability to execute an attack.

Level 2 – 10 to 49 percent likelihood of attack because the adversary has a history of attacks, but no longer has the intent, motivation, and capability to launch new attacks.

Level 1 – less than 10 percent because the adversary has no history of attacks and lacks the intent, motivation, and capability to execute an attack.

Despite a given threat rating, threats are not static, rather they are dynamic and rise or fall over time. Threats can and should be reassessed as needed and when new information becomes available. A good example might be the increased threat level near the anniversary of the Oklahoma City bombing, which itself coincided with the

Branch Davidian standoff in Waco, Texas between cult leader David Koresh and the Bureau of Alcohol, Tobacco, and Firearms (ATF).

EMERGING THREATS

Accurate threat assessments are critical for security decision makers; however, not even the best threat assessment can anticipate every possible scenario including the addition of more assets. Terrorists and criminals always adapt to and overcome updated countermeasures. In today's world of technology, state of the art counter-measures are outdated at an increasing pace and adversaries usually move at a similar pace. Security decision makers should keep abreast of the latest threat information using the best available sources of information. Using the threat infor-mation sources discussed above and adding to them where possible will assist in keeping the security professional abreast of the latest threats and the assessment report up to date.

The mitigation of emerging threats requires the ability to think and act like the adversary. Historical data, specifically studying the adversary's modus operandi (method of operation) sheds significant light on what security decision makers should watch for in the future, but truly thinking like a criminal or terrorist will allow security decision makers to think outside the current wisdom.

Maintaining a current profile of adversaries is important for the threat assessment. W. Dean Lee, Ph.D., in an article entitled 'Risk Assessments and Future Challenges' and published in the Federal Bureau of Investigation's July 2005 *Law Enforcement Bul-letin*, developed the acronym CAS-DRI-VARS to characterize adversarial tactics and methods currently being used by adversaries operating around the world.

Creative – applying innovative use of the ancient arts of unconventional warfare.
Asymmetrical – launching multifaceted physical, political, informational, and cyber attacks.
Secretive – cloaking in multiple layers and compartmented cells.
Deceptive – misleading and manipulative in their intent and behavior.
Resourceful – maximizing the use of available resources to achieve their objectives
Intelligent – capitalizing on detailed planning and orchestration.
Visionary – foreseeing the third and fourth order of effects of their actions.
Adaptable – evolving and adjusting with each new countermeasure.
Ruthless – striking with brute violence against the innocents.
Sophisticated – employing intricate ploys and strategies.

Beyond the above characteristics, security decision makers should continually study the goals and objectives that adversaries are attempting to achieve. Their motivation and intent must also be evaluated. Keeping a watchful eye on adversarial capability is by far the most important element in keeping the threat assessment current. For example, commercial businesses, retailers in particular, know that an incarcerated shop-lifter has little to no capability. Thus, they lobby for prosecution, stiffer sentence guide-lines, and strong enforcement of existing laws. The US government understands that terrorist capability is highly dependent on funding for terror operations and thus has implemented various worldwide strategies to stop the flow of funds to and between ter-rorist leaders and operations personnel.

An adversaries' skills deteriorate and improve over time as well. Without recent experience and training, some adversaries may lose their capability to successfully attack. Security decision makers, depending on the nature of the organizations they protect, can keep abreast of the latest tactics and methods of their most common adversaries. Here again, the US Government recognizes this and has also attempted to close down terrorist training camps in hopes of reducing the overall skill level of terrorists.

Asset knowledge is critical to adversaries, and moving targets are more difficult to execute successful attacks upon. While most businesses are not able to move assets to throw criminals off the track, they are able to keep information about some assets confidential and prevent adversaries from knowing exactly where they are, or how they can be accessed. While most criminals will be familiar with people who store their money under a mattress, few criminals will be privy to the knowledge of where the family's safe is located within the house. One of the more interesting home protection ideas from the past was the homeowner who posted a sign on his door which stated, "This house protected three days a week by Smith and Wesson. You pick the days." Amusing as the sign may be, one would have to believe that the unmotivated house burglar may have been deterred by the existence of such a sign.

Threats may also change depending on the availability of tools and weapons to the adversary. Arguably, the point of the now defunct assault weapons ban in the United States was to reduce the availability of high capacity weapons to criminals, in particular street gangs. Passports have long been sought after tools for terrorists and spies. In recent years, many countries have improved their country's passports to prevent duplication. Some countries have even cancelled all existing passports and reissued new ones to their citizens with better security features.

Opportunities can impact the threat level more than any other factor. Fortunately, opportunities can to a large extent be controlled by security decision makers through careful monitoring of asset vulnerabilities. An example of this is the assassination of John F. Kennedy in Dallas, Texas, in November 1963. Not only was the President traveling in an open top automobile, but the motorcade was traveling with many points of higher ground surrounding it. After that fateful day, the US Secret Service will not likely ever allow a President to travel in a convertible automobile. Reducing opportunities will be discussed in depth in the vulnerability assessment chapter.

THREAT DYNAMICS

While the daily assessment of terror threats applies primarily to security decision makers who are charged with protecting critical infrastructure assets, such as chemical plants, oil refineries, airports, and maritime ports, most security decision makers focus on terrorism as a high risk, low probability concern which needs to be addressed on an irregular basis. Once terrorism contingency plans, emergency procedures, and business continuity plans are established, security decision makers can once again turn their attention to the day to day issues that threaten the organization's assets. Everyday crimes are the most common threat facing security decision makers in protecting their assets, and a thorough assessment of the specific nature of crime and security breaches can reveal possible weaknesses in the facility's current security posture and provide a guide to effective solutions. A full understanding of everyday crime's dynamic nature allows security decision makers to select and implement appropriate countermeasures to reduce the opportunity for these incidents to occur in the future. Thus, the remainder of chapter focuses on the dynamics of everyday threats, identifying their key elements, and how to analyze these elements to block specific threats.

In discussing threat assessments thus far, ideas have been laid out in an effort to help the reader understand the conceptual perspective of threats. Everyday threats can now be discussed to enable the reader to understand the practical nature of common threats and to evaluate the threats to the organization's assets. There are a number of threat dimensions that the security decision makers should be well versed in before selecting countermeasures. As conceptually outlined previously, these dimensions include:

The facility's situational elements
Target/Asset characteristics
Adversary motivation and capability
Adversary's target selection factors
Opportunity reduction strategies.

Situational elements are those characteristics of the facility that create an environment which is more or less conducive to certain types of crimes or security violations. For example, a retirement home may suffer more from thefts within the community than from auto thefts due to the nature of the business. Another example of situational elements affecting crime may be the proximity of the facility to escape routes such as dense fields or wooded areas that can be used to conceal the offender on foot or quick escapes via highways used by the criminal in a motor vehicle. Situational elements also include the nature of the activities that occur on the property. Businesses face different problems than residential areas. The type of business that is conducted on a property may attract more crime. For example, bars and nightclubs may be more prone to assault type crimes and sexual offenses as inhibitions are lowered due to alcohol consumption. Hotel, motel, and other lodging facility customers are often victimized on or near the property because they are not as aware of the area's crime history. Criminal perpetrators know this and take advantage of the situation.

A target's characteristics are often determined by the nature of the business. Jewelry stores maintain two types of attractive assets, large amounts of money and small, easily concealed property. Sometimes, the characteristics of targets are self-evident. For example, banks can be assured that their primary concern is the money stored on-site, whereas retail stores' primary concern is usually shoplifting. Analysis of past crime data may reveal other threats that may not be evident. For example, a retail store that has a history of car-jacking robberies and assaults of customers may only be fully known by reviewing internal security reports or police crime information. Facilities with high levels of auto thefts can narrow the field of targets by using threat assessments and crime analysis to determine which cars are more theft prone. If the ideas presented in the asset identification chapter are followed, security decision makers will have identified the organization's critical assets and their attractiveness as well as past history of attack.

Adversary motivation and capability is key to understanding the nature of crime on the property. Criminals, more often than not, are rational decision makers capable of being deterred or enticed to commit their acts. In modern criminal justice, it is widely accepted that certain people can be generally deterred from committing crimes given swift and severe punishment. Specific deterrence measures can be taken at the property level by introducing countermeasures that increase the risk of detection by security personnel. For example, the presence of security dogs or closed circuit camera systems (CCTV) may deter many adversaries. By the same token, people may also be encouraged to commit crime by providing them with ample opportunity and a low risk of detection. An adversary's capability must also be considered. The same adversary who attempts to enter the property secured by security dogs may have the capability to bypass the dogs by way of poisoned treats or a distraction method. The security decision maker's goal is to reduce encouraging elements and increase the risk. For instance, hiding assets in a safe is often a good way to make valuables "out of sight, out of mind."

An adversary's ability to select specific targets is a process by which the rational criminal will select the easiest target that provides the highest reward. An open and inviting property provides a high level of opportunity for criminals. University campuses are a good example of an easy target since they are typically open environments with minimal perimeter security measures. It is quite a challenge to secure university campuses without creating impediments to the institution's primary goal of learning. Adversaries also select targets where the rewards are high. Malls, for example, provide ample auto theft opportunities for the perpetrator who specializes in stealing cars. One may think of target selection primarily as a force of opportunity. The goal, then, for security decision makers is to reduce the available crime opportunities at the facility.

Opportunity reduction strategies address the characteristics of the facility that either encourage or deter crime. Each facility will be different in terms of the solutions that are effective because each property has its own unique characteristics and unique threats. Unfortunately, what works at one facility may not work at a similar facility in a different geographic area. Opportunity reduction strategies may take the form of enhanced policies and procedures, physical security measures, or security personnel. Though the focus of this text is on cost-effective solutions to everyday crime concerns, the reader should not feel limited to using what is discussed herein, but rather is encouraged to be creative in their search for appropriate solutions for their particular concerns. While it may sound too basic, one of the fundamental opportunity reduction strategies for litter prevention is the installation of trash receptacles.

While this section is not intended to be comprehensive in addressing every possible threat, it will endeavor to cover the more common crimes that affect many facilities. Security decision makers are encouraged to study in depth the particular crimes that have historically occurred at their facilities.

Assault Type Crimes (Assault, Aggravated Assault, and Murder)

Assault, aggravated assault, and murder are evaluated together as their threat dimensions are similar. Assault type crimes can escalate, such that assault can escalate to aggravated assault and aggravated assault can escalate to murder. The facility's situational elements may either encourage or discourage assault type crimes. For example, bars, nightclubs, and other venues where alcohol is served can be prone to assault type crimes because alcohol tends to lower inhibitions and cause people to become more combative. South American soccer games, for instance, are also more prone to assaults than American football games, primarily due to the passion of the fans. European soccer fans were satirized in the 1990s in an old Saturday Night Live skit about Scottish soccer hooligans who were so aggressive and passionate about their teams that they beat each other up. It is the task of the security decision maker to determine what threats are inherent to their facility. Residential communities, such as apartment buildings, may also suffer from assault type crimes. Demographic and crime data would indicate that interpersonal, or domestic, assaults are more likely in lower socioeconomic communities.

Criminological data indicates that assault type crimes are committed by and against people who are similar in age, race, and gender. Thus, for assault type crimes, the target's characteristics will often be substantially similar to the adversary's. Schools provide a good example of this wherein the victim and offender are typically the same age and race by virtue of the inherent nature of schools. For security decision makers, threats can be identified using this information.

Adversarial motivation and capability for assaults, aggravated assaults, and murders typically lie with emotional issues. Here again, soccer games provide the emotional, passionate high wherein fans may express their excitement in violent ways. Gun control laws are society's method for reducing the capability of adversaries to commit violent crimes. While sometimes effective gun control laws are certainly not without controversy. Many schools have implemented zero tolerance policies for guns to protect students. Some have even installed metal detectors to reduce the capability of bringing a gun into a school.

Target selection methods vary for assault type criminals. While many assaults are driven by anger, some targets are carefully selected. Serial killers, for example, normally select their victims based on their characteristics. Ted Bundy's victims were attractive girls with long, dark hair normally parted down the middle, while Jeffery Dahmer's victims were young males.

How do security decision makers prevent assault type crimes? Those assaults, aggravated assaults, and murders that are not interpersonal are called stranger-initiated. Stranger-initiated assault type crimes are easier to prevent than interpersonal assaults. Opportunity reduction strategies include deterrence and response measures designed to create an environment perceived by the adversary as risky with a high chance of apprehension. Some assault type crimes are very difficult to prevent. Interpersonal assaults, for instance, which occur between two known parties, are not typically deterred by security measures. For example, an apartment community may have a security fence and gate, parking lot lighting, and high security locks on doors, yet none of these measures can prevent a husband from striking his wife.

Robbery

Robberies are a big concern for most security decision makers and adversely affect business in a number of ways, including injuries, loss of property, negative reputation, and liability. There are two primary types of robberies, robberies of people and robberies of business. Bank robberies, shoplifting escalation, and retail hold ups are business-related robberies. Personal robberies include car-jacking, purse snatching, and mugging.

A facility's situational characteristics which contribute to a robbery prone environment are easily identified by an experienced security decision maker once they understand the precise type of robbery impacting the property. Poor lighting, hiding places, and unprotected assets provide ample opportunity for personal robberies. Poor employee training, unfettered access, and easy escape routes can create an environment prone to business robberies. Among the better security concepts developed in recent years is improved parking lot designs at retail stores and shopping malls. Additional curbing has been used to control the flow, direction, and speed of traffic, all of which create a deterrence to robbery and other crimes by creating obstacles to robbers escape from the property.

Robbery target characteristics depend on the nature of the robbery. Purse snatchings obviously require an unaware female holding a purse, while car-jackings are limited to areas where cars can travel or park. Why does a convenience store experience more business robberies than another convenience store located across the street? Perhaps poor lighting and store windows cluttered with signs and posted at the robbery prone location are factors.

A robber's motivation is typically a rational balancing of risk and reward. If an asset is valuable (high reward) and unprotected (low risk), the probability of attack increases. Banks are susceptible to robbery because of the high reward for perpetrators. As such, bank security professionals institute various strategies for protecting bank assets. Capability is dependent on the type of robbery executed. Bank robberies take more skill than purse snatchings.

What does a robber look for in an attractive target? Regardless of the type of robbery, targets are rarely selected randomly. Obviously, the balancing test of risk and reward is a factor. Purse snatch robbers seek out unaware women to target with the reward being higher in higher socioeconomic areas.

Like assault type crimes, robbery opportunity reduction strategies vary with the type of robbery occurring on the property, but generally increased physical security measures, enhanced natural and artificial surveillance, and security personnel provide protection. Banks may implement silent alarms or install bullet proof glass to protect against robbery. Residential homeowners may install alarm systems with sensors mounted on all entry points and may even have the alarms monitored by a private company or the police. Convenience store owners may remove obstructive signs from windows to increase surveillance both into and out of the store. Car manufacturers have also started including automatic locks on their vehicles to prevent car-jacking. Oftentimes, simple and inexpensive changes in policies and procedures can have a positive impact on robbery reductions.

Theft and Auto Theft

Similar to robbery, there are many types of thefts. Situational elements at a facility are a primary determinant to the types of theft which occur. Retail stores are prone to shoplifting, while large parking structures experience auto thefts and burglaries of motor vehicles (BMV). Laundromats may experience high levels of theft from the coin operated machines, and schools may experience a large amount of bicycle thefts.

Each year the automobile insurance industry releases data on the nation's most frequently stolen cars and trucks. While it might surprise some readers that BMWs and Mercedes don't make the top ten list, it won't surprise most security professionals. Other cars, such as Hondas, Toyotas, and Chevrolets are easier to hide among the masses, are more easily fenced, or parted out for use in other cars. These characteristics lend certain cars to auto theft more than BMWs. What characteristics of your assets make a target attractive? Cigarettes are a good target for young men, hence their location behind the counter in convenience stores.

The motivation and capability of thieves is subject to the risk and reward balancing test. Grocery stores, for example, often suffer from high levels of baby formula and over the counter drug thefts because of the high value of both items. These items are often turned over to a fence, or middleman, who will pay decent amounts to the thief and then sell the items back to the retailers. The capability of a thief is limited only by their skills and creativity. Some thieves work alone committing petty thefts, stealthy thieves may be pickpockets, and organized thieves may band together to commit larger thefts.

Normally, what a property owner finds valuable about an asset is also the same characteristic that a thief finds attractive. Jewelry is a good example since it is valuable and easy to conceal because of its size. Financially motivated thieves will seek assets which they can later sell for a profit. Personally motivated thieves will steal assets which they can personally use, like drugs or expensive basketball shoes.

Opportunity reduction strategies for theft range from simple to the most complex, from moving an asset out of sight to installing vaults, alarms, and camera systems. Auto theft reduction may take the form of simple alarm systems to monitored tracking systems. Some grocery stores have taken to storing baby formula and over the counter drugs in locked cabinets. Clothing retailers have used electronic security tags to prevent their clothes from being shoplifted. Here again, it is incumbent upon the security decision maker to fully understand the type of theft experienced at the facility to implement appropriate countermeasures.

Political Crimes (Terrorism)

The United States will continue to face the risk of domestic terrorist attack over the foreseeable future. The Federal Bureau of Investigation defines terrorism as the unlawful use of force or violence against persons or property to intimidate or coerce a government, the civilian population, or any segment thereof in furtherance of political or social objectives.

What situational elements of a facility lend themselves to terrorism? Without delving into the politics of terrorism, it is safe to say that groups angry with a government's policies and actions can create the justification for terrorists to take action. Timothy McVeigh bombed the Murrah Federal Building in Oklahoma City because of his outrage over the US Government's actions in Waco against the Branch Davidians. Osama Bin Laden claimed that one of the reasons Al Qaeda is angry at the United States is because the United States established a military base in Saudi Arabia during the first gulf war.

Terrorist motivation and capability has been discussed throughout this chapter, but to add to that discussion it's appropriate to say that a motivated and capable terrorist provides for a high degree of threat.

Adversary's Target Selection Factors

It goes without saying that national monuments and critical infrastructure assets are likely targets. What other factors make a target attractive to terrorists? Areas where large amounts of people (targets) gather make good terrorist targets. Bus stops are frequent terrorist targets in Israel, while trains have been attacked in both the UK and Spain. In the United States, one of the biggest fears for homeland security specialists is a terrorist incident at a large significant sporting event, like football's Super Bowl or baseball's World Series. As Timothy McVeigh taught government security professionals, government buildings with a concentrated level of enforcement agencies such as the

Federal Bureau of Investigation and the Bureau of Alcohol, Tobacco, and Firearms make better targets than government buildings with other agencies such as the Social Security Administration or the Equal Employment Opportunity Commission.

Reducing the motivation and capability of terrorists are the prime methods for reducing the threat of terrorism. It might make one wonder whether or not Osama Bin Laden considered the risk and reward balancing test before launching the September 11 attacks. For now, that issue will be left to the experts to figure out. Reducing capability, as we have already discussed, is a good way to bring down the threat level. Certainly cutting terror funding and destroying training camps are good opportunity reduction strategies.

HOMELAND SECURITY ADVISORY SYSTEM

Despite its relatively short existence, the most well-known threat rating scale is the Homeland Security Advisory System. The system is qualitative in nature with color coded levels indicating the threat level. The rating scale is described below with general responses and countermeasure deployments that should be considered depending on the nature of the organization the security decision maker is protecting.

1. Low Condition (Green) – This condition indicates a low risk of terrorist attacks.

   Refine emergency operation plans and business continuity plans.
   Conduct drills of emergency responses.
   Train personnel on emergency response.
   Assess vulnerabilities and develop mitigation strategies.
   Continue to monitor threats.

2. Guarded Condition (Blue) – This condition indicates a general risk of terrorist attacks.

   Follow the responses and countermeasures described under Level 1.
   Ensure communications with designated emergency response personnel.
   Review and update emergency response procedures.
   Provide employees with information that would strengthen their ability to act appropriately.

3. Elevated Condition (Yellow) – This condition indicates a significant risk of terrorist attacks.

   Follow the responses and countermeasures described under Levels 1 and 2.
   Increase surveillance of critical assets.
   Coordinate emergency plans as appropriate with other businesses and law enforcement.
   Assess and refine mitigation strategies with the characteristics of the current threat.
   Implement additional contingency and emergency response plans as needed.

4. High Condition (Orange) – This condition indicates a high risk of terrorist attacks.

   Follow the responses and countermeasures described under Levels 1, 2, and 3.
   Coordinate security efforts with all organizational departments and law enforcement.

Taking additional precautions at public events and possibly consider alternative venues or even cancellation.

Execute appropriate elements of emergency response and business continuity plans.

Restrict facility access to essential personnel only.

5. Severe Condition (Red) – This condition indicates a severe risk of terrorist attacks.

Follow the responses and countermeasures described under Levels 1, 2, 3, and 4.

Prepare emergency response personnel.

Pre-position emergency response equipment.

Evacuate the facility.

CHAPTER 4

Crime Analysis

Karim H. Vellani

CONTENTS

Statistics for Security Management
Crime Triangle
Purpose of Crime Analysis
Data Sources
Law Enforcement Data v. Social Disorder Models
Advantages of Law Enforcement Data
Methodology
Return on Investment

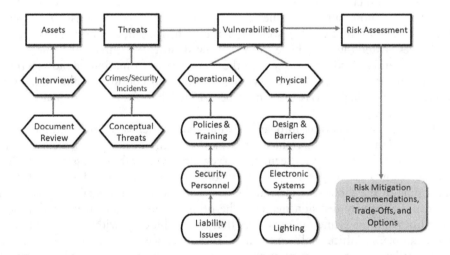

FIGURE 4.1 Strategic Risk Assessment Process, Copyright ©2019 by Threat Analysis Group, LLC. Used by permission. Additional information available from Threat Analysis Group, LLC via www.threatanalysis.com.

STATISTICS FOR SECURITY MANAGEMENT

Statistics are used in planning for the future. As a key component of a threat assessment, crime and security statistics guide the risk assessment process, help in the selection of appropriate countermeasures, monitor program effectiveness, and alleviate risks and the associated costs of risks. The use of information regarding crimes and other security incidents helps the security decision maker plan, select, and implement appropriate security measures that address the actual risks of the facility. Security decision makers, after assessing the crime problem, can select the most effective countermeasures that eliminate risk or reduce it to an acceptable level. Budget justification is also accomplished through the use of statistics since effective security measures will reduce the risk, and returns on security investments can be calculated and considered in the bottom line.

A common application of statistics in the security arena is the use of security reports and crime data to determine the risks to a facility. The security decision maker need not be a mathematician to fully utilize statistical data, rather he or she needs only a basic understanding of the various methods to use such information along with a basic knowledge of spreadsheet software (e.g. Microsoft Excel, Google Sheets, etc.).

The use of statistics extends beyond planning security at an existing facility. Statistical data may also be used to select and plan security at new facilities. For example, the real estate department of an organization may provide the security decision maker with a list of potential new sites, one of which will be selected based on, among other things, the threats or anticipated threats at the location. In this role, the security decision maker serves as an advisor to the real estate department by conducting crime analysis of the proposed sites and potentially security surveys of each site to identify vulnerabilities in an effort to select the locations that pose an acceptable level of risk to the organization. In this scenario, the security decision maker may gather and analyze crime data for similar businesses in the area surrounding each site to determine the threat profile at those similar businesses. The sites that have the least crimes can be evaluated further by means of a security survey which identifies potential or existing vulnerabilities. After the sites have been narrowed down by threat and surveys completed, the security decision maker has the necessary information to advise the real estate department on which sites to avoid and which to continue evaluating. In some organizations, even higher risk sites may be selected based on the company's overall business model.

Integrating crime analysis into an existing risk model is a fairly simple task for most organizations. Threat assessment information is the backbone of security surveys and defines the scope of the security survey and vulnerability assessment. Before embarking upon a security survey, security decision makers should have a thorough understanding of the threats, crimes, and security incidents at the facility. This information guides the security decision maker as he or she conducts the survey and looks for vulnerabilities and the crime opportunities that can be blocked with security measures.

For example, an office building security director concerned with a flood of thefts of employee wallets and purses may conduct a survey with an eye toward the opportunities that are available in the office suites. As he or she walks the offices, s/he may find that purses and wallets are readily visible from office doors and windows thus providing the opportunity for criminals to see the target property. A simple and cost-effective solution to this problem is to institute a "clean desk" policy whereby employees are encouraged to lock their personal belongings in their desks or a company locker.

A more serious security problem that the building security director may face is that of assaults and robberies in the parking garage adjacent to the office building. If the statistical information indicates that the assaults are occurring on the upper floors of the garage and the victim does not know the perpetrator, the security director will assess the security weaknesses of the parking garage. S/he may find that there are numerous unlit hiding areas that provide the necessary cover for robbers. By applying relatively low cost measures such as mirrors and lighting, the building security director can reduce the concealment areas.

It isn't that they can't see the solution. It is that they can't see the problem.

G.K. Chesterton from The Scandal of Father Brown

Crime analysis is a process in which a set of quantitative and qualitative techniques are used to analyze data valuable to police agencies and their communities[1] and for security departments and their organizations. Public sector crime analysts, those that work for law enforcement agencies, study information relevant to a police agency, including crimes, disorder, calls for service, quality-of-life issues, traffic collisions, and sometimes even fire and Emergency Medical Services (EMS) incidents.[2] In the private sector, crime analysts study similar elements for an organization's security function. According to the International Association of Crime Analysts (IACA), the crime analyst is

> absolutely necessary for identifying and specifying the problem at hand, analyzing data to understand why the problem is occurring, helping to develop when and where responses would be best implemented, and helping to assess the impact of the response on the problem.

Crime analysts in both the public and private sector assist their agencies/organizations with designing, implementing, and evaluating crime and loss control efforts.[3]

Definitions

The International Association of Crime Analysts (IACA) recognizes four major categories of crime analysis,[4] organized around several factors, including the nature and source of the data, the techniques applied, the results of the analysis, the regularity and frequency of the analysis, and the intended audience and purpose:

- Crime intelligence analysis
- Tactical crime analysis
- Strategic crime analysis
- Administrative crime analysis.

Crime intelligence analysis, the analysis of data about people involved in crimes,[5] and administrative crime analysis are not particularly relevant to the security risk management function and are not discussed in this chapter. Administrative crime analysis is touched on in the 'Security Measures: Personnel' chapter as it relates to staffing levels. Tactical and strategic crime analysis are the primary focus of this chapter. Both of these types of analysis have considerable overlap.

Tactical crime analysis, according to the IACA, is:

> the analysis of police data directed towards the short-term development of patrol and investigative priorities and deployment of resources. Its subject areas include the analysis of space, time, offender, victim, and modus operandi for individual

high-profile crimes, repeat incidents, and crime patterns, with a specific focus on crime series.

Tactical crime analysis data typically uses police/offense reports and may include repeat incident analysis, crime pattern analysis, and linking known offenders to past crimes.[6]

Strategic crime analysis, according to the IACA, is "the analysis of data directed towards development and evaluation of long-term strategies, policies, and prevention techniques." Its subjects include long-term statistical trends, hot spots, and problems. Strategic crime analysis usually includes the collection of primary data from a variety of other sources through both quantitative and qualitative methods, and includes trend analysis, hot spot analysis, and problem analysis.[7]

CRIME TRIANGLE

Reducing the opportunity for crime to occur is a strategic goal of security decision makers. The reason for this is the concept of a crime triangle, whereby three elements must exist for a crime to occur:

Motive
Capability
Opportunity.

With little or no control over a determined offender's desire, security decision makers focus their attention on the remaining elements of the crime triangle by attempting to block opportunities and remove motivation, both of which can be controlled to a large extent by an effective security program.

Motivation is created by the actual crime target. In the private sector, a criminal's motive is the asset(s) that the security program is created to protect. Here again, assets include people, property, and information. Since organizations usually require assets to operate, the removal of motivation is a difficult task, if it is possible at all. Most businesses must instead turn their attention to blocking the opportunity of crime. As seen in Figures 4.2 and 4.3, the theory states that blocking opportunities for crime leads to a reduction in crime.

The crime triangle is a simple, yet effective method for illustrating how a crime can be prevented. More complex methods for explaining crime causation exist such as the Routine

FIGURE 4.2   Crime triangle.

FIGURE 4.3   Crime triangle.

FIGURE 4.4   Expanded crime triangle.

Activity Theory developed by Marcus Felson. Part of this theory explains crime causation and may be considered an expansion of the crime triangle. There are six components that must be present for a crime to occur according to this explanation. They are:

Motivated offender – a person ready and willing to commit a crime.
Absent or ineffective handler – a person who influences the behavior of the offender. Handlers include parents, relatives, friends, teachers, employers, etc.
Suitable target – a person or asset that is of value to an offender.
Absent or ineffective guardian – a person who protects the target from harm. Guardians include police, parents, relatives, friends, and property managers.
Time – a period for the first four ingredients to come together.
Space – a place for the first four ingredients to cross paths.

PURPOSE OF CRIME ANALYSIS

Sir Arthur Conan Doyle in his Sherlock Holmes mystery, *A Study in Scarlet*, said, "There is a strong family resemblance about misdeeds, and if you have all the details of a thousand at your finger ends, it is odd if you can't unravel the thousand and first." It is on that basic premise that crime analysis is based. Whether one is working proactively to address security concerns or reactively in litigation or during the investigation of a crime, crime analysis is an effective tool. From an asset protection perspective, crime analysis is the identification of threats, actual and conceptual.

Examining crimes perpetrated at company facilities is commonplace in today's business environment. In larger companies, there may be a person or group of people who are solely dedicated to the function of crime (or intelligence) analysis usually working under the risk management or security departments. In smaller companies, the crime analysis function is carried by someone who also has other security management duties. Crime analysis may also be outsourced to a contracted analyst.

Crimes are analyzed in different ways depending on what one is trying to accomplish. Most commonly, facilities are ranked based on the crime level or rate. Generally, facilities with more crime or a higher crime rate are given a larger piece of the security budget, while less crime prone sites are given less security money. Crimes are also analyzed on a facility by facility basis allowing security decision makers to select appropriate countermeasures. The various types of crime analysis methods are discussed in depth later in this chapter.

Finally, crime analysis is used to assess and select appropriate countermeasures. Crimes that are perpetrated on a property can usually be prevented using security devices or personnel; however, it should be noted that not all measures are cost effective or reasonable. Certainly, a criminal perpetrator would be hard pressed to steal an automobile from a small parking lot patrolled by 20 security officers, though that type of security extreme is not reasonable or cost effective. Crime analysis guides security decision makers in the right direction by highlighting the types of crimes perpetrated (crime-specific analysis), problem areas on the property (spatial analysis), and when they occur (temporal analysis), among others. Using this information, it is much easier to select countermeasures aimed directly at the problem.

In summary, crime analysis seeks to:

evaluate actual risk at a company's facilities and rank facilities by risk level
reduce crime on the property by aiding in the proper allocation of asset protection
  resources
justify security budgets
continually monitor effectiveness of the security program
provide evidence of due diligence and reduce liability exposure.

Why would a security decision maker need to know how crime occurs? Understanding the factors that lead to crime, coupled with a comprehensive study of crime on the property, assists security decision makers in creating effective security programs to block opportunities for crime. Crime analysis seeks to answer the questions:

- What?
- Where?
- When?
- Who?
- How?

Answers to these questions help security decision makers better understand the particular nature of crime on a given property and formulate specific responses. The *What* question tells us what specifically occurred. For example, was the crime against a person or property, violent or not, completed or attempted? *What* also distinguishes between types of crime that require different solutions such as whether a reported robbery was actually a burglary.

Where answers the location-specific question. Did the crime occur inside the walls of the location, in the parking lot, in the alley way behind the site? If the incident occurred inside, did it occur in a public area or a controlled area? Determining the precise location assists security decision makers in creating additional lines of defense around targeted assets. For example, if the crime analysis indicates that a vast majority of loss at a small grocery store is occurring at the point of sale, then little will be accomplished by installing a lock on the back office where the safe is located. In this example, the crime analysis will rule out certain measures, but by the same token, crime analysis will also spotlight certain solutions, such as increased employee training or updated accounting systems at the point of sale.

The *When* question gives us the temporal details of each incident. Knowing when crimes are most frequent helps in the deployment of resources, especially costly security measures such as personnel. Temporal details include the date, time of day, day of week, and season that a crime occurred.

Who answers several important questions that help a security decision maker create an effective security program. Who is the victim(s) and who is the perpetrator? Knowledge of the types of criminals who operate on or near a given property assists security decision makers in selecting the best measures to reduce crime opportunities. For example, gambling casinos have used video surveillance for some time to track known gambling crooks. Also important are the potential victims of crime. Ted Bundy and Jeffrey Dahmer, like other more common criminals, select particular types of victims. Thus, an understanding of the people that may be targeted focuses a security decision maker's attention. For example, a residential apartment complex that caters to recently released psychiatric patients has larger responsibility to provide a safe environment given the fact that their clientele are not usually capable of protecting themselves. The oldest example of the *Who* question dates back to premises liability law itself where innkeepers where often found to be responsible for the safety of a guest when crime was foreseeable. People on travel are usually not aware of the area in which they are staying, and they also have little control over the security measures that they can take to protect themselves inside the hotel room.

How is the most consequential question to be answered by the crime analysis. How a crime is committed often directly answers the question *How* can the crime be prevented in the future. More specific *How* questions may also be asked. How did the criminal access the property? If we know that a criminal has accessed the property via a hole in the back fence of the property, efforts can be taken to immediately repair the fence. Other specific questions reveal the method of operation (MO). How did a criminal enter the employee entrance of an electronics store to steal a television? How did a burglar open the safe without using force? How did the car thief leave the gated premises without knowing the exit code? Obviously, the list of examples is unlimited, and security decision makers need to ask as many questions about the criminal's actions as possible to learn the most effective solutions. It is true that often the *How* will be the most difficult question to answer. This leads into a problematical area as crime sources can be divided into two categories, internal and external. Internal sources of crime can be employees and other legitimate users of the space, such as tenants. They are called legitimate users of the space as they have a perfectly valid reason for attending the location, but in the course of their regular activities, they also carry out criminal activities.

External sources of crime are illegitimate users of the space whose prime motivation for coming to the site is to conduct some type of criminal activity. Security strategies may be vastly different between legitimate verses illegitimate users of space. For example, there can be several barriers between the outside public access and a specific target. If the property or security decision maker is only concerned with someone breaking into an area, then they will be ignoring the legitimate user who may have an access control card, Personal Identification Number, password, biometric feature, or any number of other avenues of entry.

With these answers, security decision makers are better armed to attack the crime problem. Using a retail store as an example, the six questions can be applied. **What** specifically occurred? Let's assume the crime of concern is robbery. **Where** did the robberies occur? Since our example is of a retail store, we have two geographic areas – inside or outside. Did the robberies occur in the parking lot or inside the store? **When** did the robberies occur? Does the data show a trend during certain hours of the day? **Who** was involved? Were the robberies directed at individuals or the business? Were the robbers targeting victims known to them? **How** is the most consequential question to be answered by the crime analysis. How a crime is committed often directly answers the question How the crime be prevented in the future? How was the robbery committed? Was a purse snatched? Was the retail store's safe robbed? Being specific is critical to identifying the right solution to the problem. The specific type of robbery drives the decision to deploy one countermeasure over another. The differences between crimes explain why the solutions to each cannot be the same. In the robbery at a retail store, for example, the five questions make it is easy to be more specific in regard to the type of robbery occurring at the retail store:

- shoplifting escalation
- purse snatching
- car-jacking
- robbery of a person
- robbery of a business
- vehicle crime escalation.

DATA SOURCES

Security Reports

A valuable and highly encouraged source of data for security decision makers is security incident reports. As the name implies, these are reports of criminal activity and other incidents (parking, loitering, and security breaches) which are likely to be of concern to security decision makers. These reports may be generated by management directly or through contracted security companies. The validity of security incident report data is only as good as the policy which outlines the reporting and recording procedures, the quality of supervision over security personnel, and the verification process used to eliminate subjectivity and redundancy. Regardless of the quality of their security incident reports, management should be cautious not to exclude other sources of data and rely solely on in-house security incident reports. In requiring the collection of security incident reports, management can stipulate precisely what information is beneficial for their purposes and is contained within each report and useful for the subject organization.

Having said that, management should strive to include the following minimum elements:

1. Incident reported
2. Date of incident
3. Time of incident
4. Precise location where the incident occurred on property.
5. Victim(s), if any
6. Witness(es), if any
7. Modus operandi (MO), or method of operation used by perpetrator, if any
8. Follow up investigation(s)
9. Remedy.

The most successful use of security reports that the author has seen occurred in a large, multi-building apartment community. After spending over 40,000 dollars on fencing and access control systems to reduce the high level of auto thefts at the apartment complex, the apartment manager was distraught that the auto thefts continued at the complex despite the fact that the innovative access control system had been installed. As a consultant, the author was asked to analyze the situation and determine additional measures to be implemented to thwart the problem. After analyzing the crime and verifying the extent of auto thefts, a review of the apartment's resident screening policies was conducted and it was learned that management was not carrying out criminal background checks on prospective tenants as required by the policy and leases.

Apartment management immediately conducted the checks and learned that three convicted auto thieves were living in one unit of the complex. This information was corroborated by analyzing the auto theft data for the complex which showed that, though auto thefts occurred in all areas of the parking lots, they were concentrated around the particular apartment building where the three men lived. Because the men lived on property, they had full, authorized access to the complex and its parking areas. Management proceeded to have the three men evicted for failing to pay their rent on time and soon after the eviction was finalized the auto theft problem disappeared. This example shows the importance of following security policies and procedures as well as analyzing the crime statistics and other internal data thoroughly.

LAW ENFORCEMENT DATA V. SOCIAL DISORDER MODELS

Some companies have used social disorder models in place of crime analysis, though more and more are realizing the problems associated with these models. Since the publication of *Applied Crime Analysis* in 2001, the author has seen more than 90 percent of his security consulting firm's clients migrate away from using social disorder theories and toward utilizing true crime analysis. While those numbers are substantial, there are still many organizations who do not understand the concerns of social disorder models, the most problematic of which are discussed below.

Social disorder models are based primarily on criminological theory with little practical use since the primary source of their metrics is demographic data. Among the social disorder model's primary problems is the failure to publish the methodology used in arriving at the model's results. Without a published and peer-reviewed methodology, security decision makers cannot rely on the data and one can only imagine the implications of having a large part of a company's risk model rejected by the courts during litigation. Security directors have a responsibility to fully understand the risk model they use and be prepared to explain it in deposition and trial when representing their company in litigation.

Another problem with social disorder models is their reliance on demographic data. Though private firms collect demographic data more frequently, the majority of demographic data in the United States is only collected every ten years via the US Census. Because of the time lag to obtain the demographic data and subsequent time to develop the model from that data, results are not timely. Social disorder models also present some challenges in effectively removing race from the analysis since the base demographic data is based on an area's population and its characteristics including socioeconomic levels, education levels, and personal traits of the populous such as age, sex, and race. Contrary to Federal Bureau of Investigation crime reports and actual police data, large areas of the United States are considered high crime according to social disorder models, necessitating many companies to discontinue use of the model in large parts of the country. Some companies have faced charges of redlining, the private sector equivalent of racial profiling, resulting in a negative impact on corporate reputations.

ADVANTAGES OF LAW ENFORCEMENT DATA

Police data is the most widely used source data for crime analysis because it presents an accurate crime history for a property and is from an objective source. Since police departments don't have a stake in a company or any associated liability exposure, their crime data is considered reliable and unbiased. Though some instances of crime statistics' manipulation have occurred historically, rarely if ever are the statistics for specific facilities skewed. Most crime data manipulation occurs to overall city crime levels to serve various political goals. At the facility level, there is little reason for law enforcement agencies to skew the statistics.

Another advantage of police crime data is its vast availability due to extensive reporting, capturing, and maintenance of the crime statistics across most jurisdictions in the United States. While costs for the data vary from jurisdiction to jurisdiction, most fees are reasonable. The only downside to police data is the time required to obtain it from police agencies with the necessary time ranging from hours to weeks.

Various crime data and analysis methodologies have been published and used by many cutting edge companies in the protection of assets. Crime analysis methodologies have been published and subjected to peer review in various security and police textbooks, the definitive security book being *Applied Crime Analysis*.

Law enforcement data is almost always accepted by the courts, and in fact is sometimes required by the courts in determining foreseeability of crime. Though a particular methodology may be subjected to scrutiny, the data is normally admissible. The security decision maker tasked with testifying on behalf of his or her employer is safe to rely on crime data from police departments so long as the methodology used is sound.

Law Enforcement Data Sources

Law Enforcement Data Sources include Calls for Service, Offense Reports, and Uniform Crime Reports (UCR). These data sets are typically easy to obtain, and in the case of

UCR for large geographic areas are online at the Federal Bureau of Investigation website (www.fbi.gov). Local law enforcement data is normally accessible via Freedom of Information (FOIL) requests or under individual state laws regarding public information. For state laws and detailed instructions, contact the state's Office of the Attorney General.

Uniform Crime Report

According to the Federal Bureau of Investigation:

> the Uniform Crime Reporting Program was conceived in 1929 by the International Association of Chiefs of Police to meet a need for reliable, uniform crime statistics for the nation. In 1930, the FBI was tasked with collecting, publishing, and archiving those statistics. Today, several annual statistical publications, such as the comprehensive *Crime in the United States*, are produced from data provided by nearly 17,000 law enforcement agencies across the United States. Crime in the United States (CIUS) is an annual publication in which the FBI compiles volume and rate of crime offenses for the nation, the states, and individual agencies. This report also includes arrest, clearance, and law enforcement employee data.

The Uniform Crime Report, or UCR as it is commonly known, is the nation's crime measure. The UCR employs constant crime definitions across the country's many law enforcement jurisdictions and measures the following crimes:
Part I Offenses:

1. Murder
2. Rape
3. Robbery
4. Aggravated assault
5. Burglary
6. Theft
7. Motor vehicle theft
8. Arson.

Part II Offenses:

9. Other assaults
10. Forgery and counterfeiting
11. Fraud
12. Embezzlement
13. Stolen property – buying, receiving, possessing
14. Vandalism
15. Weapons – carrying, possessing, etc.
16. Prostitution and commercialized vice
17. Sex offenses
18. Drug abuse violations
19. Gambling
20. Offenses against the family and children
21. Driving under the influence

22. Liquor laws
23. Drunkenness
24. Disorderly conduct.

These crimes were selected because they are serious by nature, they occur frequently, they are likely to be reported to law enforcement, they can be confirmed by means of investigation, and they occur across all jurisdictions in the country. Developed by the Federal Bureau of Investigation, the UCR includes crime data for most geographic areas in the United States ranging from counties and cities to the nation as a whole. Intermediate areas such as state and metropolitan statistical area (MSA) crime data are also available. Though these areas are too large to be included as the primary focus of crime analysis, the methodology and classification system is what security decision makers should understand and use at the property level.

When using the UCR, it is best to examine violent and property crimes separately as they pose different concerns to security decision makers and may require the application of different security measures. To be certain, crimes should be evaluated individually and as specifically as possible. For example, the crime of robbery can be further divided into robbery of a business and robbery of an individual. Oftentimes, the security measures used to counteract these two robbery types are different.

Calls for Service

Though internal security reports and police crime data may overlap, security decision makers may consider both in developing a more comprehensive view of a facility's risk. Thus, the next step is to contact the local police department and determine what types of data are available by address. UCR data or actual crime information can sometimes be obtained by address. If available, it is often a superior source relative to Calls for Service (see UCR below). If UCR data by address is not available, Calls for Service (or 911 dispatch logs as they are referred to in some departments) should be requested from the law enforcement agency.

Calls for Service often serve as the basis for the initial crime analysis and provide for a broad portrayal of criminal and other activity at a property. Calls for Service consist of every report of crime, suspected crime, and activity called in to the police from a property. No other crime information source is as focused on a specific address for such a vast time span as Calls for Service, with the possible exception of in-house security reports generated by personnel operating on property twenty-four hours a day, seven days a week. These inclusions, by definition, omit the imprecise factor of unreported crime. Research has found that unreported crime accounts for a 10 percent higher crime index, though this is highly dependent upon the type of crime under observation. Despite the exclusion of unreported crime, Calls for Service still provide representative illustrations of criminal activity on a property.

Calls for Service are those crimes or other activity reported by a victim, witness, or other person to a local law enforcement agency via 911 emergency system and other channels. These reports may consist of actual crimes, from murder to theft, or suspicious activity, and other incidents such as missing children, motor vehicle accidents, and parking complaints. Whatever the concern, if it is reported by a person, it is noted by the law enforcement agency. The synopsis of the given incidents is included on the record along with the location, date, and time the event was reported.

January 3, 2020

Alvin Police Department
Attn: Records
1500 S. Gordon St.
Alvin, TX 77511

Re: **Public Information Request**

Dear Records:

I am writing to request the following:

Record Type: List of **all offenses/incidents** including dates, times, and case/report numbers (If a list of offenses is not available, Calls for Service may be substituted)

Record Format: Excel **spreadsheet** (If an Excel spreadsheet is not available, please substitute a different format, preferably electronic)

Date Range: January 1, 2017 to December 31, 2019

Address(es):

1234 Main Street

Please send request for payment and records to:

E-mail: kv@threatanalysis.com   **Fax:** (281) 494-5700
U.S. Mail: P.O. Box 16640, Sugar Land, TX 77496

For questions, please call (281) 494-1515. Thank you for your assistance.

Sincerely,

Karim Vellani

FIGURE 4.5   Sample request letter for calls for service.

From devastatingly influential to seemingly insignificant, these records exist as clues waiting to be examined in some Holmesian mystery, and because of their completeness of representation and maintenance by a local governing body, and as they operate independently from the security decision maker's interests, they can generally be considered objective, thus adding the first of many threads of reliability to the crime analysis conclusions. In addition to the more obvious crimes, Calls for Service add elements that may be of interest to management such as the above-mentioned suspicious activity, accidents, and parking violations which could be realized to be important in the holistic concept of crime prevention.

Being hyper-inclusive, no single set of data exists that rivals Calls for Service. As with any set of statistics, many more desirable possibilities can be derived by performing additional correlations such as sorting crimes by precise location on the property and by times at which they occurred. When more raw data is available in one's database, more meaningful cross-references and correlations are possible. One can consider that some of the fundamental ways people learn about various disciplines is through comparison, trial and error, or cause and effect methods. Calls for Service allow trends or patterns in crime activity to come to light which aid in the selection of appropriate crime countermeasures and provide for more enlightened comparisons between properties.

Among other considerations which users of Calls for Service should remember, Calls for Service data reflects the location where a complaint was made, which may or may not be the site of the incident. However, the location and precise nature of the calls can be verified and reliability enhanced when Calls for Service are used in conjunction with the local law enforcement agency's offense or incident reports, which will be discussed in depth later in this chapter.

Some newer Calls for Service systems encode data using the Federal Bureau of Investigation's UCR codification system, thus crimes can be easily differentiated from false reports and easily compared to city, state, and national crime levels. Older systems, though, must be converted to UCR through verification with offense reports.

Calls for Service are generally available from the local police department at a reasonable cost. In light of the availability and aforementioned considerations, Calls for Service data can be used effectively to produce a fairly accurate crime history of a property, distinguish any crime trends or patterns, and to compare properties.

Reliability of Calls for Service

It is important to note that Calls for Service or dispatch log accuracy varies by jurisdiction. Further, changes to incident management and dispatch systems may also impact accuracy even within the same jurisdiction. When assessing crime risk, Calls for Service and dispatch logs should not be used alone. Offense/Incident Reports are necessary to validate the Calls for Service or dispatch logs, specifically the crime type, crime location, and whether a crime actually occurred. Calls for service or dispatch logs alone, in many jurisdictions, are insufficient for these three elements.

An older study indicates that Calls for Service over a year's period would have a 90% accuracy rate for predicting future call volume and type, significantly higher than demographic data in predicting crime in the long run. However, it should be noted that Calls for Service prediction accuracy implies that one can predict future calls, not future crimes. It is absolutely incorrect to imply that the accuracy rate of Calls for Service somehow implies an ability to predict or foresee crime.

RELIABILITY OF CALLS FOR SERVICE DATA IN PREDICTING LONG-RUN RISKS

Reliability of Calls for Service data in predicting long-run risks (all calls, not just crimes):

One month of data = 50% accuracy
Two months of data = 60–65% accuracy
Six months = 80%
1 year (13 28-day periods) = 90%

Source: Spelman in *Crime and Place*, 135.

Offense Reports

Calls for Service are a listing of all reports called into the police from the property and normally include the reported incident, the date and time the call was made, and an incident number. In some cases, Calls for Service also tell us whether there was an offense report written, the disposition of the case, and possibly the UCR classification. In essence, Calls for Service disclose the initial details of crimes reported to the police from a particular location and include every report of crime, suspected crime, and other activity as reported by a victim, witness, or other person to a local law enforcement agency.

Offense reports are the written narrative of a crime investigation and are used to verify Calls for Service. This verification process is necessary as Calls for Service data reflects the location from where a complaint was made, not necessarily the incident location. Offense reports also confirm the type of crime committed as well as the date and time of the offense. In many jurisdictions, only select portions of the offense report are available; however, there is usually enough information contained in the public information section to accurately build a database of crime incidents. Generally speaking, crime analysis seeks to build the most accurate database possible using only public information. During the course of a lawsuit, complete offense reports including arrest records and final case dispositions become available by subpoena, but the goal here is to proactively address the crime situation to prevent injuries and lawsuits.

February 4, 2020

Alvin Police Department
Attn: Records
1500 S. Gordon St.
Alvin, TX 77511

   Re: **Public Information Request**

Dear Records:

I am writing to request the ***Offense/Incident Reports (Public Information only – I agree to all necessary redactions)*** for the following incident(s):

201802569
201800567

Please send request for payment and records to:

E-mail: kv@threatanalysis.com   **Fax:** (281) 494-5700
U.S. Mail: P.O. Box 16640, Sugar Land, TX 77496

For questions, please call (281) 494-1515. Thank you for your assistance.

Sincerely,

Karim Vellani

FIGURE 4.6 Sample request letter for ORs.

Offense Reports

More of an expansion of Calls for Service than an independent data source, offense reports, or incident reports as they are sometimes known, should clear up ambiguities and possible inaccuracies through verification of Calls for Service. Sometimes, however, an offense report is generated when police officers discover a crime independent from a call into the 911 emergency system. More precisely, offense reports are the written narrative of a Call for Service that resulted in an actual crime and includes the individual reports of all law enforcement agents, including officers, detectives, and supervisors who worked the case.

Although availability of offense reports may be limited by law because of inclusion of personal information, victim names, criminal methods, or ongoing investigation, security decision makers should attempt to obtain them from the local law enforcement agency while in the process of conducting crime analysis. Often, however, most states allow the report or a portion of the narrative to be released to the general public upon request. As with all information, security decision makers should seek access to as much relevant crime information as possible to help make knowledgeable management decisions. By no means should a security decision maker feel that they are in error for not including offense reports when they are not available, and on the contrary, one can only do what is reasonable and possible.

Levels of Analysis

Before delving into the crime analysis methodology, it is imperative to determine what geographic area is to be covered by the crime analysis. For the purpose of crime analysis, a hierarchy defines the geographic levels of analysis. Though one cannot mathematically quantify the importance of each level of geographic analysis, one can distinguish a relationship between, or order of importance for, each level. In defining each level, they have been listed in order of importance, and simultaneously in the order one should be concerned.

Stated another way, the geographic levels of analysis provide us with a micro view of crime and move toward a macro view of crime. The micro view of crime tells us what is happening at a specific property. The macro view of crime, on the other hand, tells us what is happening at properties like this. The micro view primarily deals with actual threats, while the macro view tells us more about the conceptual or inherent threats. The micro view tells us, for example, that .04% of the residents, visitors, and employees will become the victim of a violent crime at an apartment complex each year. The macro view would tell us that approximately 1% of the population of Houston will become the victim of a violent crime in Houston in any given year. The micro view tells us about a property's crime levels. The macro view tells about aggregate crime levels. From a public health perspective, the macro view of risk tells us that people who don't want to wear a helmet while cycling, will not cycle, and therefore may put their overall health at risk. The public health perspective from a micro view tells us that I am 70% less likely to have a brain injury while wearing a helmet and cycling.

Place (Facility or Site)

From a security decision maker's perspective, control of crime is normally limited to the organization's facilities. This geographic area is the fundamental level of analysis for

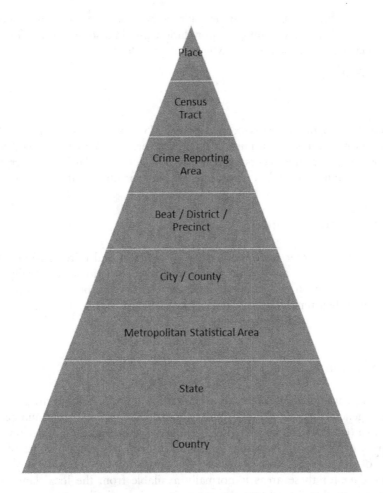

FIGURE 4.7   Hierarchy of data. Copyright ©2019 by Threat Analysis Group, LLC. Used by permission. Additional information available from Threat Analysis Group, LLC via www.threatanalysis.com.

both crime prevention and liability prevention as security personnel have the most ability to regulate most facets of its use. The primary source of crime data for this level is Calls for Service and offense reports, and inhouse security reports, if they are available. Though security may influence neighboring areas with a diffusion of benefits, a process by which security measures implemented at one property may prevent crime at another location, the goal is to prevent crime at the controlled facility. For example, a security decision maker may be able to reduce crime on neighboring properties by increasing the lighting on his or her property as the light cannot be wholly contained to one property. Thus, security measures may positively impact neighboring properties indirectly.

As we move away from the property level in the crime analysis, the geographic areas get larger and less easily influenced. The smaller areas that can be analyzed include Census Tract, Crime Statistical Reporting Areas, and Beats, Districts, or Precincts. Police departments sometimes maintain crime data for these areas and they are marginally useful in crime analysis, but they do assist us in determining how our area compares to other areas in the same city. Whenever possible, the population should also be known for these areas so we may calculate the crime rate (see Methodology below).

Census Tract

Census tracts are geographic areas defined by the US Census Bureau for population and demographic purposes. In some instances, law enforcement agencies accumulate crime statistics by census tract. Since this occurs infrequently, it is not a standard level of crime analysis but may be included if the local law enforcement agency maintains data by census tract.

Crime Statistical Reporting Area

A reporting area is another uncommon level of analysis and criteria for their creation may diverge significantly across law enforcement jurisdictions. Generally, reporting areas are small, homogeneous areas created for the sole purpose of supporting crime data collection. When reporting area data is available, it may be used to assist with the crime analysis of an individual property.

Beat, District, or Precinct

Patrol beats are common geographic zones in metropolitan areas that are created by law enforcement agencies to meet their resource allocation objectives – the number of patrol units in an area (beat). Beats are sometimes grouped together and fall under one command center, district, or precinct. The actual land area of beats, the total number of beats, and the number of districts/precincts overseeing the beats can vary considerably in different cities. Crime data for these areas is normally available from the local law enforcement agencies on an annual basis and oftentimes maintain crimes similar to those in the UCR.

Larger areas may also be considered in the crime analysis. These areas include cities and counties, states, metropolitan statistical areas, and the nation and are all included in the UCR. The advantage to these geographic areas is that population data is available; however, their sheer size creates a disadvantage.

City/County

City and county crime data is available from the UCR and encompasses crime information for an entire law enforcement jurisdiction. County data includes only the crime statistics for rural (unincorporated) areas and not the information for cities within the county.

Metropolitan Statistical Area (MSA)

Another geographic area created purely for crime statistical purposes, MSAs account for approximately 76% of the total US population. MSAs consist of core cities of over 50,000 people and the surrounding suburban regions.

State

Similar to city and county data, state data can be found in the UCR and includes crime information for the entire state. This level of analysis details crime statistics for individual states and is often available from a state law enforcement agency.

Nation

Crime statistics for the nation are primarily available through the UCR program, via actual crime information and estimations for the occasional law enforcement jurisdictions who are not involved in the program. While larger geographic areas are easier to analyze due in large part to the availability of crime statistics, crime at each facility tells the more accurate story.

METHODOLOGY

The best method for learning the true risk at a facility is to analyze internal security reports and verified police data using a computer spreadsheet application or database software program. Once this information is in a usable format, a number of basic and advanced statistical analyses can be performed. The security decision maker will adapt the analysis to best meet the needs of his or her organization. While some security decision makers prefer highly detailed charting and graphing functions, others prefer to view the raw numbers. Either way is fine as long as the security decision maker is comfortable and able to disseminate the information to those that need the data. Among the statistical tools available to the security decision maker are crime-specific analysis, MO analysis, crime rate ranking, forecasting, temporal analysis, spatial analysis, and pattern analysis.

The crime analysis methodology outlined below has been tested in the courts and in private organizations, is based on a logical foundation, and provides useful information for a security decision maker. By no means is the methodology limited to what is described, as to a large extent, security decision makers may find that the information requires customization to meet company needs. Whatever the case, this methodology provides the cornerstone from which to build a more comprehensive analysis when necessary. It should be noted that not every type of analysis is required for every organization.

Security decision makers may consider aligning their crime analysis methodology with case law on issues of foreseeability to assist in mitigating claims of negligent security. Most states use crime data to determine if crime was foreseeable (predictable) and if management is on notice of crime. If crime is foreseeable on the property, property owners and/or managers normally have a duty to protect their invitees (customers, employees, etc.) against it. Though a foreseeability analysis is a good place to start the process of crime analysis, it certainly need not be the end. To be proactive, security decision makers require more data analysis to efficiently track security deficiencies and deploy more effective security measures.

The International Association of Professional Security Consultants' Forensic (IAPSC) Methodology, a peer-reviewed and consensus-based guideline, addresses both time and distance in assessing the crime impact at a property. The methodology states, in part, that security experts should consider relevant crimes on the subject property for a three- to five-year period prior to the date of the incident. The IAPSC recognizes that criminology studies and related research have generally found that crime in the area may or may not be relevant to the subject property. Courts have typically accepted two to five years of historical crime data in premises liability lawsuits, while for security purposes, three years of crime data is recommended.

At this point, the Calls for Service and corresponding offense reports should have been requested and received from the law enforcement agencies and inhouse security reports will have been incorporated into the database or spreadsheet application. Though crime analysis can be conducted using paper and pen, software applications are recommended as it allows for quicker data entry, sorting, and analysis of the data. Software applications also allow users to easily create graphs, charts, and maps. A typical spreadsheet will start with keying in basic elements from the Calls for Service and offense reports, including:

- Site (address and/or site number)
- Reported crime – This information is located on the Calls for Service sheets and may also be listed in the offense report.
- UCR code – Since most police departments do not include this code, this may be inserted later.
- UCR description/actual crime committed – The first page of the offense report will normally have the final crime classification.
- Date – This is the date on which the crime occurred, not the date reported.
- Time – This is the time at which the crime occurred, not the time reported.
- Day of week – This may be inserted manually if not listed on the offense report.
- Offense report (or incident) number – Listed on the offense report.
- Crime location – This is a description for advanced analysis and may not be known or gleaned from the offense reports. As mentioned earlier, in reviewing a crime scene location, it is often important to determine whether the crime is internally or externally generated.

Since most law enforcement agencies use different offense report forms, at first it may be difficult to ascertain each of the elements which are to be included in the database; however, given some practice with each law enforcement agency's forms, the process is rather routine. Once all the information from the offense reports has been entered, security report information can be entered, taking caution not to duplicate entries from the offense reports. Additional codes may be created for incidents of concern to management that are not included in the UCR coding system. The crime analysis format should be versatile and expandable so when new data becomes available or when management needs change, different types of analysis may be added.

Once the data, including Calls for Service, offense reports, and inhouse security reports for the property, has been assembled, it can be translated into a standardized set of codes that denote actual crimes or plain language (e.g., theft, murder, etc.). To ease comparisons, the UCR definitions and codification system should be used as it is simplistic and other data sets already use it. If anything other than UCR codes are provided then the crimes must be transferred to UCR codes. This is required because police reports may differ in how they are worded or coded from the norm or from one another, and to simplify matters the UCR coding system is recommended as it includes a fairly complete listing of possible crimes, which will make analysis that much more complete.

Using this main database, security decision makers can sort information by site, by type of crime, by date, time, or day of week. The database will also allow the security decision maker to begin performing basic calculations such as totals for specific types of crime at each site and the average crimes per site. One may also be able to discern any patterns or trends in crime types or temporally (date, time, day).

Another piece of data that should be entered on the spreadsheet is the site's annual traffic level, which is generated from internal records. The traffic level will be used as the site's population to calculate crime rates and trends. Traffic levels may also be calculated using transaction counts or other data which reflects the number of persons at a property. For example, at an apartment complex, they may use 2 residents per one-bedroom apartment unit and 3 residents per two-bedroom apartment unit. Thus, for a 100 unit apartment building which has 50 two-bedroom units and 50 one-bedroom units, the population of the apartment building would be 250 people:

2 people × 50 one bedroom units = 100 people
+
3 people × 50 two bedroom units = 150 people
=
250 people.

Most security decision makers would add other people who are frequently on the premises including employees such as maintenance and leasing personnel.

One large fast food restaurant chain uses a standard number of customers per transaction based on historical records for the entire company. For every transaction, there are on average 2.1 people. Thus, if the restaurant has a daily transaction count of 4000 transactions, they will have had 8400 persons through the restaurant on that day.

In an effort to take geographic variables into account, some companies use a different multiplier for each region or district. Though this is more accurate, the multiplier may be difficult to discern. Security decision makers should use whatever multiple is reasonable.

Several different types of analysis make up a crime analysis as a whole. These include temporal analysis, crime-specific analysis, crime rate analysis, spatial analysis, MO analysis, and forecasting. Each of these modes of analysis examines an aspect of crime's impact at a facility, identifies crime patterns and trends, and indirectly identifies security measures that are appropriate to counter the known risks.

Crime-Specific Analysis

Though the Federal Bureau of Investigation's UCR coding system breaks crimes down into their specific legal elements, it is often beneficial to break crimes down into sub-levels for security purposes. Crime-specific analysis focuses not only on the type of crimes committed at a facility by enumerating the amount of crimes such as robberies and assaults, but also whether the robbery victim was a business or the victim was an individual. Further specificity aids management in knowing the specific type of problem, to what degree it exists, and indirectly what specific crime prevention measures can be used to reduce the opportunity for those problems, if not eradicate them completely. Another benefit of this type of analysis is that a breakdown by crime will help to indicate whether the asset targeted was a person or property, whether the crime was violent or not, the resulting loss or damage to that particular target, and the implications of that loss or damage. As already mentioned, this data should be coded in compliance to the Federal Bureau of Investigation's UCR system for ease of comparison among properties and to create uniformity among the data sets. However, further information may be included beyond the UCR code and description including victim type, asset targeted, and location of crime.

Crime Rate Analysis

Crime rates, like most statistics, exist to actively represent events which transpired or to extend that number to forecast future occurrences. Within crime analysis, crime rates assess a property's risk of violent and property crime victimization. The calculation of the crime rate is fairly uncomplicated and requires little more than two pieces of data, one a management derived figure and the other gleaned from the crime statistics. Simply stated, the violent crime rate is calculated by dividing the number of crimes by the traffic level and then multiplying by 1000, the number commonly used to compare crime rates across the various levels of geographic analysis. Property crime rates, on the other hand, use the number of property targets as the denominator. Most calculations of crime rates are not estimates of crime risk, because inappropriate measures of the crime opportunities (targets) are used for the denominator in the calculations. For example, burglary rates are calculated by dividing the number of burglary events by the population of the area being studied. The appropriate denominator is the number of buildings in the area. Crime rates should be calculated using the number of targets as the denominator. In other words, for crimes against persons, the denominator should be the number of persons. For crimes against properties, the denominator should be the number of items under consideration.

Crime rates are one of the best methods for comparing crime at various facilities. Crime rates should be used whenever possible as they offer the most accurate reflection of crime at a site by taking not only the crime level into account but also the traffic level. By utilizing the population and transaction counts discussed above, a security decision maker is able to make apples-to-apples comparisons of facilities under his or her control, to similar businesses in the area, and to larger geographic areas such as the city in which the facility is situated. Comparisons may also be made to other geographic areas for which crime statistics are available including census tracts, police beats, MSAs, states, and the nation as a whole. Again, it is important to note that the larger the geographic area, the less relevant the comparison. Crime analysis emphasizes the smallest geographic area possible, the property level.

Crime rates are calculated using the following formula:

Violent Crime Rate (VCR) = (Total Violent Crime/Population) × 1000

Note that the crime rate refers to violent crimes, which have an easily countable target via the site's traffic level (population). Other crimes, such as auto theft, will have calculable crime rates if the target count is available. For example, the auto theft crime rate can be figured using the auto theft level and the annual number of vehicles on the property (traffic level). Thus, with 17 auto thefts and an average of 3500 cars per day last year, our auto theft rate is 4.86 per 1000 autos:

Auto Theft Rate = (Total Auto Theft/Population) × 1000
Auto Theft Rate = (17/3500) × 1000

Auto Theft Rate = (0.00486) × 1000
Auto Theft Rate = 4.86

Using this formula for each site allows us to accurately compare risk levels at different sites. This formula may be applied to each year of the crime analysis to formulate trends and patterns over time which are easily discernible when graphed. Burglary rates are calculated by dividing the number of burglary events by the number of targets. In a large apartment community with 2000 units and 5000 residents, the appropriate denominator for calculating the property crime rate is 2000, while the denominator for calculating the violent crime rate is 5000. Taking this example further, if the community experienced 25 violent crimes and 200 property crimes during the preceding year, the violent crime rate is .005 [(25/5000)*1000], while the property crime rate is 100 [(200/2000)*1000]. Simply stated, for crimes against persons, the denominator should be the number of persons. For crimes against properties, the denominator should be the number of properties.

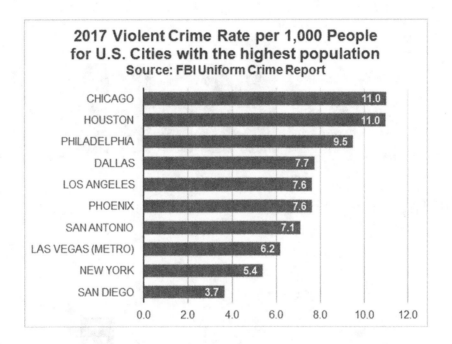

FIGURE 4.8   Crime rate graph.

Temporal Analysis

Various methods for understanding a facility's crime peaks and valleys are available to the security manager. Temporal analysis, or the analysis of time, is among the most effective tools for allocating security resources. Patterns can be considered including time of day, days of week, week of month, seasonal trends, and, on the extreme, crime trends during full moons. If there is historical evidence that particular crimes occur during certain periods, security can focus additional crime defense measures during those time periods. Deploying security measures during high crime times can save the security department money and generate cost avoidances that can be used in calculating Return on Investment.

Temporal analysis is the consideration of time periods when crimes occur. It allows the security decision maker to effectively allocate scarce security resources during peak crime periods. Though other security practices can be adjusted and modified based on temporal analysis, it's most common use is in the efficient scheduling of security and protective force personnel.

There are many ways of analyzing the temporal factors of crime, including time of day, days of week, quarters, and seasonal trends. When a temporal pattern exists, we can deploy resources during the peak times to block the opportunities for crimes. Temporal analysis can significantly cut down the cost of a security force.

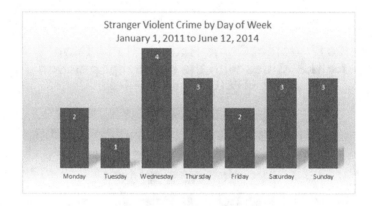

FIGURE 4.9   Temporal analysis: day.

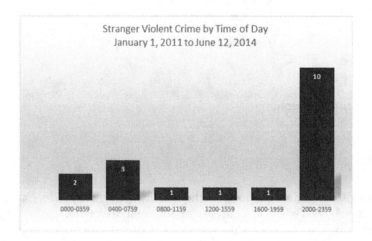

FIGURE 4.10   Temporal analysis: time.

Spatial Analysis

Crime analysis is focused on *wheredunit* rather than *whodunit*, that is where the crime occurred, rather than an offender-specific crime analysis. Spatial analysis is another critical analysis that helps deploy security resources efficiently by assessing the location of crime within the facility. For larger properties, spatial analysis can be very useful, but even for smaller facilities, an understanding of whether crimes are occurring inside the facility or outside in common areas such as parking lots can be beneficial in selecting countermeasures. Hot spot analysis is a form of spatial analysis where hot spots are small places in which the occurrence of crime is so frequent that it is highly predictable.

Crime is "seldom randomly or evenly distributed across space."[8] Identifying high crime areas, or hot spots, can be useful for the development and evaluation of security responses and to provide security decision makers with information to prevent and respond appropriately. Although there is no widely accepted definition of a hot spot, according to the IACA, it is defined as "a group of similar crimes committed by one or more individuals at locations within close proximity to one another."[9] While there is no standard threshold for what constitutes a hot spot or high crime area,[10] they are characterized by:

1. A relatively high volume of crime;
2. Evidence of spatial clustering; **and**
3. An observable pattern of time occurrence and duration.[11]

In short, there is no firm rule as to how much crime there is in a micro place before it can be categorized as a hot spot. Instead, they are defined as such only when there is an extremely high level of criminal activity relative to other places in the city. Hot spots are identified using clustering, that is repeat events or crimes at the same place.

- Specifically, where does the problem stem from?
- Through what door did an intruder enter the property?
- At what point did an attack take place between the building exit and the parking garage?
- Around what certain corner was an attacker hiding before perpetrating the crime?

Knowing the answers to these questions can help in determining the nature of defenses which are at the security team's disposal. For example, if the security decision maker of an office building realizes that the parking garage is the paramount source of crime, emphasizing security for the suites inside the building would certainly do little to address the problem at hand.

Spatial analysis focuses on specific targets within the property and the security measures that were penetrated. For example, if a crime pattern has been established at a particular location within the facility, the security decision maker can review the security measures currently in place as well as the access points to that area and mark them for improvement by way of personnel, physical measures, or simple policy and procedure changes.

Spatial analysis is aided by facility blueprints and other schematics of the site to help pinpoint crime scenes. If the security decision maker finds that a number of crimes are clustering in the same location, s/he can then look to see what opportunity there is for crime to occur there and make attempts to block the incidents in the future.

MO Analysis

Modus operandi is a term commonly heard in television crime dramas and refers to the method of operation, or MO, used by a criminal perpetrator. Crime profilers often use the term *signature* when referring to a criminal's MO. Dependent upon the availability of details culled from inhouse security reports, offense reports, or interviews with victims, witnesses, and offenders, MO analysis determines an offender's criminal tactics that separate their crimes from other criminals.

From MO analysis, certain crime features become known. Some crimes such as purse snatchings on days when people are to be paid from their jobs might make sense when one considers what has been learned about rational choice theory and routine activity theory, or that home burglaries tend to occur when the home is unattended or that shoplifting tends to occur more frequently when a business is sparsely staffed. If such a fact in a given area is known and known enough by criminals, then the seed of criminal activity can be planted and come to fruition when such times arrive. Such occurrences happen for a reason.

Forecasting

Forecasting is a useful crime analysis technique that allows the security decision maker to mathematically project future crime by using the facility's crime history. Forecasting can project specific crime concerns as well as the times, days, and locations of these future crimes. For forecasting to be accurate, larger samples of data are beneficial, typically at least three years of data. The larger the database, the more accurate are the forecasts.

Once the various statistical analyses are complete, the security decision maker finds him- or herself well equipped to make decisions about future allocations of security resources. The crime analysis results should be disseminated among as many departments in the company as feasible to obtain feedback and possible solutions. Most importantly, the information should be distributed to line security officers and supervisors so they are aware of the threats and can work toward reducing the opportunity of these crimes. Obviously, the information should be as specific as possible to enhance the detection and protection function with which the security force is charged.

RETURN ON INVESTMENT (ROI)

In today's corporate environment, it is important for all departments to show bang for the buck, and this philosophy applies to the security organization all too much as often their budget is among the first to be cut. Showing a return on investment simply means that security measures are either paying for themselves or better, adding to the bottom line. Return on security investment is important as it helps the security decision maker justify costs and obtain future budget monies. Some security programs will not pay for themselves while others actually become a profit center.

For example, crime analysis almost always pays for itself as it helps the security decision maker select the most appropriate security solutions for specific problems and efficiently deploy the resources. Without it, the effective security decision maker has little to guide him or her toward effective, adequate, and reasonable solutions. More expensive countermeasures such as CCTV systems and personnel are harder to show return on investment; however, over the long run, these measures become relatively inexpensive when compared to the financial turmoil that can occur from even just one indefensible claim of negligent security.

A case study published by the American Society for Industrial Security International in Volume 6 of their *Security Business Practices Reference* discussed a retail company that was able to generate a 7 percent saving on their projected security budget using crime analysis. In order to select and deploy appropriate security measures, the retailer outsourced their crime analysis needs to the author's security consulting firm. Using the crime data generated for each of their stores, the retailer expanded their risk model from internal security reports only to include the police crime information in assessing the threat level at each of the company's retail stores.

Since the company's retail stores cater to a diverse group of people and are normally the anchor store in strip centers, a lot of the crimes reported from each store did not actually occur at the facility. Offense reports were used to verify all violent crimes to ensure that only those that actually occurred at the property and occurred as reported were included in the database.

The security department utilized a crime analysis software application to analyze the databases of crime data for each of their stores. The database includes the time and date of each crime and the specific nature of the crime that occurred. The software allows the department to quickly determine where the violent crimes occurred on the property and identify the victim. With this information, the security personnel are able to not only determine whether a store is high, medium, or low risk, but also who is being targeted, customers or the store itself. With this specific information, the security department can deploy appropriate security measures to reduce the risk at each store specifically.

By the end of their first year with this new program, the security department was able to realize a sizable return on investment. Based on the company's 300 stores, an annual saving, or cost avoidance, of $9.2 million was gained in the first year after implementation. This saving reflects a number of changes to their security program, but primarily constitutes the redeployment of security personnel during higher risk times. Prior to this new program, security personnel were used haphazardly with no regard for actual risk levels.

Though the above example is tangible, most savings in the business of security are intangible and not as easy to assess quantitatively. One of these categories is the savings generated by reducing crime and thus the avoidance of security-related litigation. Regardless of a security measure's ability to be quantitatively assessed, security decision makers should strive to calculate a return on security investment.

REFERENCES

1 International Association of Crime Analysts. (2014). Definition and Types of Crime Analysis [White Paper 2014-02]. Overland Park, KS: Author.
2 Ibid.
3 International Association of Crime Analysts. (2015). Effective Responses: High Crime and Disorder Areas (White Paper 2015-01). Overland Park, KS: Author.
4 International Association of Crime Analysts. (2014). Definition and Types of Crime Analysis [White Paper 2014-02]. Overland Park, KS: Author.
5 Ibid.
6 Ibid.

7 Ibid.
8 International Association of Crime Analysts. (2013). Identifying High Crime Areas (White Paper 2013-02). Overland Park, KS: Author.
9 Ibid.
10 Ibid.
11 Ibid.

CHAPTER 5

Vulnerability Assessments

Karim H. Vellani

CONTENTS

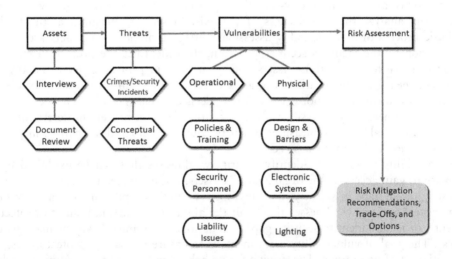

FIGURE 5.1 Strategic Risk Assessment Process, Copyright ©2019 by Threat Analysis Group, LLC. Used by permission. Additional information available from Threat Analysis Group, LLC via www.threatanalysis.com.

DEFINITION

In simple terms, vulnerabilities are opportunities. More precisely, vulnerabilities are weaknesses or gaps in a security program that can be exploited by threats to gain unauthorized access to an asset. Vulnerabilities include structural, procedural, electronic, human, and other elements which provide opportunities to attack assets. Vulnerabilities can be categorized as physical, technical, or operational. Physical vulnerabilities may include structural characteristics of the facility, geographic location of facility, location of assets within the facility, strength of access control measures, and illumination levels, among others. Technical vulnerabilities may include equipment properties, network weaknesses, susceptibility to eavesdropping and other electronic surveillance, effectiveness of locks, and the type and number of cameras. Operational vulnerabilities may include policies, procedures, practices, and personnel actions and behavior.

A vulnerability assessment, sometimes referred to as a security vulnerability assessment, is an analysis of security weaknesses and opportunities for adversarial exploitation in one or more of the above categories. The fundamental method for assessing vulnerabilities is the security survey, which is a tool for collecting information about the facility. The goal of a vulnerability assessment is to identify and block opportunities for attacks against assets. By effectively blocking opportunities, security decision makers can mitigate threats and reduce risk.

VULNERABILITY ASSESSMENTS

A vulnerability assessment is a systematic approach used to assess a facility's security posture and analyze the effectiveness of the existing security program at the facility. The basic process of a vulnerability assessment first determines what assets are in need of protection by the facility's security program, then identifies the protection measures already in place to secure those assets and what gaps in protection exist. Finally, the assessment measures the security program's effectiveness against valid security metrics and provides recommendations to security decision makers for improvements. In essence, the vulnerability assessment assists security decision makers in determining the need for additional security measures, security equipment upgrades, changes in policies and procedures, and manpower needs.

Vulnerability assessments identify security weaknesses that can be exploited by an adversary to gain access to the organization's assets. For example, a vulnerability assessment may reveal gaps in security in an investment bank's financial management system, it may reveal security weaknesses that limit the ability of a nursing home to protect its residents, or it may identify security gaps in a national monument's visitor management process. The goal of vulnerability assessments is to ensure life safety, protect assets, and the continuity of operations. The driving forces behind vulnerability assessments include new legislation, revised threat assessments with new or emerging threats, increased criticality of assets, asset loss, asset damage, asset destruction, a concern for continuity of operations, and newly recognized vulnerabilities. For many organizations, the driving force is an outcry from users of the property. For example, nurses may express concern to a hospital's leadership regarding the lack of workplace safety or shoppers at a mall may complain of burglaries of motor vehicles (BMVs) in the mall's parking lot. A comprehensive vulnerability assessment affords security decision makers and facility management personnel the opportunity to make future planning decisions based on an acceptable methodology that can be used for budget considerations, capital expenditures, personnel allocation, and establishing procedural guidance.

The vulnerability of an asset is determined by the potential weaknesses in operational processes and procedures, physical security weaknesses, and technical gaps which can be exploited to attack an asset. Vulnerability assessments are used to identify these weaknesses by way of a security survey. To paraphrase noted security author Charles A. Sennewald, "a security survey is a fact-finding process whereby the assessment team gathers data that reflects the who, what, how, where, when, and why of an organization's existing operation and facility." The purpose of a security survey is to identify and, to the extent possible, measure the vulnerabilities at a facility or to specific assets by determining what opportunities exist to exploit current security policies and procedures, physical security equipment, and security personnel. The outcome of a security survey is a report, normally written, that outlines a series of solutions which, if implemented, will reduce the short-term and long-term opportunities at a facility. Vulnerability assessments should not operate in a vacuum. They should also consider the threats (identified via a threat assessment) to which the assets are exposed. Security surveys are designed to meet the unique needs of a facility or type of facility. For example, one may use a security survey designed for a maritime port facility for other port facilities, but a maritime port facility security survey will not likely meet the needs of an office building. Even within similar type facilities, unique characteristics must be considered and included in the security survey.

Security surveys are often designed as a series of questions or checklists that are completed by the assessment team during off-site preparations and on-site inspections of the facility. Surveys may range from a few basic questions to highly detailed lists comprising thousands of questions. A typical security survey contains general information about a site and evaluates the geographic characteristics of the facility, physical layout of the facility and its unique characteristics, security and other personnel, operational requirements, security equipment capability and deployment schedules, and threats and other incidents that impact security. General information normally captured in a security survey includes:

- Vulnerability assessment team (identify by name and title)
- Date(s) of assessment
- Name of facility/site
- Emergency contacts and telephone numbers
- Law enforcement jurisdiction (agency name, address, and phone number)
- Main facility telephone numbers
- Site address
- Site description
- General purpose of site
- Public, private, or mixed use
- Normal operating hours
- Staff/employee hours
- High activity use (hours/days)
- Other tenants or users of the site
- Individuals who have access to critical, sensitive, and non-public areas
- Location of critical assets within the facility
- Known vulnerabilities.

SCOPE OF VULNERABILITY ASSESSMENTS

The scope of a vulnerability assessment depends on the goal of the security team. Some assessments are geared toward protecting only the most critical assets, such as an assessment which emphasizes only the reduction of violent crime opportunities to protect people at the facility. In this situation, vulnerabilities around the authorized user of the property are considered. Other vulnerability assessments emphasize the full range of opportunity reduction strategies for all critical assets and lesser assets.

One may wonder why there is a difference in scope among vulnerability assessments. Normally, a truncated scope is in reaction to a particular threat or the identification of a new critical asset. Sometimes, a limited scope vulnerability assessment is the result of a need coupled with finite resources, typically time and money. Independent security consultants face this often where management identifies a need for a vulnerability assessment based on a new threat and has limited funds in which to execute the assessment. The threat assessment, for example, which is normally conducted prior to the vulnerability assessment, may have identified and prioritized threats and these high ranking threats serve as the scope of the vulnerability assessment. Simply prioritizing threats may lead to a limited scope assessment. For example, a hospital which operates one main facility and several medical clinics off campus may decide to pursue the primary, most attractive target first and leave the other facilities for another budget cycle. Another example is where an oil and gas CEO was targeted and another organization recognized the need to assess the vulnerabilities of their executive leadership.

Regardless of the range of the scope, a written mission statement is often used by the assessment team to guide the vulnerability assessment. The mission statement identifies the stakeholders and outlines the assessment's objectives. The stakeholders may include the organization which owns and/or manages the facility, the organization's employees, the people that frequent the facility, and possibly the community at large or even a broader group. The mission statement identifies the key issues that are of interest to the stakeholders. A sample mission statement for a hospital vulnerability assessment may be: "To perform a vulnerability assessment which identifies security vulnerabilities, opportunities for security breaches, and hazards on the hospital's premises which can adversely affect the employees, visitors, and patients of the hospital."

Key to the vulnerability assessment is project management. The vulnerability assessment team leader is best suited to take on the role of project manager. Project management includes defining the scope of the assessment, refining the security survey for the unique needs of the facility, determining a project work plan, time line, and milestones. The project manager should also define the role of each assessment team member and arrange for all resources needed for the assessment. Project Management is discussed in great detail in Chapter 11.

THE VULNERABILITY ASSESSMENT TEAM

An important quality for the vulnerability assessment team is the ability to think like an adversary. When conducting the assessment, there are three focal points which the assessment team should consider: How can an adversary carry out a specific type of attack against a specific asset or group of assets; how effective are existing security measures in deterring, detecting, and delaying the specific attack; and what is the current level of vulnerability? This last item should have either a quantitative or qualitative value assigned.

The attack modes considered will have been developed during the threat assessment and are used in conjunction with targeted asset lists to assess vulnerabilities based on predetermined performance metrics or against accepted security guidelines.

The assessment team should include not only security personnel but also personnel familiar with the facility under assessment and specialists as needed by the nature of the facility. The vulnerability assessment team leader should be familiar with various assessment methodologies unless a particular methodology must be followed. For example, Sandia National Laboratories Risk Assessment Methodology for Water Systems (RAM-W) may be required by the facility. The team should also include experts or specialists as needed. Blast analysis specialists and structural engineers, for example, may be needed for a water system or dam. Of primary consideration to be included on the team are people with precise knowledge of the processes and procedures that occur at the facility as they relate to critical assets.

Depending on the nature of the vulnerability assessment, a team may be comprised of as few as one person or may range much higher. Typically, the assessment team is made up of three to eight people. On smaller teams, the project manager role is often shared by a general security management person, while other roles may include a technical security professional and a person familiar with the facility. Oftentimes, the assessment team includes external personnel such as consultants who have experience in conducting assessments for various types of facilities and have had exposure to other security systems. One of the greatest advantages of an outside independent security consulting firm is the range of security strategies which they bring to the current vulnerability assessment. Having had experience in different and similar facilities, and through the process of trial and error, independent security consultants usually have more experience in conducting vulnerability assessments than internal personnel.

ASSET-BASED AND SCENARIO-BASED VULNERABILITY ASSESSMENTS

Vulnerability assessments tie assets to threats in an effort to identify potential vulnerabilities and countermeasures to reduce those vulnerabilities. The level of vulnerability of each asset and threat is evaluated using either an asset-based assessment or a scenario-based assessment.

Asset-based vulnerability assessments are broad evaluations of assets and the threats that impact those assets. For example, an asset-based assessment at a jewelry store will focus on the jewelry as the primary asset in need of protection and the threats that may impact upon the jewelry. Asset-based assessments assume that every scenario cannot be imagined or those that are, are too speculative to consider.

Scenario-based vulnerability assessments, on the other hand, focus on the attacks themselves. The scenario-based assessment evaluates vulnerability by asking how targets might be attacked. This type of assessment requires knowledgeable assessment team members who have an understanding of history and can foresee the methods used by adversaries in the future. While history is a primary indicator, not all future threats can be anticipated based on the past attack modes. Certainly, the September 11 attacks were evidence of a new attack mode that was not anticipated, at least not by the general public, prior to 2001. Scenario-based assessments are advantageous in that they are better suited for assessing high value assets and high consequence attacks. Unfortunately, this advantage also creates a problem whereby lesser threats are ignored and security measures not implemented. The scenario-based vulnerability assessment process includes the following seven steps undertaken by the vulnerability assessment team:

- Selects the scenario to evaluate.
- Studies the target or asset's characteristics.
- Evaluates specific types of adversaries.
- Evaluates specific types of attack modes.
- Evaluates the likelihood of existing security measure's ability to deter, detect, or delay the attack.
- Analyzes the consequences of the asset's loss, damage, or destruction.
- Assigns a vulnerability rating.

The attack scenarios are normally selected by the vulnerability assessment team from the high consequence alternatives. While the team's objective is to be creative in assessing different scenarios, the scenarios must be sufficiently realistic. A fair assessment of the target's attractiveness, from the adversary's perspective, is critical to accurately evaluate the strengths and weaknesses of each asset. While it is easy to theorize about well trained, skilled, and properly equipped adversaries, the team should not create an infallible threat. History has shown repeatedly that adversaries make mistakes. Though not always true, it is often said during an investigation that criminals are stupid. This thought is based on the sometimes obvious mistakes criminals make during the commission of a crime. The next step is to evaluate the likelihood of existing security measure's deterring, detecting, or delaying the attack. Typically, an outside-in approach is used whereby the assessment team identifies the outer most layer of protection and works their way inside toward the assets, passing through each protection layer in the same order that an adversary would do so. The training, skills, and equipment of the theoretical adversary should be considered as each protection layer is breached. Finally, the assessment team analyzes the consequences of the asset's loss, damage, or destruction, and assigns a vulnerability rating.

An example of a scenario-based vulnerability assessment is where the assessment team selects a low grade explosion outside a government building as an attack scenario. They postulate that the explosion occurs immediately outside the building during normal business hours. What are the characteristics of the building and its assets (employees and other people would be among the critical assets) that may contribute to the loss, damage, or destruction. How would an attacker detonate a bomb in close proximity to the building? Would any element of the current security system be able to deter, detect, or delay the attack? Would the video surveillance system detect the adversaries? Is the video surveillance system monitored with direct communications to the security response force? Would the building survive a low grade explosive attack?

As seen in this example, a downside to scenario-based assessments is evident, in that these types of assessments force the team to focus on protecting against particular threats and possibly ignoring other threats. Nevertheless, both asset- and scenario-based vulnerability assessments will result in a list of recommendations for changes to the security program.

VULNERABILITY ASSESSMENT STEPS

Like threat assessments, vulnerability assessments may be quantitative or qualitative depending on the nature of the assessment and the availability of metrics. In both scenario- and asset-based vulnerability assessments, the general steps are:

1 Identify assets in need of protection.
2 Review historical security and incident information if available.

3 Prepare security survey.
4 Identify existing security measures for each asset and determine the effectiveness of each measure individually or in combination with one another.
5 Assign rating to each asset based on quantitative or qualitative vulnerability rating scale.
6 Prepare written report with recommendations for additional security measures or changes to the security program.

Step 1 assumes that the vulnerability assessment is not being conducted as part of an overall risk assessment and therefore assets have not yet been identified. If the vulnerability assessment is being conducted as part of a risk assessment, then the asset information should be readily available to the assessment team.

Step 2 also assumes that the vulnerability assessment is not being conducted as part of an overall risk assessment and therefore a threat assessment has not yet been conducted. If the threat assessment is already completed, reviewing the threat assessment report should indicate any vulnerabilities that adversaries have exploited in the past. For example, the threat assessment report indicates that security personnel have responded to an alarm generated from camera 7 repeatedly during the past year. The vulnerability assessment team determines that camera 7 surveys the right rear perimeter fencing of the facility. Upon inspection, the assessment team finds that the fencing in that area is in disrepair and is an older design relative to the fencing in the front of the facility.

Step 3 of the vulnerability assessment is to prepare the security survey. There are many sources of security surveys and are limited only by the assessment team's creativity. Previous vulnerability assessments may also be refined, updated, and used for the current assessment. There are numerous security books which contain sample security surveys and various industry organizations which have developed surveys specific to their industry.

Step 4 of the vulnerability assessment is the identification of existing security measures for each asset and the determination of the effectiveness of each measure individually or in combination with one another. As the team assesses the facility, existing security measures designed to address known security gaps are identified and noted on site diagrams or blueprints. Depending on the nature of the facility and the type of security measures in place, the countermeasures may be tested and compared to established metrics and industry standards. One of the biggest mistakes a vulnerability assessment team makes is to assume that existing countermeasures are adequate and counter the threat. Using performance testing, the team can determine if the countermeasures are doing what they were designed to do, that is, reduce the vulnerabilities. Experienced assessment teams will analyze the facility from the adversary's point of view rather than from the security decision maker's perspective. What factors may deter the motivated offender? What paths might the attacker take into the facility? What tools will be required to defeat security measures? Will stealth or deceit be necessary? Will an insider be needed? Technical security people are also beneficial to the overall evaluation of existing security measures in that they will know the limitations of electronic measures. The vulnerability assessment team conducting an asset-based assessment will spend more time in the field assessing routes to assets, points of detections, and determining lines of defense. The scenario-based assessment team will spend more time brainstorming and conducting table top exercises in an effort to assess worst case attacks and consequences to the facility's most critical assets.

Step 5 requires that the vulnerability assessment team assign a vulnerability rating to each asset based on a quantitative or qualitative vulnerability rating scale. These scales are discussed in detail at the end of this chapter. For now, it's important to understand that each vulnerability is rated by being based on the asset's value (qualitative or quantitative), the threat posed, and the security measures' effectiveness in reducing the opportunity for vulnerability exploitation. The rating will also be dependent on the consequence of loss, damage, or destruction. For manufacturing type facilities, this is measured in operational downtime and loss of revenue, both of which can be measured quantitatively.

In step 6, the vulnerability assessment team prepares a written report summarizing the assessment and recommendations for additional security measures or changes to the security program to reduce the overall vulnerability level and the vulnerability level of specific assets. The report should also include a basic cost-benefit analysis outlining the reduced vulnerability level that may be achieved after implementing recommended security measures. Some of the factors that the assessment team should consider in their report, especially for critical facilities, are:

- Facility population
- Structural integrity of facilities
- Land area of facility
- Distance to emergency services
- Redundant power supply
- Video surveillance systems
- Intrusion detection systems
- Barriers
- External lighting
- Security personnel.

VULNERABILITY RATING SCALE

Vulnerability ratings are based on the attractiveness of the target and the level of protection afforded those assets. The rating scale can be either quantitative or qualitative. Qualitative ratings are scaled by relative value to the organization's mission. Quantitative are based on life cycle costs, including the actual value of the asset, replacement cost, operational costs, maintenance costs, and costs associated with time lost while the asset is replaced or repaired. A simple example will illustrate the point. If your personal car were to be stolen, the current value would be lost, plus the cost of purchasing a new car, plus the cost of transportation between the car's loss and replacement.

Qualitative Vulnerability Rating Scale

An example of a qualitative vulnerability rating scale for facilities is as follows:
Very High – A facility with attractive targets, a history of threats, inadequate security measures, and adversaries capable of exploiting the security weaknesses. An attack

on this type of facility may include structural damage, operations may be severely hampered or completely stopped, and assets contained within the facility may be destroyed.

High – A facility with attractive targets, no history of threats, inadequate security measures, and adversaries capable of exploiting the security weaknesses. An attack on this type of facility may include some structural damage, operations may be reduced to only the most critical, and assets contained within the facility may be destroyed.

Moderate – A facility with attractive targets, no history of threats, adequate security measures, and no adversaries capable of exploiting the security weaknesses. An attack on this type of facility may affect normal operations with minimal downtime.

Low – A facility with no attractive targets, no history of threats, and adequate security measures. An attack on this type of facility will cause minimal disruption to normal operations.

SECURITY SURVEY AREAS FOR HOSPITALS

- General information
- Organizational issues
- General security
- Visitor management
- Workplace violence prevention program
- Security force
- Policies and procedures
- Emergency management
- Human resources
- Building security survey
- Perimeter barriers and controls
- Gate security and construction
- Vehicle control and perimeter entry point access
- Clear zones and signage
- Building exteriors
- Access control
- Lock and key control
- Outdoor lighting
- Video surveillance
- Duress alarms
- Intrusion alarms
- Patient safety
- Emergency center
- Infant/patient abduction prevention measures
- Medical records storage facilities
- Health insurance portability and accountability act (HIPAA)
- Information services (IS)
- Security sensitive areas
- Central plant

- Cash handling
- Parking facilities
- General
- Access control
- Personnel
- Lighting
- Physical security measures
- Crime prevention through environmental design (CPTED)
- Office area security
- Loading docks.

THE SECURITY SURVEY REPORT

The security survey report is the result of an on-site review of the facility or an asset's vulnerabilities and security measures. While the typical security survey report does not comprehensively address all facets of the vulnerability assessment, it does address the vulnerabilities, security measures, and may provide recommendations. More often, a vulnerability assessment is incorporated into a broader security risk assessment report. A typical security survey report includes general information about the facility, a review of critical assets, some form of threat assessment, an outline of existing security measures, a description of vulnerabilities, and recommendations for security changes. Noticeably absent from the preceding security survey report sections are the cost-benefit analysis and vulnerability ratings, which are not normally included in the security survey report.

Depending on the scope of work, security consultants often use a letter format for their security survey reports. According to Sennewald and Vellani, "The scope of [the consultant's] work refers to the central objective of the consulting task, or the clear focus of the effort." The time between assessments and deployment of the next phase may be very short or as much as one year.

THE VULNERABILITY ASSESSMENT REPORT

The vulnerability assessment report is a critical component of the overall risk assessment and is used to document the assessment activity. While the report may be formatted to fit the needs of the organization under assessment, a typical vulnerability assessment report includes the following sections.

Table of Contents

The table of contents is an often overlooked section of the vulnerability assessment report. Each major report section as well as subsection should be identified with its corresponding page number. A comprehensive table of contents is beneficial since an index is rarely included in a vulnerability assessment report.

Executive Summary

The executive summary is an overview document used to provide a condensed version of the entire report. It is prepared to cover the highlights of the report for those decision makers who do not have the time to read the full report. Executive summaries tell the report's audience what is significant within the report and what issues must be responded to by decision-making readers. While covering each section of the full report, the executive summary should not be longer than 10 percent of the full report and is often much shorter and should be a standalone document. Generally speaking, the executive summary should cover the scope and objectives of the vulnerability assessment, team composition, vulnerability assessment methodology utilized, the facility assessed, the date(s) of assessment, threat assessment information, critical assets assessed, conclusions, and recommendations. The assessment team should take caution with the recommendations within the executive summary since justifications for each recommendation are typically not included in this document.

Background

The background section of a vulnerability assessment outlines the scope of the assessment, critical assets, the facility characterization, and provides an overview of the assessment methodology and process. A summary of the threat assessment report is also normally included.

The vulnerability assessment team's first on-site task should be to review the facility characterization resulting from the asset identification and threat assessment risk assessment steps. This is an important step to understand the facility, what assets specifically are in need of protection, and the threats posed to those assets. The facility characterization should include a concise description of the organization's mission, the criticality of the facility under assessment, major functions and processes, and key staff used to ensure the mission is carried out. Also included in the facility characterization is the geographic location, property boundaries, access points, physical and structural characteristics and condition, and significant features of the facility. Occupant information, traffic patterns, neighboring facilities, and community demographics also should be included. The facility characterization may also address supply chain and transportation information, regulatory and legal requirements that impact the facility, and security policies and procedures in effect. A savvy vulnerability assessment team, especially a team consisting of external personnel, will also seek to understand the organization's mission so as not to trample on it.

The facility characterization will include a review of facility blueprints, site diagrams, and floor plans; identification of property boundaries; the location of authorized access points; and maps depicting facility ingress and egress paths. The characterization may also include a description of physical structures, traffic patterns, and neighboring facilities. Reviewing threat information during the facility characterization is advised. This information may come from interviews or a formal threat assessment report. Internal security records, authorized users lists, and operational logs may also be reviewed. For purposes of understanding operational vulnerabilities, the assessment team should be aware of any differences during different operational shifts at the facility. This includes an awareness of normal activities and functions occurring during each shift as well as traffic levels of employees, contractors, and visitors. Finally, the facility characterization should include a list of critical assets as identified in step 1 (asset identification) of the risk assessment process and describe the operational consequences if those assets were to be lost, damaged, or destroyed.

Blue prints, site diagrams, and floor plans should be reviewed during the facility characterization as they may be used to identify property borders, ingress and egress routes to the facility, specific vulnerable areas in and around the facility, adjacent facilities, physical structure locations, and features outside the facility such as railroads, waterways, interstate highways, and airports.

The assessment methodology and process should include the various types of assessments conducted including operational, structural, and procedural. The operational assessment may outline the types and lengths of work shifts, activities typical to each shift, security implications, and availability of protection forces. The structural assessment methodology should describe how physical structures were assessed. For example, what type of materials are the roof, walls, windows, floors, and foundation composed of? How are the heating, ventilation, and air conditioning (HVAC), sewage, and water systems secured? A procedural assessment describes the processes and procedures in place at the facility. This includes the access control procedures for employees, contractors, and other visitors such as delivery people and vendors. How are hazardous materials transported into, out of, and inside the facility? How are vehicles inspected while entering and leaving the facility?

Assessment Overview and Process

The assessment overview and process section describes the facility's critical functions, significant threats, and documentation available. The primary goal of this section of the vulnerability assessment report is to detail comprehensively the major vulnerabilities at the facility. Of primary concern is the functionality of the physical protection system.

Typical physical security measures will depend on the nature of the facility. However, many physical security measures are common across various applications. For example, fencing is appropriate at most facilities, even in open campuses such as universities where certain facilities may be fenced. The vulnerability assessment team should identify each component of the physical security system and decide what level of effectiveness is required for the facility and what risks management is willing to accept. Why would the team even consider anything less than maximum effectiveness? No physical security system can maintain maximum effectiveness. Documenting the assumed risks is part of the team's due diligence effort.

The effectiveness level of a physical protection system (PPS) is a factor of its ability to deter potential adversaries, detect those that are not deterred, and delay adversaries until the protection force can respond. Each of these functions should be built into the physical protection system, performed in order, and take less time to activate than it takes for the adversary to reach its intended target. An effective physical protection system provides protection in depth with multiple layers of security that forces the adversary to defeat each layer in order, minimizes the consequences of individual component failure by having redundancy, and exhibits balanced protection no matter which path of attack the adversary chooses.

As discussed earlier, the first thing a physical protection system should do is deter the potential adversary. Deterrence is a security strategy designed to discourage adversaries by increasing the risks to the adversary, promoting a sense of security, and instilling doubt on behalf of an adversary. Failing an ability to deter a would-be adversary, the physical protection system should detect the presence of the adversary. Detection is a security strategy designed to assess the threat and alert security personnel of an adversary's presence. Cameras and sensors are examples of detection measures. Once the adversary has been detected, the physical protection system should delay the adversary from meeting its objectives until the protection force can respond to neutralize or defeat the adversary. Delay, then, is a security strategy designed to slow the progression of adversaries into or out of the facility, and defeat is another security strategy designed to neutralize adversaries before an asset is lost, damaged, or destroyed. Barriers are an example of a delay measure. The physical protection system model described applies to most protection situations, from Fort Knox to home defense.

Here again, it is important to note that a common mistake made during the vulnerability assessment is to assume that existing countermeasures are adequate in effectively countering the threat and reducing vulnerabilities. The use of security metrics is helpful in determining if the system is optimally configured and deployed. Vulnerability of the physical protection system can be both quantitatively and qualitatively measured depending on the nature of the component. False alarm rates (FAR) and nuisance alarm rates (NAR) can be measured quantitatively and compared against industry metrics. Protection force response times can also be measured quantitatively and benchmarked against average response times for different types of threat levels.

The vulnerability assessment team should address each physical protection system area separately beginning with deterrence measures. Among the more common deterrence measures are highly visible, uniformed security personnel, lighting, signage, and other countermeasures such as fencing and natural barriers which may intimidate adversaries and tip the risk-reward balance in the favor of security.

Detection measures present in the physical protection system should be addressed next. Detection security measures should be located throughout the facility, but primarily at the perimeter to increase the time between detection and the security force's response. These measures include both interior and exterior intrusion detection systems and their individual components such as sensors, closed circuit television systems, and clear zones. Among the questions that the vulnerability assessment team should be asking during the security survey are:

- What is the key control process?
- How are packages screened prior to entry into the facility?
- Are X-ray machines and magnetometers used or are people and packages screened visually?
- What access control measures are in place to allow entry to only authorized personnel?
- Are there multiple entry points?
- Are vehicles screened when leaving sensitive areas?
- Are perimeter intrusion detection measures such as sensors operating properly?
- Do environmental factors, such as terrain and weather, negatively impact the ability for sensors to detect intrusion?
- Have any past attempts to penetrate the facility's access control systems been successful?
- Is the physical protection system adequately assessing alarms?
- Are the false alarm and nuisance alarm rates at a minimum?

- Are cameras able to adequately detect unauthorized entry at all points around the perimeter?
- Are video surveillance systems monitored by security personnel or electronic means?
- Are intrusion detection systems, video surveillance, and other electronic measures monitored on- or off-site?
- Are all video surveillance components (switching equipment, video monitors, transmission lines) working as designed?
- Are lighting systems fully functional?
- Do lighting systems meet the various codes and standards such as the Illuminating Engineering Society of North America's Guideline for Security Lighting for People, Property, and Public Spaces (IESNA G-1–16)?

The list can go on ad infinitum, but suffice it to say that the security survey items should be comprehensive to meet the needs of the facility and the assets in need of protection.

Delay, as discussed earlier, is a security strategy designed to slow the progression of adversaries into or out of the facility. Delay comes into play after detection measures have signaled an actual intrusion, effectively blocking out false alarms, and the protection force has been notified. The response team may or may not be located on site. For example, low security facilities, such as office buildings, may not have a response team on site, but rather on roving patrol for numerous facilities. Regardless of the location of the protection force, the delay security measures should slow the progression of the adversary toward its intended target, allowing enough time for the protection force to arrive and neutralize the threat. Delay measures include locks, doors, walls, fences, and barriers. The United States Army has published numerous penetration times relating to different types of delay measures and depending on the type of facility under assessment, these standards should be consulted.

The protection force is probably the most difficult security measure to address in the vulnerability assessment. Depending on the nature of the facility, there may not be a traditional protection force, but rather designated personnel responsible for responding to distress and alarm signals. The key factor to assess is response times. Response times are an excellent security metric that the vulnerability assessment team should monitor and evaluate during the vulnerability assessment. On-site personnel responsible for security should also constantly monitor response times to ensure the protection team is operating at an optimum level. The protection forces should also be evaluated for appropriate equipment and training on any prescribed equipment. Protection force equipment includes communication devices, vehicles, firearms and other weapons, incident reporting mechanisms, personal protection equipment, etcetera. The vulnerability assessment team should also evaluate policies and post orders, especially those relating to use of force. Patrol records and daily activity reports (DARs) can shed light on protection force effectiveness.

Conclusions

The conclusion section of the vulnerability assessment report is used to summarize the vulnerabilities and provide the reader with the vulnerability ratings. The vulnerability ratings may be quantitative, qualitative, or a hybrid depending on the nature of the vulnerability. Deficiencies should be noted in sufficient detail to provide justification for the recommendations to follow in the next section.

Recommendations

The recommendations section of the vulnerability assessment report includes the assessment team's suggested changes to the security program. These changes may include the deployment and redeployment of security personnel, additional physical security measures, and updates to security plans, policies, and procedures. The recommendations should be prioritized based on vulnerability ratings for each asset allowing the security decision makers to move forward with changes in an appropriate fashion. Cost-benefit analysis and cost estimates should also be included in this section of the vulnerability assessment report. Cost-benefit analyses are important since budget requests will have to be made and costs justified. Recommendations may also be made in phases with threats and vulnerabilities reassessed between phases.

Appendices

Appendices may be included in the vulnerability assessment report and usually contain facility and area photographs, blueprints, site diagrams, and floor plans. It is also helpful to the reader to include a copy of the security survey checklist and any cost-benefit analysis documentation.

VULNERABILITY ASSESSMENT REPORT OUTLINE

Table of Contents

Executive Summary
Vulnerability assessment dates
Scope of assessment
Team composition
Facility characterization
Critical asset description
Summary of threat assessment
Vulnerability assessment objectives
Summary of conclusions
Summary of recommendations
Background
Organizational mission
Criticality of the facility
Key staff
Major functions
Geographic location
Overall physical characteristics and conditions

Significant features, including history
Occupant information
Community demographics
Supply chain and transportation system
Specific critical assets
Security policies and procedures
Regulatory and legal requirements
Reviewed facility blueprints, site diagrams, and floor plans
Identification of property boundaries
Location of authorized access points
Maps depicting facility ingress and egress paths
Descriptions of physical structures
Traffic patterns
Neighboring facilities
Assessment overview & process
Identification of critical functions
Significant threats
Available documentation
Vulnerability assessment team composition and biographies
Schedule
Major vulnerability areas
Site
Environmental
Structural
Physical protection systems (PPS)
Policies and procedures
Documentation
Security plans
Security incident reports
Security personnel
Life safety and fire protection systems
Communications systems
Information technology security systems
Conclusions
Recommendations
Prioritized ranking of recommendations
Cost-benefit analysis of recommended changes
Appendices
Facility and area photographs
Blueprints
Site diagrams
Floor plans
Security survey checklist
Cost-benefit analysis documentation

CHAPTER 6

Risk Assessments

Karim H. Vellani

CONTENTS

Definition
Security Risk Assessments
Qualitative Security Risk Assessments
Quantitative Security Risk Assessments
Specialized Security Risk Assessment Methodologies
Risk Mitigation
The Security Risk Assessment Report

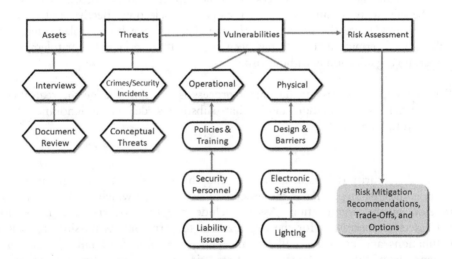

FIGURE 6.1 Strategic Risk Assessment Process, Copyright ©2019 by Threat Analysis Group, LLC. Used by permission. Additional information available from Threat Analysis Group, LLC via www.threatanalysis.com.

DEFINITION

Risk is a function of threats and vulnerabilities. It is the possibility of asset loss, damage, or destruction. Risk is the result of the likelihood that a specific vulnerability of a particular asset will be exploited by an adversary to cause a given consequence. Risk assessment is a process to identify and prioritize risks. Risk assessments may be quantitative, qualitative, or hybrid assessments that seek to determine the likelihood that an adversary will successfully exploit a vulnerability and the resulting impact (degree of consequence) to an asset. A risk assessment is the foundation for prioritizing risks in order to effectively implement countermeasures. Managing the risks identified during the assessment is a follow-on effort wherein security measures are evaluated and selected based on their ability to reduce identified risks. Further steps of the risk management process include implementing and monitoring the selected measures to ensure that the measures are effective in reducing risk to an acceptable level.

Risk management is a continual management and operational process, whereas a risk assessment is simply a component of that management process. For many organizations, risk management involves much more than security functions and also includes insurance and legal issues.

No organization is without risk. The risk assessment and risk management process seek to reduce risk to a tolerable level. The risk assessment is the culmination of the previous steps discussed thus far beginning with the identification of assets, inventorying existing security measures, defining threats, and identifying vulnerabilities. The final step of the process is to "calculate" risks and make recommendations to reduce them to a level acceptable to the organization. Reducing the risk involves identifying countermeasures that can mitigate vulnerabilities through the implementation of additional or different security measures or changing security practices and other operational protocols. Cost estimates and cost-benefit analysis can be a key component to selecting effective and reasonable security measures. Once the proposed recommendations have been implemented, risk is recalculated to determine if the risk has been reduced to an acceptable or tolerable level. Remember, no organization is without risk.

> The first step in the risk management process is to acknowledge the reality of risk. Denial is a common tactic that substitutes deliberate ignorance for thoughtful planning.
>
> *Charles Tremper*

Recapping the security risk assessment steps may be a good idea at this point. Identifying assets is the first step. This is the process of determining which assets are critical to the mission of the organization. Assets include people, property, and information. Critical assets are necessary for the organization to carry out its mission, for without them, functions and processes will fail and cause the mission to fail. The higher the consequence from the loss, damage, or destruction of an asset, the more critical the asset. Each organization has different mission critical assets; thus, no specific list is provided in this text. It is up to the security risk assessment team to determine what the critical assets are for a particular organization. Critical assets are typically determined through interviews and questionnaires of the people charged with carrying out the organization's mission. For the Coca Cola Company, the formula for Coke is a critical asset as it gives Coca Cola a competitive advantage. For a litigator, his win-loss record is a critical asset. For an athlete, her strength, agility, and energy are critical assets. For the security consultant, his integrity is a critical asset.

When determining the criticality of an asset, it is important to consider the time and money needed to replace the asset. The organization's reputation may be a critical asset and may take a considerable time to re-establish after negative publicity. A company whose critical assets include their computer network may be able to replace the functionality of that asset rather quickly, but with considerable expense. A homeowner whose house is destroyed by fire may be covered financially by insurance (risk transfer), but the time to build or buy a new house may be problematic and the fire will likely result in significant sentimental loss of the house and contents. A manufacturing firm whose equipment is damaged may suffer downtime until the equipment is restored or replaced. The airport whose metal detectors unknowingly malfunction while not terrible in and of itself, can be detrimental to homeland defense through cascading effects. Here again, asset criticality can be categorized quantitatively by value, replacement cost, etc. or qualitatively by low, medium, high, or some other relative scale.

The second step of the security risk assessment process is to inventory existing security measures designed to protect assets. The measures may include policies and procedures, physical security equipment, security personnel, or some combination of these measures. It is important to remember that security measures should not be assumed to be effective in protecting the assets. There are two effective methods for inventorying current security measures, inside-out or outside-in. In the outside-in approach, the assessment team begins at the facility's perimeter and works their way in toward the asset through each line of defense. The inside-out approach is the opposite with the team starting at the asset and working their way out to the perimeter. Commonly, assets have multiple layers of protection. This concept is known as defense-in-depth. In a hospital, for example, there are many assets in need of protection. A blood irradiator may exist in one area of the hospital while the executive suite may lie in another area. It is possible for these two assets to have multiple layers of protection, but only share one layer, e.g. the building's perimeter protection measures. In addition to the inside-out or outside-in methods, the inventory process should also include reviewing any available security documentation including security plans, policies and procedures, security officer's post orders, and physical protection system documentation.

The third step in the security risk assessment process is the threat assessment, whereby threats are identified, characterized, and rated on either a qualitative or quantitative scale. Threats are anything that can exploit a vulnerability, intentionally or accidentally, and obtain, damage, or destroy an asset. Threats are classified as either human or natural. Threat can also be defined as an adversary's intent, motivation, and capability to attack assets. Adversaries can include insiders, outsiders, or a combination of insiders and outsiders. Adversarial capability and motivation should be assessed based on their ability to steal, damage, or destroy critical assets. The adversary's past methods, equipment, skills, and training should be clearly articulated in the assessment report. Target attractiveness is a key component of the threat assessment. In commercial and residential applications, threat assessment generally employs data analysis techniques to identify patterns or trends in historical data and sometimes includes conceptual threats.

The fourth step of the security risk assessment process is the vulnerability assessment wherein weaknesses in the security program are identified via the vulnerability assessment's primary tool, the security survey. Vulnerabilities are opportunities. Vulnerabilities are weaknesses or gaps in a security program that can be exploited by threats to gain unauthorized access to an asset. Vulnerabilities may be structural, procedural, electronic, and human in nature and provide opportunities to attack assets. Existing security measures may or may not address the security program's weaknesses. Vulnerabilities may also be classified quantitatively or qualitatively.

Security risk assessment, including the cost-benefit analysis and report with recommendations, is the fifth and final step in the security risk assessment process.

SECURITY RISK ASSESSMENTS

Security risk assessments are comprehensive and rational reviews that offer a logical and defensible method for security professionals to make decisions about security expenditures and the selection of cost-effective security measures to protect critical assets and reduce risk to an acceptable level. Assessing risk is a dynamic process that involves continuous evaluation of assets, threats, and vulnerabilities. Security risk assessments are typically a staged process whereby critical assets are identified, current countermeasures are enumerated, threats are identified, vulnerabilities are defined, and prioritized recommendations are made to protect critical assets based on probabilities of attack.

Security risk assessments can be both quantitative, qualitative, or a hybrid. Qualitative assessments are based on the data available and the skills of the assessment team, while quantitative assessments utilize data to evaluate risk. Hybrid security risk assessments utilize quantitative data where available and qualitative where metrics are not readily available or insufficient. While assessing risk is more art than science, the security risk assessment methodology should be structured so that the results and recommendations can be repeatable given a different assessment team. Security risk assessments should generally be quantitative to the extent possible and recommendations for additional security measures should be the result of a cost-benefit analysis and measures should be benchmarked against industry standards.

QUALITATIVE SECURITY RISK ASSESSMENTS

Qualitative assessments are normally used when the assets in need of protection are of lower value or when data is not available. Qualitative security risk assessments may also be used when insufficient historical information or metrics exist, precluding a quantitative approach. The results of qualitative assessments depend on the assessment skills of the people involved in the assessment. Risk levels are normally given in abstract values such as high, medium, or low, or color coded like the Homeland Security Advisory System. ASIS International published a security guideline entitled, "General Security Risk Assessment," which outlined one approach to qualitative security risk assessments. The International Association of Professional Security Consultants (IAPSC) also has a qualitative approach to security risk assessments that is oriented toward premises security litigation. The full IAPSC methodology is included as an appendix to this book.

QUANTITATIVE SECURITY RISK ASSESSMENTS

Quantitative assessments, on the other hand, are metric based and assign numeric values to the risk level. Overall risk levels are derived from all available security metrics. In a physical protection system, for example, the metrics used in determining the risk level include the threat level, probability of detection, delay times, and response force times. Quantitative assessments are commonly used for the protection of business critical or high value assets. It should be recognized that security risks are notoriously hard to measure quantitatively because they involve human actions.

The general methodology for quantitative security risk assessment is to consider the probability of an attack and the expected impact on each critical asset. The probability of attack is based on the adversary's motivation, capability, and intent. Depending on the type of facility or assets being protected, historical data may also be considered, but a lack of history should not be indicative of a low or non-existent threat level. One reason a lack of history cannot be used is evident in the September 11 attacks. Had history been the only factor considered, the threat level would have been zero since no similar attacks had occurred previously in the United States or anywhere else in the world. Vulnerabilities are calculated using the probability that each specific vulnerability will be exploited by an adversary. Based on the threat and vulnerability calculations, the overall risk level is calculated. In most situations, especially during an initial security risk assessment, the risk level will not be acceptable. Thus, security measures must be identified, cost-benefit analyses performed, and the risk recalculated based on the theoretical implementation of these countermeasures. Only after a security mix has been identified and brings the risk level to an acceptable level, can the actual implementation begin. In some cases, a phased approach may be used wherein the security decision maker implements certain security measures, then allows some time to pass and then conducts another assessment to see if the measures are effective in reality. If they are not, the next phase of measures are deployed and reassessed. This is similar to the pre-test/post-test method used in the scientific and research communities.

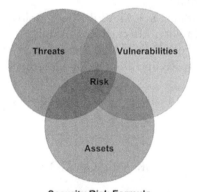

Security Risk Formula

FIGURE 6.2   Security risk formula process. Copyright ©2019 by Threat Analysis Group, LLC. Used by permission. Additional information available from Threat Analysis Group, LLC via www.threatanalysis.com.

SPECIALIZED SECURITY RISK ASSESSMENT METHODOLOGIES

A number of specialized security risk assessments exist that address the needs of particular industries or address specific threats or types of critical assets. Among these specialized security risk assessments are:

- Interagency Security Committee's Risk Management Process for Federal Facilities Standard.
- The American Petroleum Institute's "Security Vulnerability Assessment Methodology for the Petroleum and Petrochemical Industries."
- The National Institute of Justice's "A Method to Assess the Vulnerability of U.S. Chemical Facilities."
- Sandia National Laboratories Security Risk Assessment Methodology for Water Utilities (RAM-W^{TM}), for Chemical Facilities (RAM-CF^{TM}), for Communities (RAM-C^{TM}), for Transmission (RAM-T^{TM}), for Prisons (RAM-P^{TM}), and for Dams (RAM-D^{TM}).
- ASIS International's General Security Risk Assessment Guideline.
- ASIS International's Risk Assessment Standard.
- The International Association of Professional Security Consultant's Forensic Methodology.
- The Federal Emergency Management Agency's Reference Manual to Mitigate Potential Terrorist Attacks Against Buildings.
- The Center for Chemical Process Safety's Guidelines for Analyzing and Managing the Security Vulnerabilities of Fixed Chemical Sites.
- The National Institute of Standards and Technology's Guide for Conducting [Information] Risk Assessments.
- Microsoft's Security Risk Management Guide.
- Threat Analysis Group, LLC's Security Risk Assessment Methodology for Healthcare Facilities and Hospitals.
- Sandia National Laboratories' Risk Assessment Method – Property Analysis and Ranking Tool (RAMPART).
- The United States Military's CARVER Methodology (Criticality, Accessibility, Recoverability, Vulnerability, Effect, Recognizability).
- The United States Air Force's DSHARP Methodology (Demographics, Symbology, Historical, Accessibility, Recuperability, Population).

Take calculated risks. That is quite different from being rash.

General George Patton

RISK MITIGATION

Risk management is the process of anticipating future losses and using risk mitigation strategies for reducing or eliminating that risk. Generally, there are five strategies for dealing with risk:

1. Risk avoidance
2. Risk reduction
3. Risk spreading
4. Risk transfer
5. Risk acceptance.

Risk avoidance is an extreme measure since it often hampers business. An example may be a department store which chooses to stop carrying a particular brand or style of basketball shoes which are known to be stolen in great frequency. Risk avoidance is more commonly addressed in concept rather than in reality. For example, a large bank may avoid opening a new branch in a risky area. Risk reduction is typically the driving force for security decision makers whose role it is to protect assets. Risk spreading is a strategy to move assets to different geographic areas so if one area is attacked, the consequence is limited to that area. In today's business climate, it is common to have critical documents and information available electronically. Many companies store this electronic information in multiple locations so that if an attack were to occur, there is a backup of the information. Risk transfer is a strategy used to remove the risk from the owner to a third party. Insurance is the best example of risk transfer in that the business hires the insurance company to assume the risk for a fee. Risk acceptance is another strategy for mitigating risk. As the name implies, risk acceptance is simply where an organization assumes the risk to an asset.

Given a specific threat, there are many specific risk mitigation strategies available to the security decision maker. Cost effectiveness is a key component in selecting the best one for the protection of assets. A thorough security risk assessment allows security decision makers to prioritize risk reduction activities and adapt to changing and emerging threats. Risk mitigation is a security strategy that is accomplished by decreasing the threat level by eliminating or intercepting the adversary before they attack, blocking opportunities through enhanced security, or reducing the consequences if an attack should occur. Without question, the best strategy for mitigating risk is a combination of all three elements, decreasing threats, blocking opportunities, and reducing consequences. This is the homeland defense strategy used by the US government and many other governments across the globe in the war on terror. The US homeland security strategy may be characterized as the three Ps: Prevent, Protect, and Prepare, in that the Department of Homeland Security's strategy is to reduce the threat by way of cutting terror funding, destroying terrorist training camps, and capturing terrorists; to block opportunities through enhanced security measures such as increased airport and maritime security; and to reduce the consequences through target-hardening efforts which minimize damage such as window glazing and by shortening response and recovery times such as moving the Federal Emergency Management Agency (FEMA) under the Department of Homeland Security.

For the security decision maker, specific countermeasures are available for each "P" (Prevent, Protect, Prepare). Prevention measures can include psychological measures designed to deter criminals from perpetrating their acts on a given property by increasing the risk of detection and capture. Protection measures include security personnel and vaults. Preparation measures include alarm system monitoring services and corresponding personnel who respond to alarms. More than one security measure may exist for the protection of a given asset. As such, for each potential security measure, the risk reduction benefit should also be assessed quantitatively or qualitatively. The measure selected may not necessarily be the most effective, rather it is preferable to select a cost-effective measure which reduces the risk to a tolerable level. Oftentimes with security measures, the sum is greater than the parts in that multiple security measures working in conjunction with one another can accomplish reducing risk to an acceptable level. Likewise, one security measure may protect more than one asset. In either case, the overall effectiveness of security measures should be assessed to determine their net effect.

As defined above, security measures which provide maximum protection often come at a high price. While maximum protection may be warranted for critical infrastructure, maximum protection is not reasonable in most industries. Defining a reasonable level of protection to protect people, property, and information is the primary task of most security decision makers. The problem with a reasonable level of protection, however, is that reasonable minds may disagree as organizations, even within the same industry, have different risk tolerance levels.

Another security strategy is the concept of balanced protection, which simply means that no matter how an adversary attempts to reach the asset, security measures which deter, detect, or delay his or her advance will be encountered. Balanced protection is accomplished through another security strategy called protection-in-depth or defense-in-depth. Protection-in-depth is also known as security layering wherein the asset is behind multiple layers of security measures, each requiring penetration in sequence to reach the asset.

Regardless of whether maximum or reasonable protection is required, the cost of each security measure must be determined. Security equipment costs include initial costs, training costs, and on-going maintenance and repair costs. Security personnel costs include background checks, training and continuing education, uniforms, equipment, and licensing. The rule of thumb for the selection of security measures is that their total cost should not exceed the cost to replace or repair the asset being protected. Another strategy used in the protection of assets is to only provide protection for critical assets with the anticipation that other assets will be secured through a diffusion of benefits. Diffusion of benefits will be discussed in detail in Chapter 7, Crime Prevention Theories.

THE SECURITY RISK ASSESSMENT REPORT

The security risk assessment report is a comprehensive written document which incorporates all elements of the risk assessment methodology. Typical components of a comprehensive security risk assessment report include a facility characterization, a listing of significant assets, a summary of existing security measures, the threat assessment report including supporting documentation with crime analysis charts and graphs, major elements of the vulnerability assessment report with the security survey (often included as an appendix), and recommendations for security modifications with the cost-benefit analysis. The goal of the report is to highlight the findings of the risk assessment so those that hold the purse strings are able to make educated risk mitigation decisions which may include one or more of the five risk mitigation strategies (avoidance, reduction, spreading, transfer, and acceptance). The following format is suggested and builds upon the format used for the security risk assessment report.

Table of Contents

The table of contents in a risk assessment report should identify each major section and subsection and be identified by page number.

Executive Summary

The executive summary of a security risk assessment report is an overview document used to provide a condensed version of the entire report and highlights key issues for decision makers who do not have the time to read the full report. The executive summary should not be longer than 10 percent of the full report and is often much shorter and should suffice as a standalone document. The executive summary should list the major assets, critical assets, and include the facility characterization. It should also summarize the existing security measures, the threats posed to the assets including the relevant information from the crime analysis, and the major vulnerabilities. The executive summary should conclude with the recommendations and a call for action.

Background and Methodology

The background and methodology section of the risk assessment report outlines the scope of the security risk assessment and defines the methodology. The methodology may be specific to the facility or organization, an industry-specific methodology, or a general methodology. Assessment team members should also be identified along with their credentials in this section of the report. The facility characterization and security inventory are discussed along with the security philosophy of the organization, if one exists. Historical attacks will also be included in this section, along with a general threat overview. Vulnerabilities uncovered during the security survey are outlined, along with any interim remedial measures designed to deter, detect, or delay immediate threats.

Assets and Critical Assets

This section outlines the facility's assets and critical assets, with special attention to defining the extent to which assets are necessary for critical functions or are of a mission oriented nature.

Existing Security Measures

This section of the security risk assessment report contains a discussion of the current security policies and procedures, the existence of any security manuals and post orders, types of physical security measures in use at the facility, and documentation concerning the use of armed and unarmed security officers or off-duty police officers. The scheduling practices are of utmost importance in the security personnel discussion, along with hiring standards, background investigation procedures, post orders and training provided, patrol practices, security incident reporting procedures, and equipment and uniform standards.

Threat Assessment and Crime Analysis

The threat assessment section's major component is a review of historical crime data or an in-depth crime analysis. The crime analysis will include spatial and temporal trends, average and mean crime levels, descriptions of the specific types of crime that have occurred, crime totals, violent crime rates, and forecasts or mathematical projections of future crime. The threat assessment may also include a discussion of crime problems in the area and other known threats to the facility.

Vulnerability Assessment

The vulnerability assessment section of the security risk assessment report outlines the results of the security survey and identifies any opportunities for adversaries to attack. Weaknesses and deficiencies in the security program should be described in sufficient detail to assist in the identification and selection of effective countermeasures.

Security Risk Assessment and Recommendations

This section is the pinnacle of the security risk assessment report and is the culmination of a lengthy, comprehensive process. In the beginning of this section is a discussion of the current risks to the facility and to its assets based on the threats and vulnerabilities previously identified during the respective assessments. These risks may be described quantitatively and/or qualitatively. Recommendations developed by the security risk assessment teams are then included along with the cost-benefit analysis for each security measure or security mix. Anticipated risk levels after the deployment of the initial or only phase of security measures are then described. Subsequent security deployment phases are then discussed along with further risk reductions expected. The recommendations should be prioritized based on quantitative or qualitative risk ratings for each asset.

Appendices

Appendices should be included in the security risk assessment report and should specifically include asset listings and descriptions; existing security inventory documentation; facility and area photographs, blueprints, site diagrams, and floor plans; threat assessment and crime analysis information; the security survey instrument or checklist; and cost-benefit worksheets.

RISK ASSESSMENT REPORT OUTLINE

Table of Contents

Executive Summary
Background and methodology
Risk assessment methodology
Assessment scope and objectives
Team composition and qualifications
Facility characterization
Assets
Major assets and functions
Critical assets and functions
Existing security inventory
Policies and procedures

Physical security measures
Security personnel
Threat assessment
Site-specific crime analysis
Historical attacks against similar facilities
Vulnerability assessment
Security survey process
Major vulnerabilities
Other vulnerabilities
Risk assessment
Current risks
Risk ratings
Mitigation strategies
Prioritized recommendations
Cost–benefit analysis
Revised risk estimates
· Call for action
Appendices
Facility and area photographs
Blueprints, site diagrams, and floor plans
Facility personnel interview questions
Complete asset list and descriptions
Existing security inventory
Threat assessment and crime analysis documentation
Security survey instrument or checklist
Cost-benefit analysis worksheets

CHAPTER 7

Crime Prevention Theories

Karim H. Vellani

CONTENTS

The Need and Practical Application of Theoretical Study
Situational Crime Prevention
Rational Choice
Routine Activity
Crime Prevention through Environmental Design (CPTED)
Crime Displacement
Diffusion of Benefits
Problem-Oriented Policing and Problem Analysis

The time to repair the roof is when the sun is shining.

John F. Kennedy

THE NEED AND PRACTICAL APPLICATION
OF THEORETICAL STUDY

While most security decision makers are educated on common security practices and industry guidelines, the security industry at large would benefit from understanding the established and emerging crime prevention theories which formed the basis for our current security knowledge and strategies, as well as our ability to keep abreast of future protection trends. Individual elements (e.g., policies, personnel, and physical security measures) of the comprehensive security program often find their roots in well-developed crime prevention research. This chapter does not attempt to discuss the all crime prevention theories, neither does it attempt to address those covered in great depth. Instead, it serves as a primer for the major crime prevention theories in use today with the hope of enticing the reader to seek out more information from other sources. As security professionals continue on the current path of developing their security departments into legitimate business units, it is less acceptable to prescribe crime prevention measures without first determining precisely what it will accomplish and at what cost. Outcomes matter. Security decision makers that are able to justify their requirements have the best chance to obtain the scarce resources needed to fulfill their security mandate. This chapter provides the theoretical discussion for security professionals to assist them in making practical and logical decisions for a sound security program by building a bridge between crime prevention theorists and security professionals.

Reducing the opportunity for crime to occur at a facility is the fundamental goal of situational crime prevention in the private sector. However, not all crime is preventable. This is most evident when sitting in a courtroom where two security experts or criminologists opine on the preventability of a particular crime. Those with a law enforcement or criminal justice tend to evaluate the preventability of a crime based on the offender's profile and characteristics. Where the criminal is known, this security expert or criminologist will study the criminal's background and opine on whether or not the offender was deterrable, placing no emphasis on whether or not the facility could have prevented the crime through the use of crime prevention measures.

The security expert or criminologist educated in criminology and modern security practices, on the other hand, is usually more adept at providing opinions on crime causation at a facility. These individuals normally focus on well-established crime prevention theories, such as those discussed in this chapter, and often have long practiced the art of modern security through their careers as security professionals. While the courts and juries still accept the traditional criminologist as a security expert, the future of forensic security consulting belongs to the modern security professional.

CRIME PREVENTION DEFINITION

Crime prevention is the anticipation, recognition, and appraisal of a crime risk and the initiation of some action to remove or reduce it. (National Crime Prevention Institute)

What, then, is crime prevention? Crime prevention, according to the National Crime Prevention Institute, is the anticipation, recognition, and appraisal of a crime risk and the initiation of some action to remove or reduce it. This definition meets the needs of the modern practice of security. Modern security is based in situational crime prevention and can be differentiated from social crime prevention. While social crime prevention and traditional criminology won't be discussed at any great length in this book, it is sufficient to say that they generally fall within the realm of government and include such measures as unemployment insurance, welfare, vocational training, and religious institutions which provide spiritual guidance. The role of social crime prevention and traditional criminology is to be offender oriented and to assist in creating a structure for the citizenry to avoid turning to criminal activity for survival. This chapter does not view traditional criminology as useless or without merit, but rather as a parallel crime prevention construct for government and law enforcement.

Environmental Criminology

Environmental criminology, which forms the foundation for much of what we do in the security field, emphasizes the importance of geographic location and architectural features as they are associated with the prevalence of criminal victimization. According to this school of thought:

[c]rime happens when four things come together: a law, an offender, a victim or target, and a place. Environmental criminologists examine the fourth element – place

(and the time when the crime happened). They are interested in land usage, traffic patterns and street design, and the daily activities and movements of victims and offenders.

The concept of crime and place is relatively new and forms the foundation for situational crime prevention. Crime and place theories place little emphasis on the offender and instead seek to prevent crime by emphasizing crime prevention strategies and measures that may be implemented by security decision makers to control a facility.

Crime Triangle

Reducing the opportunity for security breaches to occur is a strategic goal of security professionals. The reason for this is the concept of the crime triangle, whereby the elements of motive, desire, and opportunity must all exist for a security breach to occur.

FIGURE 7.1   Crime triangle.

All three elements – motive, desire, and opportunity – must exist for a crime to occur. Capability and motive are characteristics of the criminal perpetrator. Opportunity, on the other hand, is a characteristic of the asset, or more specifically around the asset (target of crime). In the security professional, the term *opportunity* is used interchangeably with the term *vulnerability*. Eliminating or reducing opportunities (vulnerabilities) is a primary goal of most security programs. If opportunities are reduced (illustrated with a dotted line), crime risk can be mitigated as illustrated below.

FIGURE 7.2   Crime triangle.

Opportunity is closely connected to a target, in that effective asset protection will lead to an elimination of opportunity and thus target hardening. Before delving deeper into the theoretical underpinnings of modern security practice, it might be beneficial to consider the facility which the security professional is charged with protecting. What is the criminal career of the facility? Do potential offenders and potential targets coexist without crime? If so, how does this occur? Through the current use of security measures? Facilities with disproportionately high crime levels are likely to have higher value targets, have plenty of opportunities (vulnerabilities) due to an ineffective place manager, and may even encourage criminal behavior. Other places may have more opportunity for crime simply due to the number of attractive targets.

The expanded crime triangle identified an outer layer of "Controllers." Controllers are those who prevent crime. One controller can prevent a crime. For a crime to occur, all elements of the inner layer must be present at a time when all *controllers* in the outer layer are weak or absent.

FIGURE 7.3   Expanded crime triangle.

Controllers include:

- Handlers – Handlers control the offenders, typically through informal social control. Handlers may include parents, teachers, school resource officers, gang reform specialists, etc.
- Guardians – Each individual is a guardian because we protect ourselves. Guardians may also include neighbors watching over another's house. Where these fail, guardians may be police or security officers.
- Place Managers – Place managers are those that are referred to in this book as security decision makers. Place managers supervise and monitor specific places.

No problem can be solved from the same consciousness that created it.

Albert Einstein

SITUATIONAL CRIME PREVENTION

Situational crime prevention is comprised of four primary techniques: increasing perceived effort, increasing perceived risk, reducing anticipated rewards, and removing excuses. Each of these techniques has associated components as seen in Table 7.1.

TABLE 7.1   Twenty-Five Techniques of Situational Crime
Prevention

Increase the effort	1. Harden targets
	2. Control access to facilities
	3. Screen exits
	4. Deflect offenders
	5. Control tools/weapons
Increase the risks	6. Extend guardianship
	7. Assist natural surveillance
	8. Reduce anonymity
	9. Utilize place managers
	10. Strengthen formal surveillance
Reduce the rewards	11. Conceal targets
	12. Remove targets
	13. Identify property
	14. Disrupt markets
	15. Deny benefits
Reduce provocations	16. Reduce frustration and stress
	17. Avoid disputes
	18. Reduce emotional arousal
	19. Neutralize peer pressure
	20. Discourage imitation
Remove the excuses	21. Set rules
	22. Post instructions
	23. Alert conscience
	24. Assist compliance
	25. Control drugs/alcohol

Source: Clarke, 2005.

Security professionals will recognize that situational crime prevention closely follows the risk assessment methodology described in this book and common in the security industry. Situational crime prevention is executed in five steps. These five steps include the collection of data about the nature of a specific crime problem, which is basically the threat assessment and crime analysis step of the risk assessment methodology. The second step is similar to the vulnerability assessment and is the analysis of the conditions that allow or facilitate commission of the crime in question. Step three is the systematic study of possible means for blocking opportunities to commit the crime in question and analysis of cost, or the risk assessment and cost-benefit analysis step. Step four is the implementation of the best measures, which is the action taken on the security recommendations made in the risk assessment report. The final step is similar to the risk assessment methodology's feedback loop, monitoring the results. Without realizing it, many security professionals use the situational crime prevention technique during their day to day operations.

TEN PRINCIPLES OF OPPORTUNITY AND CRIME

Opportunities play a role in causing all crime.
Crime opportunities are highly specific.
Crime opportunities are concentrated in time and space.
Crime opportunities depend on everyday movements.
One crime produces opportunities for another.
Some products offer more tempting crime opportunities.
Social and technological changes produce new crime opportunities.
Opportunities for crime can be reduced.
Reducing opportunities does not usually displace crime.
Focused opportunity reduction can produce wider declines in crime.

Rutgers School of Criminal Justice professors Marcus Felson and Ronald V. Clarke developed Ten Principles of Opportunity and Crime which describes how opportunities, or vulnerabilities, are the root cause of crime. The first principle, *opportunities play a role in causing all crime*, implies that security decision makers can design facilities which either encourage or discourage crime. Their second principle is *crime opportunities are highly specific*. As discussed in the Crime Analysis chapter, the specific nature of each type of crime must be analyzed in order to select proper countermeasures, measures that are custom tailored to the crimes in question. Robberies in a parking lot of a grocery store require different security measures than a robbery of the grocery store's cash handling office. Felson and Clarke's third principle is *crime opportunities are concentrated in time and space*. This principle emphasizes that dramatic differences in crime levels can be found from one facility to the next even when both are in high crime areas. The reason for this is that crime shifts temporally (time and day) as opportunities change. The fourth principle is *crime opportunities depend on everyday movements of activity*. Expanding on principle 3, crime shifts are due to criminals and their victims moving about in time (hour of the day, day of the week) doing their routine activities of work, school, home, and recreation. Principle 5, *one crime produces opportunities for another*, is of primary concern to security decision makers. Repeat attacks by the same or different offenders leads to significant increases in risk to the facility. Principle 6 is well known to retailers: *some products offer more tempting crime opportunities*. Assets high in value and easily accessible are at higher risk than low value or inaccessible assets. Over the counter drugs, for example, are often targeted by criminals in grocery stores. *Social and technological changes produce new crime opportunities* is principle 7. A timely example of principle 7 is the theft of mp3 players, particularly the Apple iPod. Principle 8 is the basic premise behind vulnerability assessments, *crime can be prevented by reducing opportunities*. Reducing opportunities is accomplished by increasing risks to would-be offenders and reducing rewards if the crime is successful. Principle 9, which will be discussed in greater detail further in this chapter, is *reducing opportunities does not usually displace crime*. Crime displacement means that by blocking crime at one facility, security measures will force crime to another, less hardened, facility. While displacement does occur, it is not absolute. Finally, principle 10 is *focused opportunity reduction can produce wider declines in crime*. This is the concept of diffusion of benefits, which will also be discussed later in this chapter. Diffusion is a process where increased security measures at one location may also benefit neighboring facilities.

RATIONAL CHOICE

Rational choice theory suggests that offenders will select targets and define means to achieve their goals in a manner than can be explained. The task of security decisions under rational choice theory is to select crime countermeasures for the facility which cause offenders to decide that risks are too high and the rewards too low to commit the crime at that facility.

Adversaries act rationally when planning a crime by weighing the risks, rewards, and effort needed to commit their crimes. The rational choice crime prevention theory was developed in the UK by Ronald V. Clarke. This theory explains that an adversary uses a hedonistic calculus during their decision making process in selecting targets and that they will act in their own best interests. Understanding this calculus enables security decision makers to block opportunities for loss and protect assets. Rational choice theory says that, like the general public, most criminals act in a rational manner and weigh risks and rewards before taking action or committing a crime. In essence, the criminal uses a decision making process where the positive and negative aspects of committing the offense are weighed. If a crime opportunity is present and there is a reward for committing that crime (fruit of the crime), and there are low risks and low likelihood of apprehension, then they will commit the crime. The rational criminal's decision making process can be limited by time, intelligence, and accuracy of information. It is the latter element that security professionals should capitalize upon. By increasing the perceived level of security, a security professional can block the rational criminal from attacking. Note that the focus is not on the offender, but rather on the facility. Security measures, real or perceived, can force the rational criminal to believe the risk to be too high and, therefore, deter his attack.

Rational choice theory's central themes are that the human being, including the criminal, is a rational actor. Rational behavior involves a hedonistic calculus of risks and rewards and that people have free will to choose their behavior, whether it be deviant or conforming, based on their calculus. The hedonistic calculus is, in essence, a cost-benefit analysis of pleasure versus pain. Like all people, criminals will make their decisions based on maximizing pleasure and minimizing pain. Finally, security decision makers can control the rational offender's decisions by controlling the facility through real or perceived risk of detection and capture. The security professional may use all the means at their disposal, from procedures, personnel, and physical measures to psychological measures.

In summary, criminals are opportunistic, not unlike everyday people. Security professionals can block opportunities. Using the hedonistic calculus, security decision makers can force criminals to see the risks as too high and the rewards too low. If the risks are perceived to be higher than the perceived reward, the security program will be effective.

ROUTINE ACTIVITY

Routine activity theory's basic premise is that criminals, like everyone else, move among routine, daily activities that may include home, school, work, shopping, and recreation.

During these routine activities, a crime may occur if certain components come together at one point in time. These components are a motivated offender, a target, and a place without an effective guardian. The role of the security decision maker is to ensure that the place (facility) has an effective guardian.

Closely associated and complementary to rational choice theory, routine activity theory describes how crime is a function of a criminal's routine, daily activities that may include home, school, work, shopping, and recreation. Routine activity theory demonstrates the method in which motivated adversaries (threats) find suitable targets (assets) and opportunities (vulnerabilities) during the course of their routine activities. Two other elements must be present for the criminal activity to become reality. The adversary, target, and opportunity must converge in time and space in order for the crime to occur. The process of finding opportunities should be familiar to security professionals who have conducted security surveys and vulnerability assessments, as both are characterized by a search of available paths to and through an area (facility) and the targets (assets) along or just off those paths.

Those who have actively or passively studied the art of criminal profiling should find the concepts presented in the routine activities theory to be familiar. Adversarial activities are often characterized as modus operandi (MO or method of operation) and are consistent to most of an adversary's crimes. The modus operandi is typically called a signature in the profiling arena. In *Applied Crime Analysis*, the authors described how Jack the Ripper routinely chose his victims from the same London pub from where he stalked them to their homes and ultimately their deaths.

Though rather simplistic sounding, routine activity requires more than just the convergence of criminals and targets for a crime to occur. The offender must be motivated and will likely have performed the hedonistic calculus of weighing the risks and rewards. There must be a suitable target which provides the reward and a lack of guarded space which has little or no risk to the adversary. Risks can be intensified through an effective guardian. Guardians can be security personnel but are more often simply the legitimate users of the facility who provide the requisite deterrence. Offender motivation may be reduced through an effective handler. An effective handler is a person who has direct influence over an offender and may include parents, teachers, parents, friends, or employers. Most offenders do not have an effective handler and their motivation is more difficult to thwart; thus more emphasis must be placed on guardianship.

For the security professionals, one of the more common tasks in conducting a risk assessment is to determine what change in the routine of offenders, targets (assets), or guardians may have caused a sudden crime experience. Forensic security consultants, during litigation, will sometimes uncover a decrease in security coverage or an increase in available assets which led to an increase in crime.

Routine activity theory, like much that has been discussed in this book, has a specific crime emphasis. Gaining a thorough understanding of the precise nature of crimes affecting the property affords the security decision maker the ability to select and implement specific security measures which address the perpetrated crimes. Felson described four types of crime which may affect assets: exploitive crimes, mutualistic crimes, competitive crimes, and individual crimes. Exploitive crimes are predatory crimes where offenders injure or kill a person or seize or damage another's property. The Federal Bureau of Investigation's Uniform Crime Report Index Crimes are good examples of exploitive crimes. These crimes include murder, rape, robbery, aggravated assault, burglary, theft, motor vehicle theft, arson. Mutualistic crimes involve two people or a group engaged in complementary crimes such as drug transactions, prostitution, and gambling. Competitive crimes include those where two people or groups act in the same capacity and usually includes physical conflicts against each other. Gang crimes exemplify competitive crimes. Lastly, individualistic crimes are illegal acts committed by an individual. These are sometimes referred to as victimless crimes and include suicide and drug use.

CRIME PREVENTION THROUGH ENVIRONMENTAL DESIGN (CPTED)

Crime Prevention Through Environmental Design is one of the most well-known crime prevention theories. First articulated in Oscar Newman's books, *Architectural Design for Crime Prevention* and *Defensible Space: Crime Prevention Through Urban Design*, CPTED seeks to control crime through the use of natural surveillance, natural access control, and territorial concern. According to author Timothy Crowe, CPTED "expands upon the assumption that the proper design and effective use of the built environment can lead to a reduction in the fear of crime and the incidence of crime, and to an improvement in the quality of life." The role of security decision makers is to environmentally design facilities which deter and prevent crime.

The concept of defensible space, as originally conceived, called for legitimate users of residential space to act as guardians of their living areas. This entails designing the physical environment to enhance legitimate users' sense of territoriality, making it possible for them to observe their environment and communicate to illegitimate users (potential criminals) that they are under surveillance. This concept is well known to those familiar with CPTED, which expands on Newman's Defensible Space concept and incorporates the ideas of legitimate users (owners, employees, residents, tenants, etc.) versus illegitimate users (potential criminals), the effective utilization of natural surveillance, and the creation of safe communal havens for legitimate users.

THREE KEY CONCEPTS OF CRIME PREVENTION THROUGH ENVIRONMENTAL DESIGN

Key concepts of Crime Prevention Through Environmental Design (CPTED)
Natural surveillance
Natural access control
Territorial reinforcement.

The three key concepts of CPTED are natural surveillance, natural access control, and territorial reinforcement. Natural surveillance requires open areas where legitimate users can see and be seen through a visible connection. Natural surveillance is garnered by increasing visibility of and for legitimate users, and decreasing the ability of illegitimate users to hide and carry out their crime without being seen. The objective of natural surveillance is not to prevent unauthorized access, but rather to maintain observation of unauthorized users. Natural surveillance operates under the premise that some criminals do not wish to be observed. It's important to note that some criminals willingly accept the risk of identification. Locating outdoor activities within sight of the facility's windows can increase natural surveillance. For example, natural surveillance in a parking garage may entail the use of glass walls which allow surveillance and increased visibility when compared to brick or other masonry type walls. This increased visibility also increases the chances of illegitimate users being subjected to increased scrutiny by legitimate users.

The objective of natural access control attempts to keep unauthorized users out of specific areas. Natural access control encourages use of the facility or area within the facility by legitimate users while discouraging illegitimate users from staying in the area and reducing opportunities for offender concealment. Key security measures common to natural access control include well-lit walkways and other paths within the facility, and the use of thorny plants and shrubs or dense trees and waterways to keep illegitimate users out of the area.

The third principle of CPTED is territorial reinforcement. Territorial reinforcement attempts to foster ownership and responsibility of an area by legitimate users by reducing unassigned spaces. People oftentimes protect an area when they take ownership of the area. For example, a person may own a home and take measures to protect it, but they may also take measures to report suspicious activities in the immediate area around the home, such as neighborhood streets. Reducing unassigned spaces alters the perception of illegitimate users by showing that someone is responsible for the space. Some areas, by their design, have encouraged illegitimate users to take over the area and scared off legitimate users. Property owners may implement territorial reinforcement measures to discourage the illegitimate users and over time, encourage legitimate users to return to the area. Identifying unauthorized users is easier in well-defined areas.

To reiterate, CPTED attempts to design physical spaces for the normal use of that space by legitimate users and to discourage use by illegitimate users. Functionally, CPTED elements are implemented through the 3-D approach, which helps security decision makers design spaces for specific purposes for authorized users by guiding security decision makers on how to think about each space by way of the following questions:

1 Designation

   - What is the designated purpose of this space?
   - For what purpose was it originally intended?
   - How well does the space support its current use or its intended use?
   - Is there a conflict?

2 Definition

   - How is space defined?
   - Is it clear who owns it?
   - Where are its borders?
   - Are there social or cultural definitions that affect how space is used?
   - Are legal or administrative rules clearly set out and reinforced in policy?
   - Are there signs?
   - Is there conflict or confusion between purpose and definition?

3 Design

   - How well does the physical design support the intended function?
   - How well does the physical design support the desired or accepted behaviors?

- Does the physical design conflict with or impede the productive use of the space or the proper functioning of the intended human activity?
- Is there confusion or conflict in the manner in which physical design is intended to control behavior?

Broken Windows Theory

Broken Windows is a theory developed by James Q. Wilson and George L. Kelling in 1982 that theorized that disorder crimes (e.g., vandalism, public intoxication, vice crimes, etc.), anti-social behavior, and poor maintenance created an environment conducive to more serious crime and further disorder. Broken Windows postulated that reducing serious crime started with focusing policing efforts on minor crimes (e.g., misdemeanors) because eliminating the minor crimes and disorder prevented the developmental sequence for more serious incidents, such as violent crimes. New York Police Department's (NYPD) Commissioner William Bratton and Mayor Rudy Giuliani popularized many Broken Windows concepts in 1995 during a time when New York City's crime rate was already in decline. Popularity notwithstanding, Broken Windows Theory was and continues to be debated in both academia and in the public sphere, particularly due to the controversial NYPD *Stop and Frisk* practice. In response, Broken Windows' developers have argued that the theory was not designed as a zero-tolerance approach, but rather required more of a *Problem-Oriented Policing* approach, as discussed below. More recent analysis has found no causal link between Broken Windows and New York's crime rate, notably because New York's violent and street crime peaked in 1991 and was already declining. Arguably, New York's ability to maintain a lower crime rate since 1995 was the result of CompStat and *Problem-Oriented Policing*.

CRIME DISPLACEMENT

Displacement of crime is a relatively new and controversial topic in the academic crime prevention circles. Crime displacement occurs when security measures are effective in preventing crime where the security measures are and forces the criminal to go elsewhere with less security to commit their crimes. The important factor for security decision makers to remember is that only effective crime prevention can cause displacement.

There are six types of crime displacement: temporal, target, spatial, tactical, perpetrator, and offender type. Temporal crime displacement entails a shift in crime timing to different hours of the day, or days of the week when the apprehension is less risky. Temporal displacement is one of the key reasons why random security patrols are more effective than scheduled patrols. The randomness does keep the criminals on their toes by not providing them with a set time to commit the crime. Target crime displacement is where a criminal, given two equally valuable targets, will select the less risky one. Females are typically perceived as weaker or more vulnerable than males in the criminal mind and thus the criminal will likely select the female to victimize. Spatial crime displacement is similar to target crime displacement, except rather than the displacement being caused by the actual target, it is caused by the facility itself. An example is two convenience stores located across the street from one another. One is well lit and has good visibility into and out of the store, while the other is poorly lit and has signs in windows which obstruct visibility. Crime which may have occurred at the more secure store is displaced to the other store. Tactical crime displacement is where the adversary changes his or her tactics to commit the crime due to security measures in place. For example, a perpetrator who finds that windows have been secured after previous attacks at a particular facility may shift tactics and find another entry point into the facility. Perpetrator crime displacement is where specific offenders are deterred or apprehended and other offenders take their place. An example of this is where law enforcement captures a drug dealer that works a certain corner in a neighborhood and another dealer takes his or her place. Crime type displacement is rare but involves an offender who changes the type of crime s/he commits because of increase security to prevent the previous crime type. For example, a facility which has fortified itself against burglary may experience an increase in aggravated robbery against particular assets.

DIFFUSION OF BENEFITS

In some ways, diffusion of benefits is the opposite of crime displacement. Diffusion of benefits occurs when security measures taken at one facility benefit another facility. Specific diffusion occurs when a facility's security measures directly benefit neighboring facilities. Lighting is an example since it cannot be stopped at the border of the facility and overlaps to provide protection of the facilities next door. General diffusion is similar in that a facility which takes extraordinary security precautions gains a reputation of high risk to the offender and that reputation spreads to an organization's other facilities.

It is becoming more common for property owners and managers, and specifically their security departments, to work together in solving an area crime problem. For example, chemical facilities which neighbor other chemical facilities may work together to share the costs of security measures since both will benefit from the increased protection. Banks and other financial institutions also have a long history of working together to enhance their overall protection needs.

PROBLEM-ORIENTED POLICING AND PROBLEM ANALYSIS

Problem-Oriented Policing (POP) can serve as a model for security practitioners. According to Herman Goldstein, an early founder of the POP approach:

> [p]roblem-oriented policing is an approach to policing in which discrete pieces of police business (each consisting of a cluster of similar incidents, whether crime or acts of disorder, that the police are expected to handle) are subject to microscopic examination (drawing on the especially honed skills of crime analysts and the accumulated experience of operating field personnel) in hopes that what is freshly learned about each problem will lead to discovering a new and more effective strategy for dealing with it.

Security practitioners can use a similar approach to addressing site specific problems through crime analysis. POP is a strategy that calls for law enforcement to analyze and address underlying issues that contribute to chronic crime and disorder problems at specific places and in small areas. Probably the single most important element that distinguishes POP from other law enforcement techniques is that POP requires the use of community resources beyond those controlled by the law enforcement agency. For example, if bike theft is a problem at a place, law enforcement could work with the city's Parks Department or even non-profit groups in the community to obtain bike racks with built-in locks to enhance bike security measures.

Noted criminologists John Eck and William Spelman refined Goldstein's model by developing the SARA (Scanning, Analysis, Response, and Assessment) model:

- **Scanning** for problems.
- **Analysis** of problems.
- Development and implementation of **responses**.
- Follow-up **assessment** of results.

The SARA model sets forth a process for identifying very specific problems and developing responses unique to the identified specific problem. The bike theft problem above is very specific and the response is unique to that problem.

REFERENCES

Clarke, R.V. (2005). "Situational Crime Prevention: Theory and Practice". *British Journal of Criminology* 20(2): 136–147.

Cornish, D., and R.V. Clarke (1986). *The Reasoning Criminal: Rational Choice Perspectives on Offending*. New York: Springer Verlag.

Fennelly, L. and T. Crowe (2013). *Crime Prevention through Environmental Design*. 3rd ed. Boston, MA: Butterworth-Heinemann.

Goldstein, H. (1990). *Problem-Oriented Policing*. New York: McGraw Hill.

Jeffery, C. R. (1971, 1977). *Crime Prevention through Environmental Design*. Beverly Hills, CA: Sage.

Kohler-Hausmann, I. (2018). *Misdemeanorland: Criminal Courts and Social Control in an Age of Broken Windows Policing*. Princeton, NJ: Princeton University Press.

National Crime Prevention Council (1997). *Designing Safer Communities: Crime Prevention Through Environmental Design Handbook* Washington, DC: NCPC.

Newman, O. (1972). *Defensible Space: Crime Prevention through Urban Design*. New York: Macmillan.

Vellani, K. H. (2010) "Crime Analysis for Problem Solving Security Professionals in 25 Small Steps." Center for Problem Oriented Policing www.popcenter.org, https://popcenter.asu.edu/sites/default/files/library/reading/PDFs/crimeanalysis25steps.pdf.

Zahm, D. (2007). Using Crime Prevention Through Environmental Design in Problem-Solving, Problem-Oriented Guides for Police Problem-Solving Tools Series No. 8. Office of Community Oriented Policing Services. U.S. Department of Justice.

CHAPTER 8

Security Measures

Governance

Karim H. Vellani

CONTENTS

Security Awareness
Security Manual
Visitor Management Flow Chart
Emergency Management Plan
Standards

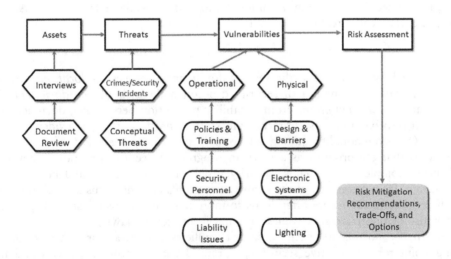

FIGURE 8.1 Strategic Risk Assessment Process, Copyright ©2019 by Threat Analysis Group, LLC. Used by permission. Additional information available from Threat Analysis Group, LLC via www.threatanalysis.com.

Measures, security or otherwise, you deploy for one type of crime are different from the types of measures that you deploy for a different type of crime. In the security field, there are three general types of countermeasures which are taken to prevent, mitigate, and eliminate risk: governance, physical security measures, and security personnel. Governance primarily consists of policies, procedures, plans, and training. Despite their relative low cost to develop and maintain, and their ability to demonstrate due diligence, policies and procedures are often the most overlooked component of an effective security program. Documentation of the security program is a critical element which includes the identification of critical assets, threats, and vulnerabilities.

FIGURE 8.2 Security program components. Copyright ©2019 by Threat Analysis Group, LLC. Used by permission. Additional information available from Threat Analysis Group, LLC via www.threatanalysis.com.

In the real estate business, the mantra for financial success is *location, location, location*. Similarly, the mantra of security decision makers should be *documentation, documentation, documentation*. From a liability prevention perspective, documentation of the security program in its entirety, from start to finish, is the best evidence of due diligence. One commonality among all security programs, regardless of industry or company, is that the program is a work in progress. A security program is never finished, never complete, never ends. Security programs often mature and become more sophisticated. Documentation of the security program's current status as well as its strategic direction into the future often leads to more mature, more sophisticated programs and can also demonstrate effectiveness in a negligent security lawsuit.

Governance documents, such as security policies and procedures, are the logical starting point for an effective security program. Lack of enforced policies and non-compliance can create weaknesses in security and reduce the effectiveness of security systems and personnel. Employee training ensures that policies are clearly understood, uniformly followed, and that employees are aware of existing security measures.

Governance may include a wide variety of documents. In the security arena, these documents can include policies and procedures, security manuals, standard operating procedures (SOPs), post orders, security standards and guidelines, security design criteria, training curriculums and standards, workplace violence prevention programs, emergency management plans, disaster recovery plans, and business continuity plans. Governance documents are often articulated in writing, but in most industries, there is no requirement or standard which requires written governance. However, formal, written governance documents save security decision makers time, assist in adequate training, increase "organizational memory," and may reduce liability by demonstrating due diligence. While the intent of security governance documents is to document appropriate behaviors, actions, and responses for and to security events, each type of governance document has a specific purpose. For example, the security manual is a comprehensive document that sets forth the strategic vision of the security organization, while emergency management plans, disaster recovery plans, and business continuity plans are specialized documents which describes the procedures and protocols used to protect assets during and recovery after specific types of incidents, such as natural disasters, data breaches, or other significant events. These types of specialized documents are unique to the industry or nature of business operations in which the organization is engaged.

The importance of security governance should not be underestimated as they serve as the backbone of any effective security program. Not only does security governance guide the day to day operation of the security program, they also move the security organization in the proper direction over the long term. On a practical level, security governance describes the security functions at a facility or for an organization, including how security functions and measures are organized, deployed, and managed. Security governance should also include methods of measuring effectiveness and/or productivity, that is, metrics. Metrics provide feedback loops that inform future changes to specific elements of the security program.

There is always more spirit in attack than in defense.

Titus Livius

SECURITY AWARENESS

Security is more effective when employees are integrated into the security program. For many organizations, security is a mission critical element of the overall risk mitigation effort. Employee buy-in of the security program, as most security professionals are keenly aware, does not come easily, but is a necessary requirement for the program to operate at an optimal level. A top-down approach, with a written policy statement from senior management, is a good first step to developing the requisite employee acceptance of the security program. The message from upper management should set the tone for the level of adherence to the security measures utilized at the facility or within the organization. While 100 percent compliance is desired, rare is the case when all employees adhere to every security policy and procedure implemented. Alternatively, absolute compliance is necessary for some of the organization's security measures. These measures should be reinforced through employee orientation, continuing education, and close monitoring by dedicated security personnel. Less restrictive measures may be supported by the organization's dedicated security personnel on a daily basis. A security manual, which will be discussed later, is important to creating an employee base which supports the security program.

Employee buy-in can be effectively garnered when return on investment and impact on the organization's financial condition are demonstrated. Non-security employees will also accept security measures when they are taught that the measures are there for their protection as well as the organization's other assets. An effective teaching tool is the case study, where employees are briefed on past events which threatened employees or assets. Showcasing past successful security interventions reduces natural employee resistance to security measures which some might feel controls their actions and behavior and limits their movements or access to specific areas within a facility. Each security measure should be discussed to ensure that employees understand that the measures are not arbitrary, but rather are designed to protect them directly and indirectly. A security program, by its very nature, can and often does create additional steps in normal business functions and operations. A security awareness program should make these additional security actions as natural as putting on a seatbelt before driving.

During employee security orientation sessions, educational material should be prepared and presented to new employees. This educational material should be designed to stress critical security issues in a manner which can be easily understood and followed by non-security employees. Educational materials may include the organization's security manual, slide decks and professional presentations, scenarios, and case studies which demonstrate a return on investment to the organization. Other means of creating awareness include tips and articles in the organization newsletters, intranet forums, internal email reminders, and security posters and memos. Regardless of the forms of communication method, the security awareness effort must be constant and continuous.

FIGURE 8.3   Example of a sign.

Whenever a security breach occurs, a thorough root cause analysis of the incident should be undertaken. Employees or departments involved should be debriefed and security awareness should be reasserted. The security breach, if created by the organization's employee, should be handled much like any other company policy infraction with all due investigation, supervision, and corrective action. Reprimands by the employee's immediate supervisor may be necessary; however, the security department employees should not be the people taking corrective action.

The remainder of this chapter discusses two major types of security governance documents. These are the security manual and the emergency management plan. While other policies and procedures are important, these two are universal among all types of organizations.

SECURITY MANUAL

While not all organizations need a security manual, those that do will often have detailed plans and policies that address various aspects of the security program. The security manual is a written document which defines the organization's security mission, provides an overview of the complete security program, and identifies methods in use for the protection of the organization's assets including policies, procedures, functions, measures, and strategies for providing a safe and secure environment and preventing crime and other security incidents. Typical security policies may address the following topics:

- Access and key control
- Active shooter
- Bomb threat
- Crime/security event reporting
- Crime investigations
- Criminal trespass
- Hostages
- Criminal background investigations for employees
- Involuntary and/or high risk terminations
- Employee identification badges
- Facility lockdown
- Security of sensitive information
- Sensitive area protection
- Use of force (security officers)
- Visitor management process/visiting hours
- Weapons
- Workplace violence.

The security manual is a living document in that it adapts as the organization's security needs change and serves as a training aid for security awareness across the organization. The security manual articulates how the security program is organized usually through personnel and function organizational charts, flow charts, and descriptions of specific countermeasures. Security manuals also describe the common security measures utilized throughout the facility or facilities, as the case may be, and how these measures operate on a daily, routine basis. Security responsibilities are clearly delineated, and regulatory compliance measures are described in detail. As described in the preceding section, the security awareness component should also be articulated in the security manual. Threat dependent measures and activities are enumerated in the security manual. The security manual also sets forth guidelines for quality control, bench marking against industry best practices, and metric development and analysis.

As a written document, the organization's security manual defines the security mission. What is a security mission? In its most basic form, the mission of any security program is the protection of assets. Depending on the nature of the organization or facility in need of protection, the mission may be more complex or unique. For example, a hospital's mission statement may encompass security for the facility, but also the maintenance of a safe environment for patients and their families. The security manual, as an overview of the complete security program, identifies the various ways in which security is provided. These methods include policies and procedures, physical security measures, and security personnel. While a proper balance is ideal, some organizations may rely more heavily on one of these general security measures and thus, the security manual will focus on that measure.

SECURITY POLICY STATEMENT

The St. John's Hospital Security Department exists to provide for a safe and secure environment in which the hospital and its associated clinics may carry out their mission of patient care, education, and research. The Security Manual is a key component of the Environment of Care program and supports the St. John's Hospital mission of providing exceptional quality in patient care and sets forth how St. John's Hospital addresses security and safety issues concerning patients, visitors, and employees.

The organization's security manual is the document which summarizes known and conceptual threats to the organization's assets, which have been identified through the formal process of threat assessment. For each identified threat, the security measures in place are enumerated, with cross-references to other policy and procedure documents which address those measures specifically. For example, in the healthcare environment, a conceptual threat is infant abduction. The security manual would identify that conceptual threat and identify the specific policies and procedures created and measures in place to reduce the risk of infant abduction.

In many organizations, different employees, at multiple levels, are responsible for various aspects of the security program. The security manual should address those responsibilities, and those groups of employees should be provided with security awareness training on key sections of the plan to ensure they understand their role in security. In the retail environment, for example, cashiers are responsible for cash handling and sometimes they are also the first responders in shoplifting thefts. These security roles, though secondary to their position and title, are vital to ensure the protection of the retailer's assets.

Organizational charts are common components of the security manual. While they do not necessarily identify security decision makers by name, they should identify them by title and place in the company hierarchy. Among the more common battles faced by the security industry is their place in the corporate structure. Where it was once common for the Security Director to report to human resources, the industry has forced a change and Security Directors are finding a place in the boardroom. While this discussion is on-going throughout the industry, for the purposes of the security manual, the reporting lines need to be identified through organizational charts regardless of to whom the Security Director reports. More importantly, the security manual should graphically portray the reporting lines within the security department. In smaller companies, this may be a one-level organizational chart, while in larger organizations, the organizational chart for the security department may indicate many layers.

Flow charts depict common functions utilized in the security program. These functions may include security patrols, access control processes, and escort procedures. Flow charts are useful in identifying how a security function is accomplished in a graphic, easy to understand manner. For example, visitor management at many large facilities is a complex issue. A flow chart may be used to demonstrate how visitors are allowed access to the facility, what security protocols are used, how tracking the visitors is accomplished, and how exit from the facility is completed.

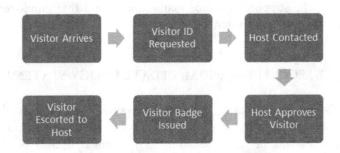

FIGURE 8.4   Visitor management flow chart. Copyright ©2019 by Threat Analysis Group, LLC. Used by permission. Additional information available from Threat Analysis Group, LLC via www.threatanalysis.com.

VISITOR MANAGEMENT FLOW CHART

If I have seen further it is by standing on ye shoulders of Giants.

Isaac Newton

In regulated or accredited organizations, adherence to security best practices, guidelines, and/or standards is required. Many companies, especially those in older, well established, and closely monitored industries, are well versed in the area of regulatory compliance since their livelihoods depend on their ability to operate within their industry's regulations. As such, their security manuals reflect policies and procedures for complying with the regulations. Newer requirements or less frequently enforced regulations, however, may not be reflected in the security manual. In the fast-changing environment of information security, security manuals are more difficult to keep up to date from the sheer growth and pace of the changes in that industry.

Threats change over time. The security manual must be able to guide the organization as threat levels rise and fall and new threats emerge. The security manual should clearly describe security changes implemented when threat conditions are elevated. The threat assessment is the driving force behind this section of the security manual. Not unlike the national threat condition responses, organizations too should have measures prepared in advance of rising threat levels.

The security manual also describes how the organization will measure its security against other similar organizations and against industry best practices. Industry-specific associations normally develop best practices and standards that relate to the security of organization's within their industry. The healthcare industry, for example, has the Joint Commission on Accreditation of Healthcare Organizations as their Environment of Care standards. The security plan should also describe the data collection and analysis process to create a relevant set of security metrics by which to measure the performance of various components of the security program. A common metric used is response time of security personnel to a high threat situation, for example.

While the security manual is intended to be a holistic document, its various components must be comprehensive enough to guide the security program. Supplementary policies may also be utilized, especially in large, wide scope security programs. Regardless of the size of the security manual, the keys to an effective plan are that it be reduced to writing, that it has the support of senior management, and that employees are trained and retrained on its contents as often as necessary.

SAMPLE SECURITY MANUAL UPDATE POLICY STATEMENT

The St. John's Hospital Security Department evaluates and revises the Security Manual on an annual basis for its scope, services, and effectiveness. Any changes in scope and services will be addressed during the annual update of the Security Manual. Effectiveness of the Security Department is assessed on a continual and constant basis with the intent of enhancing the safety and security of the Environment of Care. The effectiveness of the Security Department is assessed through a process of performance-based reviews, bench-marking, and metric analysis as defined in the Security Manual. The annual review and Security Manual updates are presented to the St. John's Hospital Board of Directors via the Hospital's General Counsel for review and approval during March of each year.

EMERGENCY MANAGEMENT PLAN

Similar to a security manual, an emergency management plan is a written document which communicates the policies and procedures to be followed in the event of an emergency. Emergency management plans are known under different names throughout the industry. In the private sector they are often called continuity of business plans or crisis management plans. Regardless of the name, the concept is the same. An emergency contingency plan, unlike a security manual, is not executed on a daily or routine basis, rather it is used only in the event of an emergency or for training purposes. Generally, and for the purposes of this text, an emergency may be defined as any event or combination of events which has the potential to negatively impact the organization's mission or components of that mission for a period of time and which require immediate response and action to continue normal mission operations. Emergencies should be defined for the specific organization or industry for which the emergency management plan is written. While not all types of emergencies can be foreseen, planning for the most predictable will move the organization a long way toward being prepared for unforeseen emergencies.

While security manuals are proactive in nature, emergency management plans are reactive in nature and should be prepared to address an emergency that is imminent or has already occurred, not to mitigate an emergency which can still be prevented. The role, then, of the emergency management plan is to reduce the effect of the emergency on the organization, also known as mitigation, identify resources to be used in the event of an emergency, or preparedness, take swift action to respond to the emergency, and to return the organization to normal operations as soon as possible, also known as recovery.

Security and risk management departments are typically the units charged with preparing and maintaining the emergency management plans. The reason for this is simple, the primary objective is the same as the overall mission of the security department, to protect assets. When developing the emergency management plan, priority must be given to protecting life and then protecting critical and other assets. When planning for the protection of life, the emergency management planner should consider evacuation routes and timing, identification of shelters, preparation for medical response, and the means to provide food and water.

An emergency management plan has several critical elements. These elements may include an organizational chart of key response personnel, resource lists, on-site and off-site shelter locations, critical asset lists, location of vital records, mutual aid agreements, and law enforcement and other emergency response contact information. Facility-specific plans should also include information unique to that facility. For example, plant emergency management plans should include plant emergency shut down procedures. The organizational chart of key emergency response personnel is essential to the emergency management plan. Since most emergencies are infrequent, the organizational chart should be updated often to reflect the current contact information of key emergency response personnel. Emergency response personnel should also meet on a regular basis to refine the plan, review their roles, and ensure the availability of resources. Resource lists should include the location of each anticipated resource, availability, and quantities. Shelters located on site should be identified. Depending on the nature of the emergency, one or more types of shelter may be necessary. Off-site shelters are more difficult to identify since their availability may change if the emergency is widespread. However, all reasonable attempts to identify that should be undertaken during the planning process. Critical asset lists are normally easily attainable from completed risk assessment reports as is the location of vital records. Mutual aid agreements are formal agreements between two or more parties who share a similar threat situation or face similar types of emergencies. Mutual aid agreements should be developed with other organizations that can assist in the response and recovery effort if an emergency were to strike one organization. These agreements should be very specific in nature and identify precisely what resources will be provided to the organization in need. While widespread emergencies draw heavily on the resources of law enforcement and other government agencies, liaison with those agencies should be maintained throughout the emergency. Complete and updated contact lists should be available in the emergency plan.

Revisions to the emergency management plan and training on the plan's procedures should be conducted frequently. The training interval will vary depending on the size and type of the organization and may be more or less frequent for individual facilities. However, there are some general guidelines on when the plan should be revised and training conducted. At a minimum, revisions and training should take place once per year. Additional training and revision may be required after an emergency to incorporate the lessons learned, when turnover is high among emergency response personnel, and when there are significant physical or environmental changes to the facility.

STANDARDS

Standards, guidelines, and best practices do not establish the "standard of care" in a legal sense as most standards, guidelines, and best practices are voluntary and often allow for implementation variances. The standard of care, on the other hand, is defined as the degree of care a prudent and reasonable person will exercise under the circumstances.[1] The standard of care does not have a specific reference document or format. It may rely on identifying security industry standards which establish criteria within the industry relating to the standard implementation of operations. The standard of care is developed by a security expert using credible sources and is based on a reliable methodology.[2] Elements for establishing the standard of care include:

- Identifying the statutes, ordinances and regulations.
- Collecting the applicable case law for the jurisdiction.
- Identifying and using adopted standards.
- Industry common practices.
- Avoiding assumptions and generalizations.
- Determining what the majority of similar security operations utilize.

It is important to note that the security industry, at least at this point, does not have a lot of standards. The standards that do exist are very broad and are not required to be adopted by organizations.

CONCLUSION

While the security manual and emergency management plans serve as the primary policies and procedures of an effective security program, other policies should be developed as needed to address security personnel and physical security measures. These policies may include a workplace violence policy, security personnel policies, and visitor management and access control policies. Other policies may be developed to address specific threats such as bomb threats, weather-related threats, and terrorist threats. Security decision makers should take full advantage of security policies and procedures, if not for their low cost to implement but also their ability to reduce liability and control other aspects of the security program.

REFERENCES

1 https://thelawdictionary.org/standard-of-care/(accessed December 19, 2018).
2 Baker, Steven T. and Alan W. Zajic (2018). "Guard Force Management Standard of Care." 34th Annual Conference, San Diego, California, International Association of Professional Security Consultants, April 30, 2018.

CHAPTER 9

Security Measures
Physical Security

Michael A. Silva

CONTENTS

Goals of Physical Security Measures
General Strategies for Good Physical Security
Site Security
Building Exterior Security
Building Interior Security
Electronic Security Systems
System Integration
Codes and Ordinances

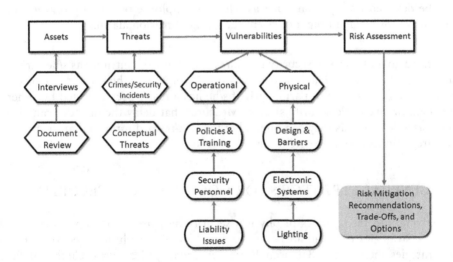

FIGURE 9.1 Strategic Risk Assessment Process, Copyright ©2019 by Threat Analysis Group, LLC. Used by permission. Additional information available from Threat Analysis Group, LLC via www.threatanalysis.com.

Of the three general types of countermeasures which are used to prevent, mitigate, and eliminate risk, physical security measures are the most tangible. Physical security measures are the physical and technical systems used to protect people, property, and information from theft, damage, and other types of harm. Physical security measures include effective site and building design; architectural elements such as physical barriers, fencing, lighting, and locks; and electronic security systems such as access control systems, intrusion detection systems, communication systems, and video surveillance systems.

GOALS OF PHYSICAL SECURITY MEASURES

There are three primary goals of physical security measures: to deter the intruder, to detect his or her presence, and to delay his or her attack. These are sometimes referred to as the "Three Ds of Physical Security", and are as follows:

Deter
The first goal of physical security measures is to deter or discourage the intruder from wanting to make an attack on the premises in the first place. Intruders want to get maximum rewards with minimal efforts. Most of all, they don't want to get caught. Things that make the intruder think that the attack will take too much time or effort, and things that make her or him think that s/he will be quickly apprehended can serve as strong deterrents to some criminals.

Detect
The second goal of physical security measures is to detect the intruder's presence as quickly as possible when s/he attempts to make her or his attack. The intruder can be detected by a person, such as when an employee or security officer sees him or her, or by an automatic system such as an intrusion alarm.

Delay
The third goal of physical security measures is to delay the intruder as s/he carries out her or his attack. The longer s/he is on the premises, the greater her or his chances of getting caught, particularly if s/he has already been detected by either a person or electronic security system. Measures that delay the intruder can also serve as a deterrent as they can often alter the risk/reward ratio so that the premises are no longer an attractive target.

GENERAL STRATEGIES FOR GOOD PHYSICAL SECURITY

Before delving into the specifics of physical security measures, it is important to understand some strategies that should be used when planning a physical security program. These strategies include the Balanced Design Approach, Concentric Circles of Protection, and Crime Prevention Through Environmental Design.

Balanced Design Approach

A good physical security program does not rely on a single type of preventive measure, but instead consists of a well-balanced combination of various types of operational, technological, and physical security elements. The successful integration of these elements creates a synergistic security program that provides effective protection of the organization's assets (see Figure 9.2).

The well-balanced security program includes the following components:

Site and Building Features

Site features can include fencing, gates, perimeter barriers, landscaping, signage, and security lighting. Building features can include doors, locks, security glazing, safes, storage cabinets, and other physical security devices.

Electronic Security Systems

Electronic security systems can include access control systems, alarm monitoring systems, closed-circuit television systems, security intercom systems, and other electronic security devices.

Operational Measures

Security operational measures can include security policies and procedures, employee security awareness training, security incident reporting procedures, security program

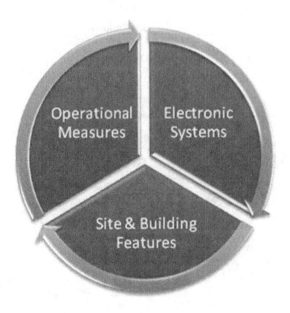

FIGURE 9.2   Balance security program.

management, and security staffing. These measures are discussed in greater detail in other chapters of this book.

It is important to note that no one element of the group can stand alone or operate independently and provide adequate protection. All elements must work together to provide effective security.

Concentric Circles of Protection

An underlying principle for providing good security involves a concept called "Concentric Circles of Protection." This principle is also sometimes called "Security in Depth" and involves the use of multiple "rings" or "layers" of security. The first layer is located at the boundary of the site, and additional layers are provided as one moves inward through the building toward the high-value assets.

This concept applies to physical security barriers. When it is not possible to provide physical barriers, other types of security measures may need to be relied upon exclusively. These can include the use of security officers, employee training, remote surveillance systems, and other types of countermeasures.

Rather than placing full reliance on a single layer of defense, these layers require an intruder to penetrate a series of layers to reach his or her goal. The more layers that exist between the outside world and a high-value asset, the better the security. The Concentric Circles of Protection concept is similar to the "multiple lines of defense" strategy employed by many military planners.

This concept is illustrated in Figure 9.3. Please note that at the boundaries of each layer, those people who belong within the next layer can be separated from those who

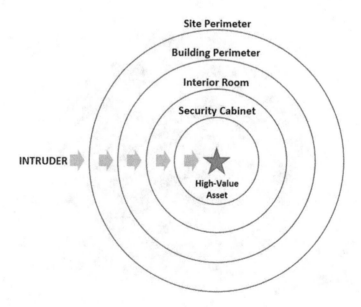

FIGURE 9.3   Security layers.

don't belong. Also, at each boundary, there is an opportunity to deter, detect, and delay an intruder. This allows intruders attempting to penetrate the layer to be detected and intercepted with an appropriate security response.

The logic behind having multiple layers of security is simple: Having multiple layers eliminates total reliance on any single layer and provides redundancy.

For example, in Figure 9.3, an intruder who "tailgated" through an exterior door would need to breach two additional layers of security before s/he could reach the high-value asset. While the chances of breaching any single layer may be good, the chance of breaching three or more successive layers becomes exponentially more difficult.

The multiple layers concept also provides redundancy in case there is a breakdown in procedures. For example, an employee may fail to lock a valuable piece of equipment in a cabinet as per established procedures, but instead leaves the equipment lying out openly on a desk. If the employee's office is locked, and access to the department is controlled, the equipment is still protected.

Conversely, if a janitor were to inadvertently leave an individual office door unlocked while cleaning, the valuable equipment would still be afforded some protection by the locked door that controls access into the department, and the secured cabinet in the office where the equipment is stored. Again, while the chance of a breakdown in any single procedure may be good, the chance of a breakdown in three or more successive procedures is considerably less likely.

An absolute minimum of three layers should exist between the outside world and any type of high-value property asset.

I used the term "asset" rather than property because I wanted it to include people and information in addition to physical property.

Basic Principles of Security Layers

- Having multiple layers decreases the probability that the intruder will be able to gain access.
- One can decrease the intruder's chance of success by adding layers, or by increasing the effectiveness of each layer, or by doing both.
- Relying on a single layer to provide security is almost never effective because it requires a level of perfection that is unattainable.
- Simple procedures, such as the locking of file cabinets and offices, can provide additional security "layers" at little or no cost.
- Employee security awareness can create an invisible, yet very effective security "layer."

Crime Prevention through Environmental Design

Crime Prevention through Environmental Design (CPTED) is a discipline based on the principle that criminal behavior can be influenced by the physical environment. While the term CPTED was first introduced in the early 1970s, many underlying CPTED principles were developed in the early 1960s. Since its introduction, CPTED has grown into one of the most widely studied and recognized methodologies in the security profession, though research on its effectiveness is limited. Existing research has provided mixed results with CPTED's effectiveness highly correlated to the criminal and their mindset. Criminals engaged in disorder crimes (e.g., vandalism) and property crimes (e.g., theft) are more likely to be deterred. Criminals engaged in violent crimes (e.g., robbery) are less likely to be deterred.

CPTED revolves around four basic principles: natural surveillance, natural access control, territoriality, and maintenance.

Natural surveillance is based on the principle that criminals do not like to be seen as they carry out their activities, and like places where they can hide and not be noticed. Techniques used to accomplish natural surveillance include designing landscaping so that it does not obstruct visibility, enclosing outdoor areas to eliminate hiding spots, designing buildings so that outside areas can be naturally observed through the windows, and providing adequate lighting so that criminals can easily be seen at night.

Natural access control is based on the principle that criminals like to easily come and go and don't like their movements to be restricted. Techniques used to accomplish natural access control include installing landscaping to define property boundaries, using landscaping rockeries and other natural barriers to create defined entrance and exit points at visible locations, and creating natural obstacles that can deter and delay an intruder.

Territoriality is a principle that clearly establishes the line between public and private property and definitively establishes ownership. Territoriality creates an atmosphere where legitimate occupants feel welcome and are encouraged to defend their space, while making intruders feel unwelcome and out of place. Territorially can be established by creating natural barriers between public and non-public spaces, creating separate spaces within the property that appear to be under the control of individual occupants, and providing signage that makes it clear that unauthorized use of the property is not acceptable.

Maintenance is based on the principle that properties that are poorly maintained attract crime while properties that are well maintained discourage crime. Having a well-maintained property sends a message that people notice and care about what goes on, establishing a strong sense of guardianship for the property. Having a poorly maintained property sends the opposite message – that no knows or cares about what goes on and that anyone can do anything.

The key to good maintenance is to regularly inspect the property and to promptly repair or replace any damaged items. This means promptly removing graffiti, replacing burned outs light, repairing damaged fencing, replacing broken windows, and removing trash and debris.

SITE SECURITY

Good physical security begins at the perimeter of the site and can set the overall tone of the security program at a facility. For example, a facility with a 12′ high chain-link fence with barbed wire can send the message that the facility is a high-security, controlled access facility, while the use of a very short decorative fence or no fencing at all suggests that the facility is open and has little security in place. It is important that the security measures displayed at the site perimeter accurately corresponds with the type of security image desired.

Fencing

Fencing is generally the first line of physical security defense for a facility. In addition to providing physical protection against intrusion, fencing serves to define the boundaries of a property, clearly marking the line between public and private property. There are three types of fencing commonly used for security purposes: chain-link fencing, wood fencing, and ornamental iron fencing.

Chain-link fencing is constructed using wires that are woven together into a metal fabric that has a distinct diamond pattern. This fabric is stretched between metal posts placed approximately ten feet apart to create the fence. Chain-link fence fabric can be constructed using different diameters of wire. The most commonly used in commercial applications is 9 gauge wire, while a heavier 6 gauge wire is typically used in higher-security applications. The spacing between the wires determines the size of the diamond-shaped openings in the fence fabric. The most common opening size used in commercial applications is 2", while smaller opening sizes of 3/8", 1/2", 5/8" are used in higher-security applications. The smaller opening sizes make the fencing more difficult to climb, and also make it harder to use a tool to cut through the fence fabric. Chain-link fence fabric is galvanized with a zinc coating to provide protection against rust and corrosion. Fence fabric can also be vinyl coated to provide additional level protection against the elements, as well as to provide coloring of the fence. Barbed wire or barbed metal tape can be added to the top of a chain-link fence to make it more difficult to climb over.

Wood fencing is constructed using posts, horizontal rails, and vertical pickets made of wood. There are a variety of styles of wood fences, the two most common being the picket fence and the full panel fence. The picket fence uses pickets that are 4" or 6" wide and are spaced 2½" or 3½" apart. This creates an open fence that provides security while still allowing direct visual observation through the fence. The full panel fence is constructed similarly to the picket fence, except that the pickets are placed almost directly adjacent to one another, creating a fence that is solid in appearance and cannot be seen through. The full panel fence provides both security and privacy. Wood fences can be constructed of a variety of species of wood, including cedar, white oak, pressure-treated pine, and redwood. Wood fencing can be stained or painted to provide protection against the elements and to improve its appearance.

Ornamental iron fencing is constructed using metal posts, horizontal metal rails, and metal pickets. Ornamental iron fencing can be designed in different styles ranging from the simple to the highly ornate. Fence post, rails, and pickets are available in different shapes and sizes. Ornamental iron pickets can be shaped outwards at the top to provide increased resistance to climbing. Ornamental iron fencing can provide good security while being very aesthetically pleasing, often making it a good choice for use at facilities where appearance is a consideration

Fencing can be installed at different heights depending on the level of security desired. For security at low to medium risk facilities, a minimum fence height of 7' is recommended, while at higher-security facilities, fencing at the height of 10' or greater is recommended. Aesthetic considerations and local building codes may prevent the installation of a fence that is at the optimum height for security. In these situations, the use of fencing may still be beneficial to define property boundaries and to control the flow of people and vehicles.

The cost of fencing varies greatly depending on the type of fencing used, the height of the fencing, and the specific materials to be used. Generally speaking, chain-link fencing is the least expensive, and ornamental iron fencing is the most expensive, with the cost of wood fencing falling somewhere in between.

Gates

Gates are used for controlling access in and out of a secured site. While most commonly used in conjunction with fencing, gates can be used alone for traffic control purposes. There are two types of gates: pedestrian gates and vehicle gates. Pedestrian gates are used to provide access for people on foot and can be controlled with a key-operated lock, or access control device such as a keypad or card reader.

Vehicle gates are used to control the entry and exit of vehicles. While vehicle gates can be opened and closed manually, they are most commonly equipped with an automatic gate operator and controlled using a keypad, card reader, or wireless radio transmitter. Vehicle gates can also be controlled by loop detectors that open the gate when a vehicle approaches, or by a manual release switch that is activated by a security guard or other attendant.

Vehicle gates are available in several styles, the most popular of which are the swing gate, slide gate, cantilever gate, and barrier arm gate. Swing gates are hinged on one side and swing open and closed like a door. Swing gates typically travel a 90-degree arc between their open and closed positions. Swing gates can consist of a single leaf or double leafs and can be in-swinging or out-swinging. The slide gate is mounted parallel to the inside of the fence and slides horizontally back and forth across the gate opening. The slide gate uses rollers on the bottom of the gate to support it. The cantilever gate is similar to the slide gate but does not use rollers that slide along the ground to support it. Instead, the cantilever gate is supported from rails that run along the inside of the fence structure. This gate gets its name from the fact that the gate "cantilevers" (hangs over) the gate opening. Barrier arm gates consist of a vertical barrier arm that is rotated in and out of the gate opening. Barrier arm gates are used to control vehicles, not pedestrians, as a person on foot can easily walk by the gate. Barrier arm gates are used primarily to control access in and out of parking facilities or to control vehicular traffic at manned security entrances.

The type of gate that should be chosen depends on a variety of factors including the width of the gate opening, space available at the gate, the volume of traffic going through the gate, level of security required, and weather conditions at the location where the gate will be installed.

At higher-security facilities, protection against the deliberate ramming of the gate is often required. This protection can be achieved by using gates that are specifically designed to provide anti-ram protection, or through the use of supplementary anti-ram devices such as hydraulically operated wedge barriers. Anti-ram gates and devices are most often rated to comply with testing standards developed by the United States Department of State. These standards establish different security ratings based on vehicle size and speed of attack.

Other Physical Barriers

While fencing is most commonly used to provide perimeter security of a site, other physical barriers can be used to provide a similar level of protection. These barriers can include berms, rockeries, landscaping, and water features. Berms are mounded hills of dirt that can be used to prevent vehicle access and provide visual screening. Rockeries are constructed using a pile of strategically placed stones of various sizes and can be used to form a physical obstacle that is difficult to penetrate. Landscaping can be used to create a variety of different types of barriers, ranging from a few shrubs planted along a walkway that can serve to direct pedestrian traffic, to a dense hedge that can serve as a wall that is nearly impenetrable. Water features, such as streams and ponds, can also serve as effective barriers to entry at a site.

Many sites are best secured using a combination of different types of barriers and fencing. For example, at a corporate headquarters campus, ornamental iron fencing might be used along the front of the campus, while chain-link fencing was used along the back of the campus, and a combination of berms, rockeries, and landscaping was used along the sides of the campus.

Lighting

Exterior lighting along roadways, pathways, and in parking lots is crucial in providing effective security. There are five basic considerations when planning lighting systems for security purposes:

1. The intensity of the lighting: How bright does the light need to be?
2. The uniformity of the lighting: How consistent does the light level from place to place throughout the lighted area need to be?
3. The color of the lighting: How accurately does the lighting need to render colors?
4. The efficiency of lighting: How much light per watt of electricity should the lighting system deliver?
5. The amount of maintenance required: How long do lamps or light-emitting-diodes (LED) last before they must be replaced?

The amount of lighting provided to illuminate an area is specified in foot-candles, or its metric equivalent, the lux. Equally important is the uniformity of lighting throughout the illuminated area. Uniformity of lighting is expressed as a ratio between the lowest light level reading and the average light level reading taken throughout the area. For example, if the average light level reading was 50 lux, and the lowest light level reading was 10 lux, the uniformity ratio would be 5:1.

Unfortunately, there is no general consensus as to what constitutes adequate illuminance levels in outdoor areas. One guideline commonly used by security professionals is *G-1–16 Guideline for Security Lighting for People, Property, and Critical Infrastructure*, published by the Illuminating Engineering Society of North America (IESNA). This document establishes different illuminance levels and uniformity ratios depending on the type of facility and location. For example, this standard suggests a minimum illuminance level of 30 lux and a maximum 4:1 uniformity ratio in parking areas at public parks, schools, and hotels and motels, while an illuminance level of 50 lux and a maximum 4:1 uniformity ratio is suggested for close-in parking at major retail establishments.

It should be noted that the G-1–16 Guideline is based on providing lighting at facilities where security is of concern. The illuminance levels stated within this document can often exceed those actually used by engineers when designing lighting systems for new facilities. The current trend towards designing environmentally friendly buildings and achieving LEED (Leadership in Energy and Environmental Design) certification can often be in conflict with the need to provide lighting that is optimum for security purposes.

TABLE 9.1 Comparison of Commonly Used Lighting Fixtures

Fixture Type	Energy Efficiency	Lifespan in Hours	Color Rendition	Installation Cost
Metal Halide	70 to 100 LPW	6,000 to 10,000	70–90 CRI	Medium
High-Pressure Sodium	50 to 140 LPW	18,000 to 24,000	20–25 CRI	Low
LED	60 to 150 LPW	50,000 to 100,000	70–90 CRI	High

The most popular types of fixtures used for outdoor lighting are the high-intensity discharge (HID) lamp type and the LED type. Within the HID category, there are two types of lamps most commonly used, the metal halide type and the high-pressure sodium type. HID lamps have been around for decades and produce light using an electrical arc. LED light fixtures are a relatively new technology and use a solid-state light source rather than a lamp.

Three of the most important considerations when choosing outdoor light fixtures are the efficiency of the light source, the lifespan of the light source, and the ability of the light source to accurately render colors. The efficiency of light fixtures is measured using a metric known as lumens per watt (LPW), which is the amount of light produced for each watt of electricity consumed. The higher the LPW rating, the more efficient the fixture is, and the less it costs to operate. The lifespan of light fixtures is the amount of time that the light will operate before requiring replacement, measured in operating hours. The ability of a light fixture to accurately render colors is measured using a metric known as the Color Rendering Index (CRI). The index uses ratings from 1 to 100, with 100 indicating that colors under the light source appear identical to how they would appear under sunlight, which is the perfect light source for accurate color rendition. Having a high CRI is especially important in security applications, where obtaining an accurate description of the color of a suspect's clothing or vehicle can be essential.

Table 9.1 provides a comparison of the efficiency, lifespan, color rendition accuracy, and relative cost of the commonly used types of lighting fixtures.

The LPW rating for LED light fixtures stated in Table 9.1 does not accurately portray the overall energy efficiency of LED lights. This is because LED fixtures, unlike their metal halide and high-pressure sodium counterparts, direct almost 100% of the lumens that they produce on their desired target. Other types of fixtures waste light by directing lumens in unintended directions that provide no useful illumination of the target. The net result is that LED light fixtures provide considerably more lumens on target than their counterparts and are therefore the most energy efficient type of light source in most applications.

BUILDING EXTERIOR SECURITY

Doors

Doors are the primary means that people use to enter buildings and play an important role in providing physical security at a facility. Doors are often chosen based on their architectural appearance rather than the need to provide physical protection and so sometimes are less than optimum for security purposes. There are two general types of doors, pedestrian doors and overhead doors. Pedestrian doors are used to control access by people, while overhead doors are primarily used to control access of vehicles and for the loading and unloading of material and equipment.

Pedestrian doors are available in both the swinging and sliding type. Pedestrian doors can be constructed of wood, hollow-metal, aluminum, and glass. Here are some important considerations when choosing pedestrian doors for security purposes:

- Hollow-metal doors within a hollow-metal frame generally provide the best physical protection and should be used in all applications where security rather than appearance is the primary consideration.
- Solid wood doors are the second-best choice for security purposes if adequate reinforcement of the door frame is provided. This can be accomplished by using a wood door within a hollow-metal door frame, or by using supplementary devices to reinforce the door frame. Hollow-wood doors provide almost no protection against attack and should not be used for security purposes.
- Aluminum storefront doors are available in narrow stile, medium stile, and wide stile versions. Wide stile versions provide the most strength and the best protection against physical attack.
- Sliding aluminum storefront doors with automatic openers often lack positive locking mechanisms and rely solely on the automatic opener to stay closed. Standard versions of these doors generally provide very little security and are difficult to use with electronic access control systems. To address these issues, many door manufacturers now offer a security version of their product that include features such as solenoid operated locks specifically designed for use with access control systems.
- All-glass doors constructed of thick tempered glass are commonly used at building lobbies when appearance is important. While relatively strong, these doors shatter into thousands of small pieces when broken. The types of lock hardware that can be used on these doors is limited, often making it a challenge to use them with electronic access control systems.
- Doors over 8' in height can be difficult to properly secure and should be avoided if possible. Many tall doors that are only locked at the top or bottom can be pulled open a considerable distance even when locked. This eventually causes the door to warp and prevents it from operating reliably.
- All doors should be equipped with door closers that allow the door to automatically close and lock.

Overhead doors are available in two common types, the sectional door and the coiling door. Sectional overhead doors are constructed using multiple hinged panels made of wood or sheet metal. Sectional door panels often have sections of foam installed within them to provide insulation against the weather. Coiling overhead doors, sometimes called curtain doors, are constructed using interlocking metal slats. Here are some important considerations when using overhead doors for security purposes:

- Overhead doors can be easily damaged by forklifts and other vehicles. Protective devices such as bollards should be installed on both sides of the door opening to protect the overhead door tracks.
- The standard factory lock hardware provided with most overhead doors provides very little security. Install supplementary locks on overhead doors to provide

increased protection. On doors that are wider than 10′, install lock hardware on both sides of the door to prevent intruders from lifting up the unsecured side of the door.

- Overhead doors that are at grade level and that have drive-up ramps can be subject to attack by vehicles. Driving a vehicle through an overhead door is a popular technique used to commit "smash and grab" burglaries. To prevent this, install removable bollards that can be locked in place in front of the door at the end of the business day.
- If overhead doors must be left open for ventilation purposes on a regular basis, provide folding metal security gates to protect the door opening when the door is left open.

Windows and Exterior Glazing

Windows and other exterior glazing used at the exterior of the building can pose a security vulnerability.

Using glass of any kind on the exterior of a building makes it more vulnerable than if it had no glass. If physical security were the only consideration, a building would have no glass. However, since this is rarely practical in the real world, the following ideas should be considered.

Breaking a window to gain entry is a common method used by burglars and windows can easily be broken by vandals. Here are some tips for providing improved security for windows:

- Minimize the use of exterior windows at facilities where security is of concern. Avoid placing windows in concealed, out of the way, locations. Try to keep windows as high off the ground as possible.
- Consider the use of security window film to reinforce glass. This film consists of one or more layers of polyester film, laminated together with special adhesives. Security window film typically ranges in thickness from 4 mils (100 micron) to 14 mils (350 micron) or more. Security window film is typically installed on existing glass by a professional installer. Glass with window film can still be broken, but the film holds glass shards together, which can delay or prevent entry by a burglar. Security window film can also reduce injuries caused by flying glass when the window is shattered because of an accident, act of vandalism, or bomb blast.
- For higher security applications, consider replacing glass windows with polycarbonate plastic glazing materials such as Lexan™. These materials are highly resistant to impact and difficult for an intruder to penetrate.
- Window bars can be used on the interior or exterior of windows to discourage entry by an intruder. While traditionally thought of as unattractive, industrial appearing devices, window bars can be constructed of stainless steel, acrylic plastic, or other materials in a manner that is aesthetically pleasing while at the same time providing good security.

Mechanical Locks

While electronic locking devices are becoming increasingly popular, mechanical locks remain a fundamental component of physical security at most facilities. Even when electronic access control systems are provided, they are most often used in conjunction with, not in place of, traditional mechanical locks.

There are four popular styles of mechanical locks. These include the cylindrical lock, mortise lock, deadbolt lock, and exit device.

The cylindrical lock consists of a round shaped lock unit that is installed in a large hole drilled within the door. Cylindrical locks are the least expensive type of lock and are commonly used in residential and light commercial applications when a heavier duty type of lockset is not needed.

Mortise locks are rectangular lock units that are installed in a cavity in the side of the door. Mortise locks are more expensive than cylindrical locks and more difficult to install. Mortise locks are commonly used in commercial and industrial applications where a heavier duty lockset is needed.

Deadbolt locks are available in both cylindrical and mortise versions and are most commonly used to supplement another lockset on a door. One exception is aluminum storefront doors, where the deadbolt lock is often the only locking device on the door.

Exit devices are locking devices installed on doors that are intended to be used for emergency egress. Exit devices are often required by building codes in certain types of occupancies and when the total number of occupants in a building exceeds a certain number. Exit devices consist of a horizontal bar, sometimes called a "crash bar", installed across a portion of the width of the door. Pressing this bar causes the door to immediately unlock from the inside.

Mechanical locks consist of two distinct parts: the lock cylinder and the lock body. The lock cylinder is the part of the lock in which the key is inserted. Lock cylinders are usually designed to work with only one specific brand and type of key but can generally be installed in any type of lock body. This allows different types of mechanical locks to be used on different doors, but so long as a common type of lock cylinder is used, a single key can be used on all doors.

The most common type of lock cylinder in use today is the pin tumbler lock cylinder. Originally developed more than a century ago, pin tumbler lock cylinders served their purpose well, but have several security vulnerabilities that make them less than optimum for modern use. These include the ability for the pin tumbler to be "picked" or "bumped" open, and the ease of which the keys used with pin tumbler lock cylinders can be duplicated by unauthorized parties.

The picking of locks involves the use of lock picks, while the bumping of locks involves the use of a special bump key. Lock picks and bump keys can be readily purchased from online sources, and instructions for making and using these devices can be found freely on the internet. These techniques are now used by more knowledgeable intruders to gain entry to buildings.

The keys used with pin tumbler lock cylinders can be readily duplicated without authorization from the facility owner. Most locksmiths or hardware stores will duplicate keys for anyone, despite any "Do Not Duplicate" warning that may be printed on the key. There are automated key duplication kiosks at many shopping malls that allow keys to be duplicated, as well as online services that will produce a copy of a key based on an uploaded picture. Once a key has been issued to a contractor or employee, it is unknown how many unauthorized copies of the key may have been made.

To overcome the vulnerabilities associated with standard pin tumbler lock cylinders and keys, high security lock systems have been developed. These systems utilize a mechanical design that is specifically designed to resist picking and bumping. High security lock systems are also constructed to resist drilling and other physical manipulation of the lock. The keys used with high security locks are patented and available only through limited distribution channels. The lock manufacturer has procedures in place so that only authorized people can order duplicate keys.

Here are some suggestions for the use of mechanical locks:

- Mortise locks provide better protection against forced entry than cylindrical locks do and should be used when a higher level of security is desired.
- The use of high security lock cylinders rather than standard pin tumbler lock cylinders is highly recommended. If budget restrictions prevent the use of high security lock cylinders on all doors, consider using high security locks on exterior doors and doors to critical interior rooms, while using standard lock cylinders elsewhere.
- The use of master key systems where a single key can open everything can increase the complexity of the lock system, make locks more vulnerable to picking and bumping, and increase exposure to loss if a master key is lost. Carefully weigh the convenience of using a master key system against the security risks.
- Have good procedures in place so that only the people who need them receive keys. Keep good track of who is issued each key and when. Encourage users to promptly report lost or missing keys. Quickly rekey locks when it is suspected that an important key may have fallen into the wrong hands.

BUILDING INTERIOR SECURITY

Building Lobbies

The lobby is the primary point where visitors and other members of the public enter a facility. As such, it is one of the most critical areas to design properly from a security standpoint. Having a poorly designed lobby makes it difficult to properly control access into the building, requiring that additional security measures be provided at the interior of the building. A poorly designed lobby can also increase operational costs by requiring that additional staff be provided to overcome the security weaknesses created by the lobby.

Many lobbies are designed primarily with aesthetics and convenience in mind, with little or no thought given to security. Often, this is because the architect and owner lacked an understanding of basic security concepts or failed to consider security during the architectural planning process. Here are some guidelines that should be used in designing an effective lobby for security purposes:

- A physical wall or barrier should be provided between the lobby and the secured portion of the building. Within this wall should be a door, gate, or turnstile that controls employee and visitor access into the facility. The receptionist should not be expected to serve as the security barrier.
- It should not be possible for visitors to enter the secured portion of the facility without passing by the reception desk. Doors, stairways, and elevators that provide access from the lobby to other portions of the building should be located behind, not in front of, the receptionist.
- The receptionist's desk should face directly toward the exterior entrance to the lobby, allowing the receptionist to see who is entering, and making it obvious as to where visitors should go once they enter.

- Providing a restroom that is directly accessible from the unsecured portion of the lobby can eliminate the need for visitors to enter the secured portion of the building just to use the restroom.
- Providing a small conference room that is directly accessible from the unsecured portion of the building can allow employees to conduct short meetings with vendors and other visitors without requiring then to sign in or enter secured portions of the building. This conference room can also be used to conduct terminations, particularly of potentially hostile persons.
- When possible, the lobby should not be used as a primary employee entrance point. If practical, provide a separate entrance point for employees and discourage them from entering through the lobby. Reducing traffic through the lobby makes it easier for the receptionist to observe activity and reduces the chances of an intruder "tailgating" in behind an employee.

Shipping/Receiving Areas

Shipping and receiving areas are a common point of security vulnerability at most facilities. Here are some ideas for providing improved security at shipping/receiving areas:

- Try to separate areas used for shipping away from areas used for receiving. When possible, provide physical barriers between these two areas.
- Where possible, provide a separately fenced yard area that encloses the warehouse shipping and receiving doors. Establish a policy that prohibits personal vehicles from being driven into the shipping and receiving yard area. Keep the gate to the exterior yard area locked at times when the warehouse is closed.
- Do not allow employee or visitor parking near warehouse shipping and receiving doors.
- Do not allow truck drivers to wander through the warehouse. If possible, provide a dedicated "driver lounge" for use by drivers. The driver lounge should contain restrooms and other amenities that can be used by drivers while they are waiting for their trailers to be loaded or unloaded. Access to the driver lounge should not require travel through interior warehouse areas.
- Exterior trash and recycle containers should not be directly accessible from the inside of the warehouse. If possible, locate exterior trash and recycle containers away from the building. Keep trash and recycle containers locked. Establish procedures for trash removal that requires at least two employees to be present when trash is being removed from the building.
- When possible, the warehouse manager's office should be located so that direct visual observation of the shipping and receiving bay doors from the office is possible.
- Avoid stacking merchandise directly in front of shipping and receiving doors – try to maintain a "clear zone of at least ten feet."
- Provide separate areas for the storage of valuable or highly desirable items, such as computer and electronic equipment, cigarettes, liquor, baby formula, expensive clothing, etc. If possible, create separately lockable "high-value" cages or rooms for the storage of these items.

Mail Rooms

Mail rooms are used for the sending, receiving, opening, sorting, and distribution of mail and small packages. Mail rooms often contain sensitive information and other valuable assets. Mail rooms are also one of the more likely locations where letter or packages containing hazardous substances or explosives could pose an immediate danger. Here are some thoughts on providing improved security for mail rooms:

- Mail rooms should be physically segregated from other portions of the building. Access to mail rooms should only be allowed when authorized mail room personnel are present.
- Consider the potential for a letter or package bomb to be detonated in the mail room. Avoid placing mail rooms directly adjacent to critical structural elements or building systems such as mechanical, electrical, and fire protection systems.
- The heating, ventilation, and air conditioning system (HVAC) for the mail room should be separately zoned so that contaminants introduced in the mail room when a hazardous package is opened are not circulated into other occupied portions of the facility.

Interior Rooms Requiring Extra Security

Most facilities have rooms that contain valuable assets or critical infrastructure that requires an additional level of security. These rooms can include computer server rooms, main distribution frame and intermediate distribution frame (MDF/IDF) closets, mechanical and electrical rooms, generator rooms, and other such spaces. To provide improved security for these high-security rooms, the following is suggested:

- High-security rooms should be located on the interior of the building if possible. If located on the exterior of the building, the room should have no exterior windows.
- All walls of the room should extend from floor to structural ceiling. Partition walls that only extend to the bottom of a suspended ceiling should not be used as they could allow an intruder to enter by climbing over the ceiling.
- The doors to high-security rooms should be hollow-metal doors or solid wood doors installed in hollow-metal frames. There should be no windows or glass panes in, above, or beside the door.
- High security lock cylinders should be used on all doors.
- All walls of the room should be constructed of concrete or masonry blocks if possible. If framed walls are used, they should be covered with ¾" thick plywood in addition to sheetrock to prevent forced entry through the walls.
- Signs that provide a description of what is inside of the room should not be used. The people who need access to these rooms should already know where they are, and there is no need to unnecessarily advertise the location to other parties. If desired, a sign with just a room number can be used.

File Cabinets and Safes

File cabinets and safes are used to provide physical security of documents containing sensitive information, and high-value assets such as cash, precious metals, and other valuables. In addition to providing protection against theft, file cabinets and safes can be used to provide protection against fire.

Burglar safes are designed to provide protection against forced entry. Burglars use a variety of tools to break into safes, including common hand tools, power tools, cutting torches, chemicals, and explosives. A burglar safe can be designed to resist each of these types of attacks, but specific materials and construction techniques must be used to protect against each type of threat. It is important to note that no safe is burglar-proof – any safe can be opened if the burglar has the right tools, the proper skills, and a sufficient amount of time. The purpose of the safe is to deter burglaries, prevent thefts by unskilled thieves, and delay the skilled burglar. When used with other security measures, such as intrusion alarm systems, a safe can provide a delay that increases the chances that the burglar will be apprehended or flee the premises before the burglary is completed. Performance ratings rank safes according to written standards developed by an independent testing laboratory. The preeminent testing laboratory in the United States is Underwriters Laboratories (UL). A written standard, called UL 687, provides rigorous requirements that safes must conform to in order to display a UL rating. UL 687 provides specific ratings based upon the types of burglary tools used and the amount of time that a safe can delay an attack. These ratings are designated using an alphanumeric code, such as "TL-15," "TRTL-30," etc.

Fire safes and fire file cabinets are designed to provide protection of the container's contents against damage caused by fire. Just as burglar safes are not burglar-proof, fire safes and file cabinets are not "fire-proof" – they only provide resistance to a certain type of fire for a certain period – hopefully long enough for the fire department to arrive and extinguish the blaze. UL also has a comprehensive system for the rating of fire safes. This rating system classifies safes based upon the assets that they are designed to store, the expected temperature of the fire, and the time that the assets are to be protected.

Here are some things to be considered when choosing a file cabinet or safe:

- To protect highly sensitive information and high value assets against burglary, a UL Burglary Rated safe should be purchased. A safe with a minimum rating of TL-15 (tool-resistant safe, fifteen-minute rating) should be used. Safes with ratings of TL-30 (tool-resistant safe, thirty-minute rating), TRTL-15 (torch-and-tool-resistant safe, fifteen-minute rating), TRTL-30 (torch-and-tool-resistant safe, thirty-minute rating), or TXTL-60 (torch, explosive, and tool-resistant safe, sixty-minute rating) can be used when higher levels of security are needed or when dictated by regulatory requirements.
- To protect paper documents against fire, a UL Class 350 Fire-Rated Safe or File Cabinet should be used. If the container will also be used to store electronic media such as tapes, CDs, and DVDs, the safe or file cabinet should have a UL Class 125 or UL Class 150 Rating.
- Unless specifically stated otherwise by the manufacturer, Class 350, Class 150, and Class 125 safes are not rated to resist burglary. While a fire safe that is equipped with a high-security lock does provide some protection against an amateur thief, a professional burglar can open most fire safes in just a matter of minutes.
- Most safes sold through office supply stores and wholesale clubs are fire-rated (if rated at all) and provide minimal protection against burglary. Some safes sold in office supply or retail stores have a UL RSC (Residential Security Container) rating. This rating provides protection against tool attacks for only five minutes and is not recommended for commercial use.

ELECTRONIC SECURITY SYSTEMS

Access Control Systems

Simply defined, the term "access control" describes any technique used to control passage into or out of any area. The standard lock that uses a brass key may be thought of as a simple form of an "access control system." Over the years, access control systems have become more and more sophisticated. Today, the term "access control system" most often refers to a computer-based, electronic card access control system. The electronic card access control system uses a special "access card," rather than a brass key, to permit access into the secured area.

The purpose of an access control system is to provide quick, convenient access to those persons who are authorized, while at the same time restricting access to unauthorized people.

Access control systems offer many advantages over manual key systems. Some of the features provided by an access control system include:

- The ability to custom tailor the specific doors to which each user has access.
- The ability to custom tailor the specific days and times that each user can gain access through each door.
- The ability to establish a "start date" and "stop date" for each access card.
- The ability to provide real-time reports that show which user entered through what door and when.
- The ability to modify or terminate access privileges of access cards on a real-time basis.
- The ability to automatically lock and unlock doors based on a time schedule.
- The ability to immediately lock and unlock doors based on manual command.
- The ability to monitor doors to determine if they have been forced open or propped open and send an email alert when an abnormal condition is detected.

Access control systems vary widely in type and complexity. However, most card access control systems consist of at least the following basic components:

Access Cards
The access card may be thought of as an electronic "key." The access card is used by persons to gain access through the doors secured by the access control system. Each access card is uniquely encoded. Most access cards are approximately the same size as a standard credit card and can easily be carried in a wallet or purse. There are a variety of different types of access card technologies available, including proximity and contactless smart cards.

Card Readers
Card readers are the devices used to electronically "read" the access card. Most card readers used today are the no-contact proximity type, which can read cards held at a distance (usually 2" to 6") from the card reader. Card readers are usually mounted on the exterior (non-secured) side of the door that they control.

Access Control Keypads

Access control keypads are devices which may be used in addition to or in place of card readers. The access control keypad has numeric keys which look like the keys on a touch-tone telephone. The access control keypad requires that a person desiring to gain access enter a correct numeric code. When access control keypads are used in addition to card readers, both a valid card and the correct code must be presented before entry is allowed. Where access control keypads are used in place of card readers, only a correct code is required to gain entry.

Electric Lock Hardware

Electric lock hardware is the equipment that is used to electrically lock and unlock each door that is controlled by the access control system. There are a wide variety of different types of electric lock hardware. These types include electric locks, electric strikes, electromagnetic locks, electric exit devices, and many others. In almost all cases, the electric lock hardware is designed to control entrance into a building or secured space. To comply with building and fire codes, the electric lock hardware never restricts the ability to freely exit the building at any time.

Access Control Field Panels

Access control field panels (also known as "Intelligent Controllers") are installed in each building where access control is to be provided. Card readers, electric lock hardware, and other access control devices are all connected to the access control field panels. The access control field panels are used to process access control activity at the building level. The number of access control field panels to be provided in each building depends on the number of doors to be controlled. Access control field panels are usually installed in telephone, electrical, or communications closets.

Access Control Server Computer

The access control server computer is the "brain" of the access control system. The access control server computer serves as the central database and file manager for the access control system, and is responsible for recording system activity and distributing information to and from the access control field panels. Programming of the access control system can be done at the server computer, or remotely over the network using workstation software installed on another computer.

Cloud-Based Access Control Systems

Cloud-based access control systems allow management of the access control system over the internet using a standard web browser. Cloud-based access control systems eliminate the need for an access control server computer to be installed on the premises. Access control field panels are connected to the internet and programmed directly by a web browser or managed centrally by a server computer located at a remote service provider's facility.

Cloud-based access control systems can be managed entirely by the user, just as if a server computer were installed at the facility; or can be fully or partially managed by the remote service provider on a paid subscription basis. When a service provider is used, the user simply needs to call or email the service provider when access cards need to be added or deleted or other programming changes are desired, and the service provider takes care of the rest. The use of a service provider can be ideal at smaller facilities where dedicated security or facilities management staff is not available to manage the system.

Standalone Access Control Devices

Standalone access control devices provide an alternative to the traditional access control system described earlier. Standalone access control devices provide some of the features offered by the traditional access control system, but at a reduced cost. Standalone access devices are typically self-contained units that are installed in place of the regular lockset on the door. Standalone access control devices contain their own internal processor and memory and are usually battery powered. Some simpler standalone devices must be programmed individually at each door, while more advanced devices can be programmed remotely over the network using a wireless connection.

Standalone access control devices can be ideal for use at smaller facilities that have a limited budget. However, they can become unwieldly when used at larger facilities or when users need advanced access control or reporting features. At larger facilities, the labor required to travel to each door to make programming changes and replace batteries on an ongoing basis can quickly outweigh any cost savings enjoyed when the devices were initially purchased.

Intrusion Detection Systems

Intrusion detection systems, sometimes called burglar alarm systems, are used to detect the presence of an intruder in a building. The typical intrusion alarm system consists of the following basic components:

Detection Devices
Detection devices are the components used to detect the entry of an intruder into the building. There are dozens of different types of detection devices, each of which uses a different method of detecting the presence of an intruder. The most commonly used types of detection devices at commercial facilities are:

Contact Switches   Contact switches are installed on doors and windows to detect when the door or window has been opened. Contact switches are most commonly installed on doors and opening windows at the exterior of the building but may also be installed on interior doors. There are different types of contact switches available for installation on wood and metal doors, windows, gates, hatches, and other types of openings.

Motion Detectors   Motion detectors are used to detect the presence or movement of people within the building. Motion detectors are most commonly installed in hallways, corridors, and within rooms that contain a high concentration of valuables. The most common type of motion detector in use today is the "passive infrared" (PIR) detector.

The PIR detector detects the body heat of a person as he or she passes within the viewing area of the detector.

Glass Breakage Detectors   Glass breakage detectors are used to detect the breakage of glass. Glass breakage detectors are normally installed near accessible glass windows and doors at the exterior of the building. Glass breakage detectors listen for the sound of breaking glass and activate the alarm when glass is broken.

Signaling Devices
Signaling devices are the devices that the intrusion alarm system activates when intrusion is detected. Signaling devices notify the intruder that s/he has been detected, causing her or him to flee from the premises, or to at least spend less time in the building. Signaling devices also notify employees, neighbors, and passersby that the intrusion alarm has been activated.

There are both audible and visual types of signaling devices. Audible signaling devices include bells, electronic sirens, and voice announcement systems which broadcast alarm messages using a recorded human voice. Visual signaling devices include revolving lights, blinking lights, and electronic strobe lights. Signaling devices are normally installed on both the interior and exterior of the building.

Arming Stations
Arming stations are the devices used to "arm" (turn on) and "disarm" (turn off) the intrusion alarm system. The most common type of arming station is the keypad arming station. The keypad arming station consists of a numeric keypad with indicators lights and an alphanumeric display. The alphanumeric display uses letters and numbers to display system status information using plain language messages. If a door in the building has been left open, the alphanumeric display can tell the user exactly which door has been left open. Alphanumeric displays can also indicate system troubles, alarm activity, and many other conditions. To use the keypad arming station, the user must know the correct code. In addition to allowing the user to arm and disarm the system, the keypad arming station provides the user with the ability to arm only a certain portion of the system while leaving other parts disarmed, and the ability to perform system diagnostic and maintenance functions.

Arming stations are the primary device that the user uses to interact with the building's intrusion alarm system. Arming stations are usually installed inside the building near the doors that are used by employees to leave and enter the building

Intrusion Alarm Control Panel
The intrusion alarm control panel is the heart of the intrusion alarm system and is used to process all system operations and activity. All detection devices, signaling devices, and arming stations connect to the control panel, using either a hardwired or wireless connection. Modern control panels are a specialized form of computer that include a microprocessor, computer memory, and data communications capabilities. Intrusion alarm control panels are fully programmable to allow the operating characteristics of the intrusion alarm system to be custom tailored to meet the needs of the building in which it is installed. Because the average user of the intrusion alarm system usually never needs to interact with the control panel, these panels are normally installed in a closet or equipment room.

Alarm Monitoring

In addition to sounding a local alarm on the premises, intrusion alarm systems can be monitored by an alarm monitoring center located off-site. When the intrusion alarm system is activated, the monitoring center will typically notify the police, on-site security staff, and facilities staff that an alarm has been triggered and that an intruder may be on the premises.

The intrusion alarm system may use several methods to communicate the alarm signal to the off-site alarm monitoring center. These include data communications over the internet, cellular, and long-range radio. The intrusion alarm system may also communicate using a landline telephone connection, although this once popular communications method is gradually becoming obsolete.

Most intrusion alarm control panels contain built-in alarm communication capabilities. In some cases, the use of a plug-in module or an external communications device may be necessary to provide the type of communications desired. To provide an additional level of security, intrusion alarm systems can be designed so that they use two separate communications methods, a primary and a backup. If the system is unable to communicate using the primary method, it then attempts to communicate using the backup method.

Remote Control of Intrusion Alarm

Many alarm monitoring companies offer a service that allows the intrusion alarm system to be monitored and controlled remotely using a smartphone app. This app may be used to remotely arm and disarm the system and allows users to quickly determine the status of their system at any time. The app may also be used to change user codes and to modify other system settings.

Panic Buttons

Panic buttons, or duress buttons, can be added to the intrusion alarm system to provide a means for users to summon help in an emergency. Both wired and wireless panic buttons can be used. When a panic button is pressed, it sends a silent signal to the alarm monitoring center notifying them that help is needed.

Video Surveillance Systems

Video surveillance systems are used to allow the visual observation and recording of events. The video surveillance system can be used on a real-time basis to monitor activity, detect abnormal conditions, and assess security threats. The video surveillance system can also be used to provide video recording of events that can be used to investigate security and safety incidents, identify suspects, and provide evidence of improper activity and crimes. Video surveillance systems are made up of the following components:

Cameras

Cameras are the devices used to capture video images to allow them to be viewed or recorded. For many decades, analog cameras were used in video surveillance systems. These cameras simply produced a video signal that was then connected to external equipment that allowed it to be viewed or recorded. Most cameras installed today in commercial applications are the IP (internet protocol) network type. These cameras are actually small computers that can intelligently process data in addition to capturing video images. Unlike their analog predecessors, IP network cameras can evaluate and enhance the video image, control the area that the camera views, and detect motion in the camera scene. The program settings on IP network cameras can be changed remotely over the network, and IP camera images can be viewed using a standard web browser. Many IP network cameras can use a memory storage card that allows them to store recorded video images directly on the camera.

There are many different styles and types of IP network cameras. The most popular type is the fixed-position camera, which is designed to view a single preset area which is determined by the camera's lens. Fixed-position cameras are commonly used to view building entrances, hallways, corridors, and special high-security areas of the building.

When it is necessary to view a larger area, pan-tilt-zoom (PTZ) cameras are often used. PTZ cameras are movable and are normally designed to view a wide area of coverage. PTZ cameras can "zoom" in and out, can "pan" left and right, and can "tilt" up and down, allowing a single camera to cover a large area. PTZ cameras are commonly used in parking lots and to cover large outside areas. It is important to note that while a PTZ camera has the potential to view a large area, it can only view a small portion of its total coverage area at any one time.

To provide continuous viewing of larger areas, panoramic cameras are available that allow the viewing of a 360-degree area. These cameras can be used in conjunction with software that allows only specific portions of the scene to be viewed, allowing them to be used as a virtual PTZ camera. However, because the panoramic camera's viewing area is spread so widely, it may not provide the same level of detail or picture quality that would be provided by a PTZ camera viewing the same scene. Panoramic cameras are often a good choice for use in locations such as building lobbies or retail showrooms where 360-degree coverage of a defined area is needed.

Multi-imager cameras are available that contain two, three, or four separate video imagers. Multi-imager cameras are essentially several fixed-position cameras combined into one package. This reduces the number of individual devices that are needed and minimizes cabling requirements. Many multi-imager cameras include software that allows the views of the individual imagers to be combined to form a 180-degree, 270-degree, or 360-degree continuous coverage pattern. Multi-imager cameras are often a good choice for use at intersections in corridors where the ability to view down each hallway is desired. Multi-imager cameras also work well at the exterior corners of buildings to allow the viewing of the building perimeter in both directions.

IP network cameras are available in several different physical configurations or form factors. The most common form factors are the dome camera, bullet camera, and box camera. Dome cameras consist of a semicircular shaped housing that encloses both the camera and camera lens. Dome cameras can be directly attached to a wall or ceiling or can be mounted from a bracket that allows the camera to be mounted to the wall, ceiling, or pole. Dome cameras can be rated for indoor use only, or indoor/outdoor use.

Bullet cameras consist of a tubular camera housing with a mounting bracket. The camera housing contains both the camera and camera lens. Bullet cameras are primarily intended to be wall mounted and are usually rated for indoor/outdoor use.

Box cameras consist of a camera body that is used with a separately attached camera lens. While box cameras can be installed by themselves in indoor applications, most box cameras are installed in some type of camera enclosure to provide protection of the camera and lens. Depending on the type of enclosure used, box cameras can be used both indoors and outdoors.

IP network cameras are connected to the network using a data network cable. Cat 5e and Cat 6 cables are most commonly used. Most IP network cameras are the Power-Over-Ethernet (POE) type, which allows them to be powered through the network without requiring an additional power source.

IP network cameras are available with a wide range of different features and at different price points. The most important characteristics that are used to define a camera include resolution, frame rate, sensitivity, and light processing abilities. The following is a brief description of each of these characteristics:

Resolution   The resolution of IP network cameras is defined by the number of pixels in the camera imager that are used to make up the video image. These pixels are arranged horizontally and vertically, and resolution is typically stated by specifying the number of horizontal and vertical pixels used. For example, one resolution commonly used today is 1920 horizontal pixels by 1080 vertical pixels. To simplify things, the resolution of a camera is usually stated using the total number of pixels in the scene, which can be obtained by multiplying the number of horizontal pixels by the number of vertical pixels. Using the example above, 1920 would be multiplied by 1080, which would give a result of 2,073,600 pixels. This number would be rounded to 2,000,000 pixels and stated as 2 megapixels (millions of pixels), or 2 MP.

IP network cameras are available in resolutions of 1 MP, 2MP, 3 MP, 5MP, 10MP, and higher. Resolution can sometimes be specified in television broadcast industry terms rather than MP. For example, the term Full HD may be used instead of 2 MP to describe 1920 x 1080 resolution, and 4K UHD may be used instead of 8 MP to describe 3840 x 2160 resolution.

In general, the greater the number of MP that a camera has, the more detail it will provide. However, this comes at a cost, both in terms of initial purchase price, as well as the bandwidth necessary to transmit and record the video image. Simply speaking, bandwidth is the amount of data that must be sent over the network and stored on the recording device. The key is to select a camera resolution that provides the necessary level of detail without unnecessarily consuming bandwidth.

Frame Rate   Video images are made up of multiple still pictures, known as frames. The term "frame rate" defines the number of frames that are displayed per second to create the video image. Frame rate is specified in frames per second, or FPS. Early television broadcast standards established a frame rate of 30 FPS as the standard for real-time video in the United States. The 30 FPS standard was quickly adopted by the video surveillance industry and became the benchmark for real-time security recording.

Although 30 FPS was the standard, it was eventually discovered that perfectly usable video recordings could be obtained using considerably lower frame rates. For example, the difference between 30 FPS and 15 FPS is barely detectable by humans, and recordings at rates as low as 5 FPS are acceptable for most security purposes.

One exception is when cameras are used to observe activity at casino tables or other locations where actions occur quickly and missing even a tenth of a second of detail would be unacceptable. In these applications, frame rates of 30 FPS or greater can be required. To meet this need, some manufacturers now offer cameras that provide frame rates of 60 FPS or higher.

Most IP networks allow frame rates to be individually set for each camera, allowing frame rates of 1 FPS to 60 FPS to be chosen based on user preferences. The exception is some multi-imager, panoramic, and high MP cameras, which may use a maximum frame rate that is less than 30 FPS.

Intelligently selecting the appropriate frame rate, combined with selecting the proper camera resolution, can greatly reduce bandwidth requirements and can significantly reduce costs of the overall video surveillance system.

Sensitivity   Sensitivity refers to the camera's ability to provide an acceptable video image at various levels of light. Camera sensitivity is generally specified in lux and refers to the amount of illumination required at the scene to produce a usable picture. Because most cameras provide a color image when adequate lighting is available and revert to a black and white image when it is not, separate sensitivity ratings are usually specified for both color and black and white.

The availability of lighting at each location should be considered when selecting cameras to ensure that cameras have the appropriate level of sensitivity.

Light Processing Capabilities   Almost every camera will provide a satisfactory image when used to view an indoor area that has an adequate amount of lighting that stays consistent throughout the day. However, cameras that are used to view outdoor areas must deal with lighting conditions that may vary from total darkness to bright sunlight, and endure weather conditions such as rain, snow, and fog. Outdoor cameras must also be able to handle the glare produced by vehicle headlights or the setting sun. Indoor cameras that are pointed toward outdoor areas, such as cameras used at building entrances, can face the same challenges.

There are numerous features available to allow cameras to handle these varying lighting conditions. These features include systems that automatically adjust the iris in the lens based on the level of light available, automatically operated light filters, and light technology that adjusts exposure levels, enhances contrast, lowers noise, and increases the level of the image signal.

Cameras that include advanced light processing capabilities generally cost more than cameras that don't but are the best choice for use at locations that have challenging lighting conditions.

Camera Lenses

The type of cameras lens used determines what the camera can see. This is known as the camera's field of view, specified as the horizontal angle of the view. Lens are available that provide standard angle (80 to 25 degree) or wide angle (100 to 50 degree) fields of view. Lenses are available in versions that have a fixed field of view that cannot be changed, and in varifocal version lenses that allow the field of view to be adjusted by the installer. Zoom lenses are also available that allow cameras to see an extended distance. Specialty lenses such as fisheye lenses and pinhole lenses are also available for special applications.

Most IP network cameras contain integral lenses that are built into the camera and cannot be changed. When selecting a camera, choose one that includes a lens that provides the field of view that is desired. The exception is box cameras, which allow the use of a separately provided lens. This often makes box cameras the camera of choice when the use of a specialty lens is required.

Infrared Illuminators

To operate correctly, cameras must have an adequate amount of light. While high-quality cameras can operate at very low light levels, there are situations where existing light levels are simply too low to allow the camera to produce a useful video image. In these situations, additional illumination is needed. To meet this need, devices known as infrared (IR) illuminators have been developed. IR illuminators use light waves just beyond the visible spectrum of light and are specifically designed to work with video surveillance cameras. Two types of IR illuminators are available, those built into cameras and external IR illuminators. Illuminators built into cameras typically provide coverage of distances up to 100′. Exterior IR illuminators allow coverage of distances of 500′ or greater.

It should be noted that while IR illumination is useful, it has several disadvantages when compared to visible light source. One disadvantage is that it is only capable of producing camera images in black and white. The other disadvantage is that images produced under IR light can appear washed out and have areas of glare. These adverse effects can often be minimized by correct placement of the camera and external IR illuminators.

Video Management Systems

Video management systems (VMSs) are used to manage the video surveillance system and to record and view images from video cameras. The size of VMSs can range from very small systems that consist of only a few cameras to large enterprise class systems that can include tens of thousands of cameras worldwide.

VMSs consist of special video management software installed on a server computer. This computer is connected to the IP network cameras over the network. Camera images are typically stored on disk drives located connected to the server computer. Live and recorded cameras images can be viewed on the server computer, or on other network computers on which special video viewing software has been installed.

Larger VMSs typically use more than one computer server and use external disk storage systems such as DAS (Direct Attached Storage), NAS (Network Attached Storage), and SAN (Storage Area Networks).

The features provided by VMSs typically include:

- The ability to record images from IP network cameras at a variety of different resolutions and frame rates.
- The ability for authorized users to view live and recorded video from any network connected personal computer or mobile device.
- The ability to control PTZ, panoramic view, and multi-imager cameras.
- The ability to use motion detection to reduce storage requirements when there is no motion in the camera's field of view.
- The ability to search recorded video by time, date, motion, and alarm event.
- A digital zoom feature to allow portions of recorded video to be enlarged.
- The ability to create and export recorded video "clips" to enable distribution to the police or other agencies.

Data Network

Video surveillance systems require network connections between the IP network cameras, VMS server, and video viewing workstations. These connections can be made using the organization's regular enterprise data network, or by using a dedicated security data network that has been specifically created for use with the video surveillance system.

The advantage of using the regular enterprise data network is that it is already in place and supported by the organization's IT department. Using this network generally results in cost savings because entirely new equipment does not have to be purchased and existing cabling and other infrastructure can be reused. The disadvantage of using the regular enterprise data network is that video surveillance cameras can consume large amounts of network bandwidth, possibly reducing the bandwidth available to meet other business needs. Putting security devices on the enterprise network can also sometimes create friction within the organization as the people responsible for managing the network don't understand the needs of the people managing security and vice versa.

The advantage of using a dedicated security network is that it can be specifically designed to meet the needs of the video surveillance system. Cameras and other security devices connected to it have no potential to impact the network used to operate the business. The other advantage of the dedicated security network is that it is more secure – there are no outside systems connected to the network that can be used to breach the network security.

The disadvantage of using a dedicated security network is that it usually costs more to install and maintain. The organization's IT department may also be unwilling to support a network other than its own, requiring the use of a separate outside vendor to support the dedicated security network.

NVR Appliances

Network Video Recorder (NVR) appliances are self-contained units that allow the viewing and recording of video. NVRs are purpose-built computer servers that have VMS software pre-installed on them. Many NVRs contain a built-in network switch that allows IP network cameras to be directly connected to them. NVRs are commonly available in 8, 16, and 24 camera versions. NVRs can be ideal for use at smaller sites that have a limited number of cameras and can be used to quickly implement a video surveillance system using a minimum number of components.

Video Encoders

Video encoders are devices that allow older analog cameras to be used within a network-based video surveillance system. Video encoders convert the analog video signal into an IP (internet-protocol) data format to allow the signal to be transmitted over the network. Video encoders are ideal when an existing analog video surveillance system is being upgraded by allowing a gradual transition between analog and network cameras. Video encoders are available as single camera units, or as rack-mounted units that can support 8 or 16 cameras.

Video Analytics

Video analytics is the capability of a video surveillance system to analyze what is seen within a camera scene and to make intelligent decisions about it. Simply put, video analytics makes the video surveillance system smart and capable of making decisions and acting on its own, without the need for human intervention. This capability has the potential to greatly improve the efficiency of the security monitoring operation – people no longer must continuously watch video monitors to detect unusual events – the system can do it for them.

Video analytics systems are most commonly used to detect motion within a camera scene but can detect many other types of events. These events include objects leaving or entering an area, objects stopping within an area, objects moving in the wrong direction, objects being left in or removed from an area, objects loitering, and many more.

Video analytics software can be directly installed on many IP network cameras allowing decisions to be made at the camera. Video analytics software can also be installed at the VMS server or on a separate server or appliance specifically installed to support analytics.

While video analytics can be useful in many applications, it does have its limitations. Many manufacturers have oversold the capabilities of their video analytics systems, leaving users disappointed. It is recommended that any video analytics systems being considered be tested in the actual environment in which they will be used before they are purchased.

Security Intercom Systems

Security intercom systems are used to provide voice communications between two or more locations for security purposes. Security intercom systems are frequently used between a locked building entrance door and a constantly attended location in the building, such as a manned security control room. In this application, the security intercom system gives visitors a means to contact someone in the building when they arrive at the entrance door. Other common locations where security intercom systems are used include loading dock doors and vehicle gates that provide entrance to the property.

Security intercom systems typically include an intercom master station at a central location, and intercom substations located at the remote entrance points. At a smaller facility, the intercom system may have just one or two substations, while on a larger campus, the system may have hundreds of substations.

Some security intercom systems also include a video capability where the substation includes a video camera and the master station includes a video monitor. This capability allows a visitor standing at the intercom substation to be seen.

Security intercom systems are available in standard versions that use dedicated cabling to interconnect the stations, and IP-network-based versions that allow communications over the network. These network-based systems are often ideal for use at larger campuses.

SYSTEM INTEGRATION

While individual electronic security systems each provide value on their own, they can be especially powerful when interconnected as a cohesive, fully integrated system. When security systems are connected to other systems such as building automation systems, employee database systems, and point-of-sale systems, the benefits can be even greater. When systems are connected, they can interact with one another, causing actions to occur automatically. This can save precious seconds when an emergency occurs and reduces the opportunity for human error. Systems can also share data with one another, eliminating the need to manually enter data and increasing the accuracy of the information provided.

Here are some real-world examples of successful system integrations:

- Visitor drives up to gate and presses button on intercom substation to contact security command center. When button on intercom is pressed, the camera viewing the gate is automatically displayed, and officer is presented with screen that allows him or her to open gate and make log entry of visitor's arrival.
- Intruder forces open gate in fenced utility yard area. Security command center is alerted and PTZ camera at perimeter of property automatically zooms in on utility yard area.
- Panic button is pressed at reception desk. Security command center is alerted and camera that views reception is automatically displayed. Doors between reception area and interior office area automatically lock. Coded voice message that alerts employees to the presence of an intruder in the lobby is automatically broadcast over the facility's paging system.
- New employee is hired and entered into human resources database system. Employee's name, photos, address, job title, and other information are automatically entered into access control system to allow access card to be issued to employee.
- Employee comes to facility on weekend and uses access card to enter. Access control system sends signal to building automation system to turn on the lights and the heating/cooling system on the floor on which the employee works.
- Customer goes to checkout counter to purchase merchandise. VMS automatically records both the camera viewing the checkout counter and the data being displayed on the point-of-sale terminal to allow all details of the transaction to be captured.

Systems integration can occur at two levels, low-level integration and high-level integration. Low-level integration occurs when two or more systems are simply wired together. This involves connecting dry-contact relay outputs from one system to alarm inputs on another system. For example, outputs from an access control panel could be connected as inputs to a network video recorder to allow the automatic display of a nearby camera when an access-controlled door is forced open. While low-level integrations can work well in very small installations, they quickly become unmanageable in larger installations.

High-level integrations occur when two or more systems exchange data with one another, usually over a network data connection. For example, instead of using the low-level integration method described earlier, the access control system could be configured to send data to the network video recorder when a door was forced open. The network video recorder could then be configured to automatically display the appropriate camera when it receives this data. With high-level integrations, connections are established through software rather than through wiring.

High-level integrations generally require cooperation between equipment manufacturers to make them happen. Manufacturers must share the data protocols that they use and allow other manufacturers to have access to certain internal portions of their system. Often, the challenges associated with high-level integrations are as much political as they are technical – some manufacturers simply refuse to cooperate with other companies that they consider to be their competitors. High-level integrations are also dynamic and require continual maintenance. When one manufacturer upgrades the software on a system, this may have a negative impact on the other systems integrated with this system, causing them to have to upgrade their software also. When multiple different systems are connected, this can cause the need for almost continuous changes and upgrades.

Another difficulty in providing high-level integrations is finding a responsible party to implement them. Often manufacturers will provide the data protocols necessary to integrate with their products but will expect someone else to write the actual software code. In many cases two manufacturers will point their fingers at one another, each expecting the other party to write the code and take responsibility for making the integration happen.

To overcome the challenges associated with large integrated security systems, a class of products known as Physical Security Information Management (PSIM) systems have been developed. PSIM systems are a separate platform that are used to manage each of the underlying security systems. Rather than the individual security systems talking directly to one another, they each talk to the PSIM system, which translates the data, makes decisions, and passes along the appropriate commands. Most PSIM systems are custom developed for each user and can be very expensive.

The bottom line: Security system integration can be extremely valuable but comes with many challenges. The key to successful system integration is to carefully define what type of integration is needed, how it will operate, who will be responsible for installing and maintaining it, and what it will cost, both initially and on an ongoing basis.

CODES AND ORDINANCES

There are many building codes, life safety codes, and local ordinances that can have an impact on the implementation of physical security systems. In the United States, these can include the International Building Code, International Fire Code, National Electrical Code, Life Safety Code, and many others. In almost every case, nationally recognized codes such as the ones described will be adopted by local government agencies but may be amended to meet local preferences. For example, a state may adopt the National Electrical Code as law but amend certain portions of it to include less stringent or more stringent requirements. Examples of ways in which codes can have an impact on the design of the physical security program include:

- Building codes may limit the height of the perimeter fencing, dictate how far it must be set back from the street, and restrict the use of barbed wire on top of the fence.
- Life safety codes may prohibit the locking of certain doors and prevent the use of certain types of lock hardware.
- Building codes may prevent the installation of walls to secure the elevator lobbies because they would obstruct a require path of egress between the lobby and the exit stairways.
- Local light-pollution ordinances or energy code may limit the amount of lighting that can be provided in the parking lots.

- Local traffic codes may prevent the installation of gates at the entrances to the site because it could cause traffic backups.

Because codes and ordinances can vary significantly from place to place, it is important that local requirements are checked when planning the physical security systems. The implementation of something in one city does not imply that another city will allow it. Even if something is done at a neighboring facility doesn't necessarily mean it is legal. Always check with local officials before proceeding. Because of the complexity and ambiguity of many codes, it can sometimes be helpful to obtain the services of a licensed architect or other design professional to help with planning efforts.

CHAPTER 10

Security Measures

Personnel

Karim H. Vellani

CONTENTS

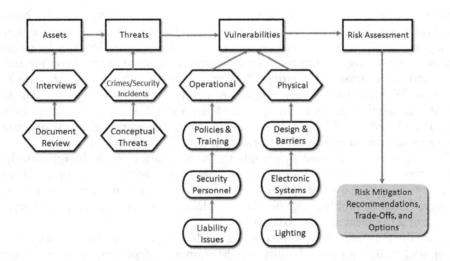

FIGURE 10.1 Strategic Risk Assessment Process, Copyright ©2019 by Threat Analysis Group, LLC. Used by permission. Additional information available from Threat Analysis Group, LLC via www.threatanalysis.com.

INTRODUCTION

Security personnel are quite easily the most expensive countermeasure available to security decision makers. However, security personnel have one key characteristic which separates them from other types of security measures: The ability to reason. Reasoning is the ability to think, infer, and comprehend in a rational manner. The ability to reason is a prerequisite for a security officer's primary task of observing and reporting. Beyond their primary task of observing and reporting, the security force's secondary responsibilities typically include controlling access by both pedestrians and vehicles to the facility, patrolling the grounds, inspecting physical security measures to ensure proper operation, and special assignments. The ability to reason is also critical to responding and controlling situations, such as crimes. As the eyes and ears of management, security officers may be stationed at fixed posts or patrol various locations within the facility.

As there are many books published which discuss security personnel management, this chapter will focus on the more difficult management issues and the latest concepts in security force deployment. Among the issues and concepts addressed in this chapter are metric-based deployment and redeployment of security forces, quantitative and qualitative performance evaluations, security force training, security quality control, increasing professionalism, the use of off-duty police officers, and the differences between contract security forces and proprietary security force.

Organizational culture has an impact on the security program and must be considered by security decision makers. Is the culture conducive to intrusive security measures, such as security personnel? Do other organizations within the same industry utilize security personnel?

SECURITY OFFICER TRAINING

Currently, there are no national standards for training security officers; however, many states have minimum training requirements and there is a push within the industry for a national standard from various entities including the International Foundation for Protection Officers, which provides standardized training for security officers and certification as a Certified Protection Officer (CPO) and the *Private Security Officer Selection and Training Guideline* published by ASIS-International. At the time of this book's publication, no standards exist for security officer training. National standards would be beneficial today due to the increased threat of terrorism and to provide consistency in the security industry.

Training is primarily used to provide the security officer with the requisite knowledge to carry out their protection duties in a legal and professional manner. However, the benefits do not end there. Anecdotal evidence suggests that training increases performance, enhances problem solving ability, reduces turnover, and mitigates liability in the event of a negligent security lawsuit.

Typically, there are two specific training needs for a security officer, general security training and facility training. Facility-specific training criteria may include familiarization with the facility including critical assets and functions as well as the facility's policies and procedures and physical security measures. General training may include the following topics:

- ethics
- Professionalism
- Legal aspects
- Use of force
- Communications
- Observation
- Report writing
- Basics of physical security measures
- Policy and procedures
- Life safety
- Workplace violence
- First aid and CPR
- Conflict resolution
- Security awareness
- Information protection
- Fire prevention
- Traffic and crowd control
- Emergency management
- Bomb threat and hazardous material response
- Public relations.

General training is more diverse and may be completed through classroom sessions, computer-based training, and self-study courses. Facility-specific training is normally accomplished through an initial orientation and on-the-job training. Depending on the facility's dynamics, continuing training may need to be provided on an ongoing basis, with refresher training provided as needed based on changes to the facility's needs.

Security officer training provides accountability in different ways. Security departments and contract security firms demonstrate commitment by providing training. Officers demonstrate aptitude by passing competency tests and responding appropriately to events. Other accountability measures include:

1. Recording security radio transmissions.
2. Recording phone calls to the security operations center (dispatch).
3. Use of Computer Aided Dispatch (CAD) systems.
4. Global Positioning System (GPS) patrol vehicle tracking.
5. Foot patrol audit systems (e.g., guard tour systems).
6. Detailed daily activity reports and security incident reports.
7. Post orders. Post orders provide guidance on expectations and instructions on performing security duties for each shift and each post and may include the following:

   - Reporting on and off duty.
   - Patrol frequency and locations.
   - Conducting escorts (if applicable).
   - System monitoring (if applicable).
   - Visitor management (if applicable).
   - Perimeter and sensitive area inspections.
   - Documentation (daily activity reports and incident reports).
   - Rotating with other posts (if applicable).

RISK-BASED SECURITY DEPLOYMENT

Security personnel are commonly used to reinforce a security program where policies and procedures and the physical security system and measures are unable to counter an elevated risk situation alone. Risk, as discussed throughout this book, is the possibility of asset loss, damage, or destruction as a result of a threat exploiting a specific vulnerability. Risk is often the most significant factor driving the deployment and redeployment of security forces. Duties and functions may be another driver for security personnel. Functional security deployment is discussed below.

Practically speaking, the most difficult issue facing security decision makers is how and when to deploy and withdraw security officers. What is the decision process used by a security professional to deploy security personnel? What factors affect the decision? Are security personnel deployed based on gut instincts or assumptions? Are they deployed based on end users who scream loudest? Security force deployment based on gut instincts can be ineffective and costly. Security personnel, because of their cost, should be deployed based on an objective understanding of risk and/or function. While quantitative deployment guidelines and models are not absolute, they can provide a foundation based on reliable measures (e.g., security call volume, area patrolled, etc.), yet remain dynamic and flexible as needs change and risks evolve.

The reality in the security management world is that security personnel are rather easy to deploy with the only major obstacle being cost. Once deployed, however, the withdrawal of security officers can be more challenging for the security decision maker. While cost was a consideration when deploying security personnel, it is risky to withdraw security personnel based on cost concerns. Security decision makers with deposition or trial experience and subjected to cross examination by a good attorney representing a person victimized on the security decision maker's property will recognize this danger.

A number of quantitative factors can be used in risk-based deployment of security personnel. The quantitative factors may include historical security breaches, calls for service frequency, past crime types, and crime rates. Other metrics may include size of the facility and population (employees, visitors, etc.). These quantitative factors must be tempered with more qualitative considerations including organizational culture, industry norms and practices, liability and insurance issues, end user and customer expectations, and the security decision maker's preferences.

Liability and insurance issues are also a qualitative consideration for security decision makers. Has the organization been subjected to legal scrutiny in the past for not deploying security personnel?

While taking the qualitative factors under advisement, the ultimate force behind security personnel for risk-based deployment is the mathematically measurable factors. Crime history, crime rates, past security breaches, and calls for service are among the metrics that can be utilized in establishing a security personnel deployment protocol. While no magic number exists, each security decision maker may have a threshold of crimes, security breaches, or threats that determine precisely when security personnel are to be used and withdrawn. To err on the safe side, many security professionals use a liberal approach to deploy, and a conservative approach to withdraw. That is, they deploy before threats are actually at the threshold and withdraw only after threats have fallen below the established threshold and for a period of time.

When determining the threshold, the security decision maker must evaluate two factors. What policies, procedures, and physical security measures can be implemented to reduce risk before security personnel are considered? The other factor is what is the manageable threat norm for the facility or the organization. Even with the deployment of security personnel, crimes can and do occur. What is the normal and manageable amount of crime and other risks for the facility? As we've seen since the Department of Homeland Security introduced the Threat Advisory System, a middle threat level is considered normal for the United States. A more practical application will be beneficial to illustrate this point. Take the example of a retail store located in a metropolitan area which experiences two violent crimes on the premises each year even with security personnel present. When security personnel are removed does crime decrease? After extensive testing and monitoring, it may be found that, even after a reasonable level of security personnel deployment has occurred, crimes will still be perpetrated on the premises. An understanding of the threat norm is critical to a reasonable and effective security program.

As discussed above, security decision makers will typically deploy personnel before the threshold is reached, but wait longer after the threat has declined below the threat level before pulling out the increased security coverage. What length of time is appropriate? The easy answer is the security officers are withdrawn only after a reasonable amount of time has passed with no further threat increase. This ensures that the decrease in threat level is not an anomaly. For each organization, the length of time will vary. On a practical level, the effort to constantly monitor threats can be difficult and time consuming. Thus, most organizations monitor threats on a calendar or fiscal year basis.

FUNCTIONAL SECURITY DEPLOYMENT

Functional deployment means that officers are needed not based on risk, but rather a need to perform a specific task, such as traffic control in a parking lot or visitor screening at a public entrance. End users and others who visit the facility have expectations as well. Is the expectation that security personnel will be present to control access, to contribute to a feeling of safety, or to provide escorts? The opposite might be true as well. Do customers and end users expect an open and friendly environment with no desire to have intrusive security personnel? Can the security personnel be dressed in softer uniforms, such as slacks and blazers, rather than more traditional uniforms?

OTHER SECURITY DEPLOYMENT METHODS

Depending on the industry where security officers are deployed, the industry's regulatory bodies, accreditation organizations, and/or trade groups may have specific guidance on security staffing levels for facilities that fall within each specific industry. For example, the United States Department of Housing and Urban Development (HUD) provides the following guidance, though no specific requirement, for HUD subsidized apartment buildings:

> The number of security personnel needed for a particular project is subject to too many variables to permit use of a general formula for manpower estimates. In practice, ratios range from a high of four persons (160 manhours per week) to a low of two persons (80 manhours per week) for each 1,000 residents.

A single lobby guard cannot be expected to provide screening for more than about 200 apartment units.[1]

The healthcare industry has historically used interior square footage as a primary driver for determining the number of security officers needed to patrol a hospital. Recent models[2,3,4] have been developed to provide a more sophisticated method for determining staffing benchmarks at hospitals. For example, the most recent iteration of the model identified several factors that drive security staffing in hospitals. These factors included:

1. Total interior square footage of the facility for which security officers were responsible for patrolling.
2. Annual number of officer-hours spent patient sitting (close or one-to-one observation of patients, usually violent or suicidal patients).
3. The number of licensed hospital beds.
4. The presence of an inpatient psychiatric/behavioral health unit.
5. The presence of a trauma center (a hospital equipped and staffed to provide care for patients suffering from major traumatic injuries such as falls, motor vehicle collisions, or gunshot wounds).
6. Total number of facility employees.
7. The previous year's security call volume.

This particular modeling effort resulted in algorithms to benchmark security staffing at hospitals across the United States.:

- For total security force FTEs: FTEs = $e^{\wedge}[(9.76 \times 10^{-8})$ × (total interior square footage) + (1.53×10^{-5}) × (total number of hours spent patient sitting annually) + (1.0775×10^{-3}) × (number of licensed beds) + (0.1460488) × (1 if a psychiatric/behavioral unit but no trauma unit) + (0.2391474) × (1 if a trauma unit but no psychiatric/behavioral unit) + (0.4102736) × (1 if both a psychiatric/behavioral unit and a trauma unit) + 2.404032]
- For patrol-and-response FTEs: FTEs = $e^{\wedge}[(2.2 \times 10^{-7})$ × (total interior square footage) + (1.4×10^{-5}) × (total number of hours spent patient sitting annually) + (8.8×10^{-5}) × (total number of facility employees) + (9.1×10^{-7}) × (total number of security calls in previous year) + 1.978012]

LAW ENFORCEMENT OFFICERS VERSUS SECURITY OFFICERS

Security decision makers have a variety of choices when it comes to the type of security personnel to utilize at their facilities. Increasingly, the debate about one of these options has grown in recent years because of the dire consequences associated with its use and recent events. This option is the off-duty law enforcement officer. Law enforcement officers provide a high level of *perceived* security when working off-duty on private property. More often than not, they are in full uniform, armed, and carry other law enforcement equipment. Sometimes they are able to use other police resources such as patrol cars which provide additional perceived value to the security decision maker utilizing their services.

Prevention is a key element of a security program. Crime prevention is *the anticipation, the recognition, and the appraisal of a crime risk and the initiation of action to remove or reduce it.*

Law enforcement officers also have the power to arrest for any crime, including minor crimes not committed in their presence. Despite their advantages, off-duty law enforcement officers are not without their shortcomings, some highly consequential to those who contract for off-duty police services. Security decision makers need to be aware of these issues before selecting police officers to provide the personnel for their entire security force or to supplement contract or proprietary security staff.

Among the first considerations when selecting off-duty law enforcement officers is the type of facility or organization in need of protection by security personnel. Unless the threat level is significantly high and the organization is seeking to enforce more than "house rules," for most apartment buildings, office buildings, hotels and motels, retail stores, and shopping centers, off-duty law enforcement would be overkill and costly. For industrial facilities, hospitals, and government buildings, law enforcement personnel may be the preferred choice for security; however, absent an inordinately high and prolonged threat level, off-duty police officers would not likely be a cost-effective solution.

The threat level of a given facility may be high enough to justify the use of law enforcement officers to provide protection. However, security decision makers who utilize off-duty law enforcement officers to provide security for their facilities have increasingly become aware of the hazards posed by this type of personnel during wide scale emergencies such as a terrorist incident or a natural disaster. In most law enforcement departments (e.g., Police Departments, Sheriff's Departments), their officers must be available twenty-four hours a day and must be prepared to return to their primary duty on short notice. Security decision makers must recognize that off-duty police officers are not dedicated security personnel and can leave the facility unprotected in the event of such an emergency. Beyond emergencies, other wide scale events which require every available law enforcement officer to return to duty can thus leave the private organization unprotected. Examples include Mardi Gras in New Orleans, the Olympics held in a US city, or Spring Break in South Padre Island, Texas.

Even without a wide scale emergency or special event, a police officer may be required to leave his or her security post to respond to a crime off the property. A relevant example of the danger created when a law enforcement officer leaves his or her security post occurred at a retail store in Texas. A sheriff's deputy moonlighting as a security officer for a grocery store was patrolling the parking lot when a young woman entered the store. While the woman was in the store, the sheriff's deputy was called away to a gang-related crime miles away from the store. Since the deputy served on the county's gang task force, he responded without informing the grocery store's management. The young woman exited the store after the deputy left, walked through the parking lot to her car, and was abducted and raped repeatedly during the night. The grocery store was subsequently sued by the victim.

Some organizations have attempted to hire off-duty law enforcement officers to protect their assets under the belief that the organization can cloak themselves with government powers. This, however, is not the case. The reality is that those government powers can be the source of increased liability exposure. The selection of law enforcement officers to fill a gap in security exposes the organization to additional liability where they are held to standards normally reserved only for government entities. That standard is Section 1983 of the United States Code and defines constitutional violations committed by the government against individual people. In recent years, this federal statute has been applied to law enforcement officers acting under "color of law" who injure or kill an alleged criminal while employed by a private company. In these instances, the alleged criminal may sue the private company under normal premises liability theories, but may also claim constitutional rights violations by the company who employed the officer. In some instances, courts have found that a privately employed law enforcement officer wearing a police uniform, displaying a police badge, driving a police vehicle, or yelling, "stop, police!" is acting under "color of law," and thus the private entity may be held liable (civil and constitutional) for the law enforcement officer's actions.

The repercussions for a jury finding in favor of the plaintiff, that is violating a person's constitutional rights, could put many companies in financial jeopardy and harm their reputation. For a private company to hire law enforcement officers to protect their assets, a conscientious separation of the law enforcement and security functions is required. In a perfect world, the organization's policies and procedures would dictate that the off-duty law enforcement officers are acting independent of their public function and would not hold themselves out as a government official while working the security detail. Unfortunately for the private organization, many law enforcement departments have changed their policies on how their officers may work extra employment.

The policies and procedures of many law enforcement agencies have been revised in recent years that restrict their officers from providing security in the purest sense. These newer policies only allow their officers to work extra employment jobs in their capacity as law enforcement officers. This is a significant change in that the security decision maker can no longer expect the off-duty law enforcement officers to enforce the organization's policies and procedures and other house rules. For the organization whose entire security force is composed of off-duty law enforcement officers, the result of these department policies is clear. Off-duty officers are at the facility acting in their official capacity as law enforcement officers, no longer able to enforce the organization's policies which may include writing daily activity reports or conducting inspections of physical security measures such as lighting and alarm systems. This means that the organization must have other personnel assigned to these tasks.

When hiring a private security contractor or using a proprietary security force, security decision makers can dictate the level of security intervention at their facility, in other words to what degree of scrutiny will their customers, employees, and other visitors be subjected. This is a critical determination as a careful balance must be drawn between protection of assets and a customer service orientation. Off-duty law enforcement officers provide more protection than customer service. With their enforcement of law function, they cannot overlook minor infractions that the organization does not want enforced from a customer service perspective. For example, if a non-handicapped customer parks in a handicap parking spot and is given a ticket by the off-duty law enforcement police, the organization does not have the discretion to prevent the officer from writing a ticket. Many organizations would prefer to take a customer service approach and provide a verbal warning to their customer rather than take a unconditional law enforcement approach. In this instance, a private security officer would have the discretion to enforce the company's rules.

Similar to other products and services, the cost of private security labor is market driven and subject to competition and other market forces which help to regulate the rates charged by a security services provider. Law enforcement labor rates are at a premium for two reasons. First, competition is almost nonexistent because there are typically only a handful of law enforcement agencies that serve a community and thus only a handful of service providers. The other reason is that there is a strong demand for law enforcement protection for special events such as sporting events, political rallies, funeral processions, and other crowd management events. In some jurisdictions, off-duty law enforcement officers can cost the organization upwards of $30 per hour for their services, while private security companies may charge less than half that amount for an unarmed, uniformed security officer and in the neighborhood of $15 - per hour for an armed, uniformed security officer.

From the security industry perspective, the financial costs of unequal competition from law enforcement agencies can be detrimental to business, and security experts realize that the training given to public police officers does not relate to security. From the departmental standpoint, police managers have voiced concerns over departmental liability, conflicts of interest, loss of focus on primary duties, and officer fatigue which may hinder their ability for normal duty.

Training is another important factor in the security professional's decision making process in determining whether to use off-duty law enforcement officers or private security officers for the protection of assets. As discussed earlier, no national level training requirements exist for security officers and the same is true for public law enforcement officers. Training standards do exist for law enforcement officers at the state level and for each law enforcement agency. The general public, including many security decision makers, usually believe that law enforcement officers are better trained. Better trained for what is the critical question. Surely, law enforcement officers are better trained to be police officers, but are they better trained to be security officers?

Law enforcement officers, by profession, are charged with the primary duty of apprehending criminal perpetrators. Obviously, that is an important responsibility that requires a significant amount of training to carry out that responsibility effectively and within the guidelines of the Constitution, state law, and departmental policy. It should be noted that apprehension is a reactive measure once a crime has already been committed. Reaction is not the goal of an effective security program. Proactive prevention of crime is the goal.

In general, law enforcement officers do receive more training than security officers; however, their job preparation often includes such topics as constitutional rights, criminal law, traffic law, drug law, use of force, the penal code, arrest, search and seizure, family violence, patrol procedures, and criminal investigation. Although some law enforcement training would be valuable for security officers, the majority is superfluous. Unlike law enforcement officers, security officers typically receive training in security specific issues such as risk management, physical security planning, alarm and CCTV operation, labor relations, theft of asset deterrence, workplace violence prevention, crisis intervention, and customer service. When considered training item by training item, it becomes evident that law enforcement officers are not adequately trained to execute the duties of a security officer. It should be recognized that the security industry has grown into a diverse profession, with training and certifications available in well-defined and highly specialized areas.

When a security professional is faced with the decision to use law enforcement officers or private security personnel as the primary protection force, they should fully understand the implications of each alternative as this pivotal decision may have unwelcome repercussions and a major impact on the organization's ability to protect assets, provide customer service, and limit liability. Should the security decision maker decide to use private security officers, another question must be answered. Should a contract security force be utilized or should a proprietary security force be created?

CONTRACT SECURITY FORCES VERSUS PROPRIETARY SECURITY FORCES

Among security professionals, there exists an ongoing, always interesting, and sometimes heated debate about the advantages and disadvantages of contract security forces and proprietary security forces. Which security force provides better protection? Which provides better value? These are difficult questions to answer and there is no right answer since the answer lies within the needs of each specific facility or organization which uses security personnel.

In his book, *Security Management: Business Strategies for Success*, Dennis Dalton discussed three myths which characterize some security buyers' feelings about the difference between proprietary and contract security officers. The myths are quality of the workforce, loyalty to the client, and turnover rates. It is typically assumed that a proprietary security force is of higher quality than a contract force. While this may be evident on the surface when assessing various security forces, a more thorough analysis yields a number of factors which contribute to a higher level of quality. These factors, which will be discussed in the next section, include higher compensation, more training, more experience, and work environment. This last factor may stand out to some readers as the work environment does not change depending on whether there is a proprietary security force or a contract security force. Or does it? Obviously the physical environment does not change but may be different due to other factors such as whether a security force is contracted or are actual employees. Does a contracted security officer get treated the same way as other employees of the facility? Is the same sense of ownership harnessed? Very likely, this is not the case with contracted employees unless management makes a concerted effort to treat a contractor's employees the same as their own employees. Security force loyalty is another myth in the proprietary versus contract security force debate. By setting the same standards for training, professionalism, and compensation for the contracted force as they would a proprietary force, security decision makers can harness the same level of loyalty to their facility and the organization from contracted security personnel as they can from a proprietary security force. Turnover among security officers is a significant cost to an organization, and its control can lead to considerable cost savings to the security department's budget. With a high quality and loyal security force, contract or proprietary, security decision makers can also reduce the turnover rate. By working closely, in partnership, with the contract security company, the organization can reduce turnover to a manageable rate and build upon the quality and loyalty.

As discussed, the contract versus proprietary security force debate does not actually revolve around whether or not a security force is contracted or proprietary. The real issue is professionalism. In today's world, there are actually three types of security personnel. Entry level security officers, professional security officers, and para-military security officers. The next section will discuss the differences and what the industry should do to move toward a more professional officer and a more professional image in the future.

QUALITY CONTROL INSPECTION CHECKLIST

Visit Type (Announced/Unannounced):
Date & Time of Inspection:

Facility Type and Address:
Officer(s) on Duty:
Latest Supervisor Inspection:
Post Orders:
Log Books:
Timesheet:
Occupant Emergency Plan:
ID Badge:
State License No and Expiration:
CPR/First Aid Card Expiration:
Post Order Knowledge:
Security Patrols:
Supervisor Interaction:
Customer Interaction:
Equipment Serviceability & Procedures:
Radio Operations:
Firearms Safety (Visual check only):
Uniform:
Other Equipment:
Security Area/Office Appearance:
Appearance/Hygiene:
Security Officer Morale:
Additional Comments:

CRIME PREVENTION EFFICACY

Do security officers deter or prevent crime? This is a question that does not get asked often. Instead, society assumes that uniformed officers, whether police or security, do in fact prevent crime. As discussed in general throughout this book, not all security measures are effective and security measures provide varying degrees of effectiveness in different environments, under shifting conditions, and with changing priorities. Security officers and other uniformed personnel are subject to the same obstacles to effectiveness.

Based on studies conducted by the International Association of Professional Security Consultants (IAPSC) and with the assistance of the Rutgers School of Criminal Justice in 2010 and 2017, there are limited studies regarding police and security officer effectiveness overall and no research studies regarding armed or unarmed security officer capabilities for preventing violent crime and assaults. Some criminologists believe that violent crime is harder to prevent because of the impulsive, expressive nature of violent crime and the rarity of violent crime in small areas.[5] The IAPSC study identified nine studies which addressed police officer effectiveness on preventing violent crime. Key findings from the nine studies include:

- Proactive policing does not decrease shootings.[6]
- Increasing police has very small effect on violent crime.[7]

- COMPSTAT[8] is less effective on violent crimes relative to property crimes.[9]
- Foot patrols and problem-oriented policing did not result in reductions in violent crime relative to controls.[10]
- Police foot patrols decrease violent crime, but the impact decayed quickly.[11]
- Problem-oriented policing[12] was associated with a 33% reduction in street violence. Saturation/directed patrols did not result in any crime reductions.[13]
- Directed patrol resulted in a sizable decrease in non-domestic firearm assaults, but no impact on firearm robbery.[14] The researchers speculated that the decrease in non-domestic firearm assaults was due to certainty of arrests and occupied vehicle checks.
- Police foot patrols reduce violent crime.[15]
- The Safe Street Team (SST) program which used problem-oriented policing concepts was associated with a statistically significant reduction in violent index crimes at the treatment places relative to the comparison places.[16]

One of the nine studies addressed *decay*, that is, diminishing returns after treatment is implemented. This study found that the deterrent effect quickly decayed. More specifically, crime reduction was greatest after the initial implementation of foot patrols and dissipated quickly during the treatment period when foot patrols were deployed. During the latter part of the treatment period, violent crime rates rebounded in the foot patrol areas, doubling from the initial early treatment low point during the latter eight weeks of treatment. Violent crime rates had already returned to pre-treatment levels while foot patrols were still deployed. The results presented indicate that any treatment benefit is relatively short-lived and, according to the researchers, these findings were consistent with previous observations.[17]

Given the lack of empirical evidence, security decision makers should temper expectations regarding the ability for security officers to prevent violent crime especially over a long period of time. As security professionals know, security is situational. The effectiveness of an individual security measure is situational. The same holds true for security officers. Security officers can be more effective at preventing violent crime when focused on specific, known threats within a short timeframe.

QUALITY CONTROL AND PERFORMANCE EVALUATION

The quality control function of a security program provides an independent inspection of security force performance. The goal of quality control inspections is to maintain a high level quality, performance, and compliance with legal and the organization's regulations to ensure that deficiencies are detected before they become too widespread and jeopardize the security of the organization or facility where security personnel are deployed. As stated, quality control inspections are independent evaluations and should be conducted by someone who can perform the inspections at arm's length, preferably an independent unit of the organization or a separate company contracted to provide quality control inspections. Quality control inspections also ensure that senior management provides the necessary planning and organization to allow the security force to satisfy the needs of the facility. The quality control function also strives to achieve continuous improvement of quality in all security related activities and maintain compliance with all applicable laws and regulations.

Quality control inspectors should be intimately familiar with the duties and responsibilities of the security force, including the officer's general orders and post orders. For a contract security force, the quality control inspectors also ensure compliance with each contractual obligation and other client mandates, such as training, licensing, uniform, and other hygiene issues. In this regard, a standardized quality control inspection checklist should be utilized to ease the inspection process. While the quality control inspection checklist is used during the inspection, some information that can be gathered during the inspections may not fit the mold of a checklist. For example, morale of the security force is an issue that is not easily captured on the checklist and can be written up in a text-based summary at the end of the report.

The quality control inspections should take place at regular intervals, with typical intervals monthly or quarterly. These inspections may be announced and/or unannounced depending on the needs of the facility or organization. In some cases, covert quality control inspections are necessary. The quality control reports provide evidence of due diligence in the event of a later dispute and should be maintained in a file. However, the reports should be acted on immediately to correct and prevent deficiencies before they become problems. For example, the quality control inspection may reveal that a security officer's CPR training expires in two months, but he or she has not yet taken a refresher course to re-certify that credential. The quality control process identifies this issue and the security officer's supervisor can take the necessary action to schedule the officer's training in advance of the certification expiry. Regardless of the type of deficiency, each one must be reported within a reasonable time, though major infractions should be reported immediately so the problem can be rectified quickly through corrective action.

Quality control reports are the result of the inspection and should be submitted through the proper channels as soon as they are complete. It is also common to provide the reports to the client in a contract security force arrangement as well. This allows the client to recognize the security service contractor's diligence as well as provides the client with the opportunity to provide feedback on the security force's performance.

After a deficiency is noted on the quality control report, the inspection should suspend the item until the next inspection and follow up to ensure that the deficiency is corrected. Corrective action can include additional training, and verbal or written reprimands.

During the quality control inspection process, the inspector ensures that each officer has in their possession all required credentials, including badges, identification cards, training cards, and any other documentation required by the organization. Each security post should have a duty book, often a three ring binder or folder, which contains necessary paperwork and forms, such as time sheets, daily activity reports, patrol logs, and incident reports. Post orders, general orders, occupant emergency plans, and threat advisory's should also be maintained in the duty book. The quality control inspector will ensure that all forms are complete, detailed, accurate, and legible. The security officer's uniform should be inspected to ensure all gear is present and that their overall appearance is professional and within the guidelines of the organization. Security related equipment, such as CCTV monitors, X-ray machines, and handheld metal detectors, are inspected during the inspection as well. The quality control inspector should also question the officers on specific post order requirements to ensure that the security officer thoroughly understands their duties. The inspector may even patrol the facility with the security officer.

GENERAL ORDERS

POST ORDERS FOR UNARMED SECURITY OFFICERS
DEPARTMENT OF ENVIRONMENTAL SERVICES (DES)
ANYTOWN, NORTH CAROLINA

SECURITY FORCE

Security Force. The Security Force for this operation consists of 2 uniformed, unarmed security officers (2 part-time/reserve officers). These officers will be responsible for manning one visitor screening post at the main entrance of the Mecklenburg County Department of Environmental Services (DES) facility located at 1240 Government Center Road, Charlotte, N.C.

In additional to performance of the primary duty of personnel screening and access control, the security officer assigned to the post may also be employed from time-to-time, based upon visitor flow and/or as may be directed by the Director, DES or their representative, to execute the following additional security functions:

Roving Patrol – random walking patrol throughout the interior of the facility, around the exterior perimeter of the building, and through the parking areas immediately adjacent to the facility

Security Escort – accompany client employees, case workers, and other government officials to designated interview areas and/or office spaces to provide a physical presence for deterrence and control of disgruntled, violent, or uncontrollable visitors or personnel who have a known or presumed potential to create disturbances to the normal operation of the facility

Provide Assistance/Information – officers will possess a basic knowledge of the Department of Environmental Services, its operations, key staff personnel, and rules/regulations to the extent that they can provide basic assistance and information to the general public and visitors in order to direct them to the appropriate locations and personnel within the facility

Law Enforcement Interface and Cooperation – while not charged nor vested with the jurisdiction to enforce any civil laws, security officers may observe, report, and document breaches of security within the facility and refer the same to local authorities as may be warranted by the severity of the incident and as consistent with the guidance provided by the Director of the facility or their designated representative

POST OPERATIONS

Post Description. Security officers will man one fixed post located inside the front doorway at the entrance foyer into the facility where a single public access point into the facility has been established. This post is designated as Post #1.

Post #1 – VISITOR SCREENING POINT, MAIN ENTRANCE FOYER, CCDES BLDG

The officer assigned to this post has the primary responsibility for performing all aspects of access control for visitors. Functional tasks associated with access control through this post encompass:

Visitor Screening – The officer will operate a client provided Garrett Model CS5000 walk-thru magnetometer screening system for screening and clearing visitors into the lobby area of the facility. The officer will use the magnetometer to identify and locate any concealed weapons, contraband, or dangerous items that a visitor may be attempting to unlawfully introduce into the facility. In addition to operation of the magnetometer screening system, the officer may also be required to use a hand-held screening wand to conduct detailed inspections of personnel who may require a more thorough inspection than that afforded by the walk-thru screening portal.

Inspection of Bags and Personal Effects – The officer will also be responsible for conducting a limited inspection of all bags, briefcases, backpacks, purses, and similar items being carried into the facility by visitors. If a prohibited or dangerous item is discovered during this inspection process, the visitor will be afforded an opportunity to remove the item from the premises. A list of items prohibited from being introduced into the facility will be provided by the Director, DES or their designated representative and will be periodically updated as may be required but at least on an annual basis.

Hours of Operation. Post #1 will be manned from 08:15 until 17:30, Mondays through Fridays, excluding holidays.

Post Equipment

The client will provide the magnetometer, hand-held screening wands (to include batteries), and a table for the inspection of bags at Post #1. Additionally, the client will, within their capabilities, provide the following support:

   a small office area, cubicle, or at a minimum a lockable storage container (e.g., file cabinet or locker-style cabinet) in close proximity to Post #1 so that officers may store necessary administrative supplies and contractor provided post equipment
   a telephone with local service connection at Post #1 or in close proximity for use by the security officer in emergency situations
   either a dedicated or designated workspace with computer access so that security officers may complete required reports, timesheets, and official paperwork associated with the performance of security duties in support of the client
   make available a designated break area out of public view where the officer may take relief and eat lunch away from their post of duty

The contractor will provide the security officer with the uniforms and personal equipment listed in Appendix 1 to these post orders. In addition to these items, Post #1 will retain the following post equipment for use by the officer assigned to this post:

   First Aid Kit with latex gloves and CPR masks
   Extra batteries for flashlights (contractor provided) and search wands (client provided)
   Pens, pencils, notepads, report forms, timesheets, and similar administrative items necessary for the orderly and efficient performance of security duties

OFFICER DUTIES

The officer serves as a uniformed, unarmed security officer and will perform his/her duties in a professional manner in accordance with the contractor's Protective Forces Policy and Procedures Manual.

The officer will log in/out using a contractor provided "Record of Time of Arrival and Departure" and record all hours worked on a contractor provided Non-Exempt Employee Timesheet. These forms will be completed in a timely and accurate fashion on a daily basis by the officer.

The officer will record all significant events using a contractor provided "Security Officer's Operations Log". This form will be completed daily and serves as a chronological record of any significant events or unusual activity (e.g., alarm system activation, fire/EMS response, etc.) that occurs during the officer's tour of duty.

The officer will visually screen visitors to the agency. The officer will answer questions as appropriate and offer assistance where practical. The officer will not conduct any Department of Environmental Services related business or answer agency specific questions. Visitors carrying visibly prohibited items will be asked to remove the items from the agency facility. If the officer discovers that a visitor has a dangerous weapon or item, such as a firearm or explosive device, he/she will take practical steps to secure the visitor and dangerous item. The officer will immediately notify the Mecklenburg County Sheriff's Department and the Director, DES or their designated representative.

At the discretion of the Director, DES or their designated representative, personnel making deliveries may be required to present valid company or state issued identification and may be required to submit packages for inspection. Additionally, when directed by the Director, DES or their designated representative, delivery personnel may be logged in/out using the "Record of Time of Arrival and Departure" during periods of increased threat or heightened security operations. The officer will not open sealed packages unless specifically requested by the Director, DES.

In the event of an emergency evacuation of the building, the officer will assist with the evacuation of DES visitors and personnel as appropriate.

The officer will report all significant security issues to the Director, DES or their designated representative. Based on the urgency of the situation, the officer may contact the appropriate law enforcement agency if, in the judgment of the officer, a situation requires an immediate law enforcement response in the interest of preservation of life or property. In such urgent situations, the officer will contact the Mecklenburg County Sheriff's Department and then, as soon as possible thereafter, notify the Director, DES or their designated representative. The officer will record all security issues on the "Security Officer's Operations Log" form and will complete a "Security Officer Incident Report" on all incidents that require either physical intervention by the officer and/or response by local law enforcement authorities. Other reportable incidents may include any unusual or serious event that occurs within the DES facility or its adjacent parking areas and include but are not limited to the following:

  all incidents requiring emergency response (i.e., law enforcement, ambulance or
     fire/rescue)

verbal or physical altercations

building alarm events

observations of unusual activity to include suspicious persons/packages

the failure of client or contractor provided equipment

As it is not possible to give complete guidance or written instruction for every possible situation which might arise, the officer must conduct himself or herself in an appropriate manner at all times. Common sense and professionalism should govern all decisions, actions, and communications.

Benchmarking is also a key quality control function that can help security decision makers determine baseline performance measurements by which security officers can be assessed. Quality control inspectors can analyze the performance of security personnel by identifying the security force's critical duties and responsibilities, and identifying the best practices used by superior security officers in executing their duties. This information can then be used to set performance objectives for other security officers to strive for.

The functions that can be benchmarked depend on the nature of the duties and responsibilities of the security officers. Security personnel assigned to monitor CCTV monitors can be benchmarked by the frequency of correct response procedures used when alerted by the CCTV system. Officers assigned to an X-ray machine can be similarly benchmarked by the rate at which they catch prohibited items from passing through security via the X-ray machine. Response times after being alerted to an intruder is also a common benchmark for security personnel. Regardless of what is measured, the benchmark system should follow the S.M.A.R.T. method described in the Data Driven Security chapter.

S.M.A.R.T. METRICS

Good metrics are attainable when security professionals strive for S.M.A.R.T. metrics. S.M.A.R.T. stands for Specific, Measurable, Actionable, Relevant, and Timely.

Specific – a metric must measure a specific variable.

Measurable – a metric measures what is measurable. Not all components of a security program are measurable. For example, morale among security forces is often "measured," but would not be in a quantitative manner.

Actionable – a metric should not measure variables which cannot be acted upon. If a security decision maker cannot remedy a problem, there is not much sense in wasting time on that variable.

Relevant – a metric that fails to provide any information to improve the security program should be avoided. If the metric cannot tell us where we can improve, it is not relevant.

Timely – metrics have expiration dates. Historical data is an excellent indicator of the future; however, the older the data, the less important it may be. A metric system incapable of assessing the latest data is useless.

INCREASING PROFESSIONALISM

In recent decades, the security industry as a whole has uplifted itself from a blue-collar occupation to a legitimate profession. Through the difficult process of earning certifications, education, and demonstrating value to their organizations, security directors have earned their proper place in the corporate boardroom, and their departments have followed suit as profit centers through cost avoidance. While a distinct level of professionalism has been earned and granted to security directors and managers, the same cannot be said for the specific role of the security officer, still relegated the title in many places of the guard.

What follows is not a discussion of how the role of the security officer must elevate to a white-collar profession as that would be unrealistic and would leave a significant gap in the security of all organizations who utilize a security force. No, what follows is a discussion to open a new line of thought, of logic, of reason, of why the guard of old must be replaced with security officers of tomorrow. What follows, hopefully, will also open the door to how a new level of professionalism can be reached.

While it is hoped that most in the security industry know why a new level of professionalism is sought for line security personnel, it might be beneficial to discuss the reasons, the altruistic and the economic. The security officer is the most visible member of the security department and is a reflection, a product, of the security management. When the security officer is seen on the same level as the janitor or maintenance personnel, it speaks poorly of the professionalism of the department. When the security officer is viewed as a valued member of the organization, it reflects well on the security management team. Economically, security officers are the most expensive element of a security program and often the most difficult to justify. The return on investment of a security officer is not easy to calculate in many situations, yet security directors are forced, based on their risk assessments, to request funding for additional or new security personnel deployment. However, when a security decision maker can adequately calculate a return on investment, the return can be even greater to the security department in terms of its growth as a business unit. With the larger business unit comes a larger budget, additional management personnel, and higher salaries for all involved. Ultimately, once the dollars have been spent on security personnel, the next biggest cost is security officer turnover. If turnover can be brought down to manageable levels, the cost savings can be significant for the department, who can then use those dollars to fund other security projects. The other economic factor is that which came to light on September 11, 2001. On that fateful Tuesday morning, the security industry was changed forever ... for the better. As difficult as it is for most security professionals to admit, but which is known in the back of the industry's collective mind, the industry benefited by being forced to the forefront of the anti-terrorism effort, to prevent future attacks. And at the ground level, security is provided on a minute to minute basis by what are hopefully trained, professional security officers.

How does the security industry accomplish the task of enhancing professionalism among the lower ranks in a post September 11 world? The first and most basic concept is for the industry, and eventually its client base, to accept the title of security officer. The term guard should be dropped from its collective vernacular, and people outside the industry who use the term should be corrected. This small, seemingly insignificant change will accomplish two things. First, calling a security officer by that title raises morale, and with morale comes loyalty and professionalism. For those in the security industry who have not called a security officer in this way, try it. Second, once a client organization's employees, the ones in need of protection, witness the use of the formal title, Security Officer, they too will follow suit and give the respect due to the industry's most visible participants.

Fundamental fairness has long been a concern among rank and file security officers. Those that come into the industry with a good amount of optimism and hope for their futures are often left jaded and skeptical after only a short amount of time on the job. This is the inevitable result of extraordinarily long hours, be they at an X-ray machine or sitting in front of a bank of CCTV monitors, fewer breaks, and low wages. A general decline in morale is common as a result of the lack of fairness, and a larger drop in morale is fueled by the all too prevalent militant (not military) management style of many security supervisors.

Security officer training is also a force which drives a lack of professionalism in the security industry. Security departments of some organizations do not require any training beyond what the contractor already provides, and most contractors rarely provide any more training than what is required by law. Though it is commonly accepted that proprietary security forces receive more training than their contract counterparts, the level of training is still low overall. With a hint of optimism, the industry may turn this problem around since its major associations are now pushing forward with training guidelines and standards.

The final factor in the professionalism equation is compensation. For most of the security industry, pay rates for security officers are not much higher than for those who flip burgers for a living. As the old adage goes, you get what you pay for. Security officers, even those who protect critical infrastructure, are not compensated as well as they could and should be. The idea of total compensation goes beyond their hourly wage, and also takes into account their other benefits such as a retirement plan and health insurance. While most security operations manager would argue that many security officers would prefer to take their benefits as cash, that is short-term thinking on the part of both the officers and the management. Fairness, training, and total compensation are critical issues that, if addressed by the security industry as a whole, can raise the level of professionalism and work ethic of the ground level security officer, and in turn, raise the true security of the United States.

REDUCING SECURITY OFFICER TURNOVER

The Problem

The rate of turnover in the contract security industry is legendary, with annual turnover rates averaging 200% or more at many client sites. High turnover results in increased costs for recruitment and training on an ongoing basis and increases administrative expenses for both the client and the contract security company.

More importantly, high rates of turnover decrease the overall effectiveness of the contract security force. It can take six months or more for security officers to become fully proficient at their duties, and having constant officer turnover means that there is a good chance that some or all officers on site during any given shift may be new and inexperienced. Inexperienced officers have less ability to detect unusual activity because of their unfamiliarity with the site, and are less able to make good decisions about what to do or not do.

Constantly having new and inexperienced security officers on site also reinforces the negative perception that many people have of security officers and can prevent employees from taking them seriously.

Isn't This the Security Company's Problem?

Many clients feel that reducing security officer turnover is entirely the responsibility of the contract security company. While the contract security company certainly has an important role to play, they cannot do it alone. In fact, many of the steps necessary to improve security officer retention can only be done by the client company. Only by working together can the client and the contract security company get a handle on the turnover problem.

It's the Low Pay, Right?

The rate of pay that security officers receive in some parts of the country is ridiculously low, with some officers being paid at the minimum wage or just slightly above. In many areas, security officers are paid less than any other class of worker, including food service and janitorial employees.

While improving the rate of officer pay is one important factor in reducing turnover, it is by no means the only factor. Security officers who are dissatisfied with their jobs often say that other issues are as important to them, or even more important to them, than the rate of pay that they receive. When examining these issues, most revolve around the conditions under which the security officer must work.

Some of the issues of importance to security officers include:

- Being treated with respect by employees at the site where they are assigned to work.
- Receiving clear direction about what they are supposed to be doing.
- Having a professional work environment and properly functioning equipment.
- Being supported by management when they enforce an established policy or procedure.
- Doing work that they feel is important and valued.
- Receiving acknowledgment when they are doing a good job.
- Having a realistic schedule that allows them to get enough rest between shifts and gives them enough hours of pay to live on.
- Having medical and retirement benefits.
- Feeling that they are being listened to.

As you can see, many things of importance to the security officer revolve around the way that they are treated rather than what they are paid. Many of the changes that can greatly improve working conditions for officers center around improving the way that they are managed, and can be implemented at little or no additional cost.

Things That Can Improve Working Conditions for Security Officers

The following are some suggested changes for improving security officer working conditions at your site:

Treat Security Officers with Respect

Security officers are treated as second-class citizens at many sites, and often are insulted or ignored by the company's regular employees. Senior management at the client company should set the tone for treating security officers with respect and make it clear that abuse of security officers will not be tolerated.

Get to Know Your Officers

Client company employees, especially at the management level, should make a point to introduce themselves to the security officers and if possible, try and remember their names. Something as simple as saying "hello" to a person by name can go a long way in improving working conditions for a security officer.

The person responsible for security at the client company should attempt to personally welcome new security officers to the job when they are first assigned to the site. This should be done for every new officer, including those that work at night and on weekends.

Provide Security Officers with Clear Direction

Security officers should be provided with clear written instructions that describe their job responsibilities and the policies and procedures that they must follow. Adequate training should be provided to officers and this training should be consistent with the written instructions. All verbal directions given to officers should be consistent with the written instructions. Security officers should never be asked by employees of the client company to deviate from written procedures without the request going through the proper channels.

Stand Behind Security Officers When They Do the Right Thing

Security officers should receive the full backing of the client company's leadership team when the officer follows established procedures, even if this offends a client company employee. For example, if procedures require that all visitors to a facility sign in, the officer should not be reprimanded when s/he insists that the company president's wife also follow this procedure.

Having written instructions that are constantly being overridden by a set of "unwritten rules" is a surefire way to frustrate even the best security officer and should be avoided at all costs. If there is a legitimate reason to have an exception to a rule, it should be clearly documented in the security officer's written instructions.

Acknowledge Excellent Performance

Security officers who do an excellent job should be immediately acknowledged. For example, if an officer spots a water leak in the computer room and reports it before it can cause damage, s/he should receive an acknowledgment of this from a member of the client company's senior management team. A simple written note costs little to send, yet can mean a great deal to the individual security officer receiving it.

You should also consider adopting a "Security Officer of the Month" program where officers who perform above and beyond the call of duty can be officially recognized. Officers who win this award should be given a certificate and some type of small gift (such as a gift card for a local restaurant).

Provide a Professional Working Environment

Many security offices and guardhouses are cramped, cluttered places that don't appear to have been cleaned in years. Patrol vehicles issued to officers are often beaten up wrecks that don't run dependably. Flashlights, two-way radios, and other equipment issued to security officers are often in poor condition and are unreliable.

Security officers perform best when they are given a professional working environment that includes professional-grade tools and equipment. In order to get an officer to act as a professional, you must first treat him or her as one.

While security offices and guardhouses don't have to be built like the Taj Mahal, they should be clean, adequately-sized, and provide a professional working environment for your security officers. Security workspaces should be serviced by your janitorial staff and cleaned regularly just like any other workspace in the company.

The tools and equipment used by your security officers should be up-to-date and in good working condition. The costs of routinely repairing and replacing equipment should be included in your annual security budget.

Encourage Open Lines of Communication with Security Officers

The security officers at each site should meet as a group at least twice per year. Officers should be paid to attend these meetings to encourage full participation. The primary purpose of these meetings is to provide updates to officers on security procedures for the site and to give officers an opportunity to air their grievances and express their ideas and opinions.

The person responsible for security at the client company should regularly attend security officer meetings so that he or she can directly hear security officer opinions without them being filtered through the contract security company's site supervisor or branch manager.

Educate Security Officers About Your Business

Efforts should be made to educate security officers on the client company's business: what it does, who it serves, what types of operations are involved, etc. This information should be included in the initial training curriculum for each officer, and reinforced through ongoing continuing educational activities.

Managers from various departments at the client company should be asked to periodically attend security officer meetings and provide a brief presentation explaining to the officers what their business unit does.

Create Realistic Schedules

Creating a schedule that meets the security needs of a business at a reasonable cost can be challenging, but responsibility for solving scheduling problems should not be placed on the backs of individual security officers. Asking a security officer to drive all the way across town to cover a two-hour shift, or asking an officer that got off duty at 2:00 am to report back at 8:00 am the same day, is unrealistic and inconsiderate to the needs of the security officer.

It is recommended that officers not work more than 12 consecutive hours in any 24 hour period, and for not more than 60 hours in any seven-day period. Off-duty periods should be scheduled to provide for an uninterrupted eight-hour sleep cycle.

Officers should receive a minimum of four hours of pay anytime that they are called in. Schedules should be balanced so that all officers receive an adequate number of hours to live on. Attempts should be made to accommodate any special scheduling requests of individual officers when it can be done so without impacting the business.

Make Company "Perks" Available to Security Officers

Many client companies offer a range of perquisites to their employees, including things such as free parking, health and fitness clubs, cafeterias, and company stores. In most cases, these company "perks" are for company employees only, and are off limits to the employees of contractors, such as contract security officers.

It is suggested that the client company rethink this policy, and consider offering at least some perks to security officers for free or at a reduced cost. The financial impact of doing this can be minimal to the company, while adding a few benefits will be appreciated by the security officers and can greatly change their perception of their job.

Security Officer Pay

Quality contract security officers prefer to work at the sites that offer the best pay and the best working conditions. Once assigned to such a site, officers want to stay there, and generally perform at a high level so that they can maintain their position. The result is much lower officer turnover and better quality officers.

Trying to cut corners on officer pay can be a false economy. Paying the absolute lowest rate may appear to reduce costs, but in actuality costs more because of increased administrative and training expenses.

Often paying only one or two dollars per hour above the median market rates can attract the best quality officers and greatly reduce officer turnover. Increasing the rate of officer pay by a dollar or two usually only increases the total annual cost of providing security services by 10% to 20%. In our opinion, this is a small price to pay for improved security officer performance.

It is recommended that clients conduct a survey of the rates that security officers are being paid in their community. Information on pay rates can be obtained by talking with your peers at other facilities, and by looking at recruiting postings on job boards and on services such as Craigslist.

Once rates of pay in your community have been established, create a chart that allows you to see how the rate that your company is paying compares to that being paid at other sites. If the rate that you are paying is significantly below that being paid at other sites, this is something that should be further evaluated.

The value of any benefits provided should be included in your pay rate evaluation. Many people working as security officers greatly value things such as medical benefits, and may be happy working for a lower rate of pay at a site that provides such benefits.

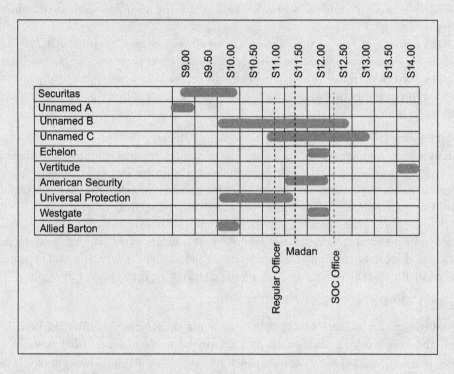

FIGURE 10.2   Reducing security officer turnover. Copyright ©2019 by Silva Consultants. Used by permission. Additional information available from Silva Consultants via www.silvaconsultants.com.

REFERENCES

1 www.hud.gov/sites/documents/74604C5PIHH.PDF.
2 Vellani, Karim H., Robert J. Emery, and Nathan Parker (2012). "Staffing Benchmarks: How Many Security Officers are Enough?" *Journal of Healthcare Protection Management*, 28(2), International Association for Healthcare Security & Safety.
3 Vellani, Karim H., Robert J. Emery, and Jennifer M. Reingle Gonzalez (2015). "A Data-Driven Model for Estimating Industry Average Numbers of Hospital Security Staff." *Journal of Healthcare Protection Management*, 31(1), International Association for Healthcare Security & Safety.

4 Vellani, Karim H. and Sadie H. Conway (2019). "How Many Security Officers Do You Need? An Evidence-based Approach to Determining the Industry Average Number of Hospital Security Officers." International Association of Healthcare Security and Safety, Orlando, FL, May 20, 2019.

5 Taylor, B.G., Koper, C.S., and Woods, D.J. (2010). "A Randomized Controlled Trial of Different Policing Strategies at Hot Spots of Violent Crime." *Journal of Experimental Criminology*, 7(2):149–181.

6 Wells, W. and Wu, L. (2011). "Proactive Policing Effects on Repeat and Near-Repeat Shootings in Houston." *Police Quarterly*, 14(3):298–319.

7 Carriaga, M.L. and Worrall, J.L. (2015). "Police Levels and Crime: A Systematic Review and Meta-Analysis." *Police Journal: Theory, Practice and Principles*, 88(4):315–333.

8 COMPSTAT is a combination of police management, philosophy, and organizational management tools.

9 McElvain, J.P., Kposova, A.J., and Gray, B.C. (2012). "Testing a Crime Control Model: Does Strategic and Directed Deployment of Police Officers Lead to Lower Crime?" *Journal of Criminology*, 2013:1–11.

10 Groff, E.R., Ratcliffe, J.H., Haberman, C.P., Sorg, E.T., Joyce, N.M., and Taylor, R.B. (2015). "Does What Police Do at Hot Spots Matter? The Philadelphia Policing Tactics Experiment." *Criminology*, 53(1):23–53.

11 Novak, K.J., Fox, A.M., Carr, C.M., and Spade, D.A. (2016). "The Efficacy of Foot Patrol in Violent Places." *Journal of Experimental Criminology*, 12(3):465–475.

12 Problem-oriented policing is an approach to policing in which discrete pieces of police business (each consisting of a cluster of similar incidents, whether crime or acts of disorder, that the police are expected to handle) are subject to microscopic examination (drawing on the especially honed skills of crime analysts and the accumulated experience of operating field personnel) in hopes that what is freshly learned about each problem will lead to discovering a new and more effective strategy for dealing with it. Problem-oriented policing places a high value on new responses that are preventive in nature, that are not dependent on the use of the criminal justice system, and that engage other public agencies, the community, and the private sector when their involvement has the potential for significantly contributing to the reduction of the problem. www.popcenter.org/about/?p=whatiscpop. See also www.popcenter.org/about/?p=elements.

13 Taylor, B.G., Koper, C.S., and Woods, D.J. (2010). "A Randomized Controlled Trial of Different Policing Strategies at Hot Spots of Violent Crime." *Journal of Experimental Criminology*, 7(2):149–181.

14 Rosenfeld, R., Deckard, M.J., and Blackburn, E. (2014). "The Effects of Directed Patrol and Self-Initiated Enforcement on Firearm Violence: A Randomized Controlled Study of Hot Spot Policing." *Criminology*, 52(3):428–449.

15 Ratcliffe, J.H., Taniguchi, T., Groff, E.R., and Wood, J.D. (2011). "The Philadelphia Foot Patrol Experiment: A Randomized Controlled Trial of Police Patrol Effectiveness in Violent Crime Hotspots." *Criminology*, 49:795–831.

16 Braga, A.A., Hureau, D., & Papachristos, A. (2012). "An Ex Post Facto Evaluation Framework for Place-Based Police Interventions." *Evaluation Review*, 35:592–626.

17 Novak, K.J., Fox, A.M., Carr, C.M., and Spade, D.A. (2016). "The Efficacy of Foot Patrol in Violent Places." *Journal of Experimental Criminology*, 12(3):465–475.

CHAPTER 11

Project Management

Karim H. Vellani and Andrew Rubin

CONTENTS

INTRODUCTION

Security decision makers invariably need to manage large security projects. While some will have the luxury of dedicated project managers inside their organizations or the ability to hire consulting project managers, many will need to manage projects themselves. Organizations may have several projects underway simultaneously, and those projects may or may not be related to a common business goal. Knowledge of project management is an essential tool for a well-rounded security professional: they will need this knowledge to either manage projects directly, or to oversee the work of a project manager and understand the concepts by which projects are managed on their behalf.

A project is a *temporary* endeavor to create a *unique* capability. *Temporary* means that the project has an end; usually this is followed by use of the project's output in ongoing operations. For example, a project may entail implementing a patrol audit system to record Security Officer roving patrols. The scope of the project might include selection and installation of the system and training the organization's employees to use it. Regularly analyzing the logs recorded by the system and presenting the results to management would be an ongoing operation after the project's conclusion, and not part of the project scope. Recognizing the difference between a project and ongoing operations is important so the project can be successfully concluded.

The other aspect of a project is that the capability it provides is *unique*. Upgrading video surveillance cameras in a facility could be a project, as the unique capability would be the added features of the new cameras. Upgrading each individual camera, even though they are different units from each other, would not be a project as the units are substantially similar.

Successful project management can result in great cost savings and increased operational benefits to an organization. Project management entails the planning and execution of all aspects of a project, management of the project's resources, and the application of skills, knowledge, and methods to achieve the project's objectives. The project's objectives are typically the financial and operational benefits that the project's output provides to the organization. Successful project management may be defined in a number of ways, but the most common are (1) completion of the project's full scope, (2) completion of the project on time, (3) completion of the project on budget, and (4) that the project's deliverables have an acceptable level of quality.[1]

SECURITY PROJECT JUSTIFICATION

Few organizations have unlimited resources, so proposed security expenditures typically compete against other proposed expenditures to enhance profitability or to directly further the organization's mission. Because a security program must make business sense, the organization's leaders need practical assessments of the possible returns on security investments in order to create an effective security program. The organization's senior management needs valid metrics that provide evidence that any expenditure positively impacts the organization's profit or directly affects its success in other ways. When determining the impact of the security program on profit and mission success, the organization's senior management will want some critical questions answered during the process of selecting which projects to fund. These questions may include:

- What is the financial impact to the organization of inadequate security?
- On average in our industry, what is the cost of losses without adequate security?
- What is the worst case scenario of financial loss without adequate security?
- How does the organization protect its property, both physical and intellectual?
- How much security is appropriate?
- What security measures are most cost effective?
- What types of security measures are needed?
- What impact will security have on the productivity of the organization's employees?

Even when a project has been justified and work started, project justification is sometimes revisited. This is particularly true in the security industry, where security is sometimes reduced out of larger construction projects to make the overall project more financially appealing. Rather than begrudge this situation, the security project manager should relish the opportunity to provide a return on investment analysis for the security portion of the overall project. For the security consultant, the willingness to provide this analysis will set them apart from other consultants and will often provide the foundation for opportunities to serve the client on other security projects. For the security professional who is internal to an organization, conducting a return on security investment analysis increases trust and support from their own senior management.

RETURN ON SECURITY INVESTMENT

Most organizations view expenditures as affecting either revenue or cost. Revenue expenditures, sometimes called "top line" items, are those that increase sales. Security typically is viewed as a cost center or "bottom line" item, since purchasing decisions in most industries do not consider which provider has the best security. Only when a security project is required for entry into a market is it considered a "top line" item.[2]

A company's financial analysts typically look at standard financial measures to justify which projects merit the company's resources. A common measure is return on investment (ROI). This is a measure of the net benefit of the project (its return) divided by the cost of the project (the investment). As an example, if a project will cost $5000 and save $6000, then the return is $1000 (the savings minus the cost), and the ROI is 20% (or $1000 divided by $5000). This project will be judged against other projects with their own ROI values, and the relative ROI of each project will be one factor in deciding which projects to fund. The importance of ROI with respect to other factors will vary from company to company.

While conceptually simple, ROI can be difficult to calculate for real projects. Security projects are often justified on the basis of improved security or safety. The real benefit would require counting things that will not happen: burglaries that won't occur, or the value of items that will not be stolen as a result of the improved security. While difficult, these benefits can be estimated based on industry statistics applied to the organization's own incident reporting data from recent reporting periods. Shrink and loss rates, asset recoveries, and employee productivity are all factors that are appropriate for this type of estimation.

Security projects that reduce the cost of security operations are more easily quantified. For these projects, it is easy to present the total cost of an operation as it is today, and the total cost envisioned after the project's completion. For example, if implementing a patrol audit system that automates the recording of individual foot patrols and compilation of those records, one can easily identify the administrative tasks that the system will eliminate and assign a cost to those tasks. Security personnel hours and rates, the cost of physical security measures and packages, liability insurance costs, and property insurance costs are factors for which accurate before and after costs can be ascertained.

The single largest cost in most security programs is that of deployed security personnel, so reducing this cost often represents the largest potential savings to a security program. The cost of physical security measures can rival the cost of security personnel, and risk assessments can help security decision makers determine and deploy the ideal security package for their facilities. The productivity of employees outside of the security function can also be a significant factor in achieving a return on security investment. These employees are often compensated at a much higher rate than security personnel, and directly serve the company's clients, so loss of their time due to security related incidents can cost the organization substantially. For example, if a law firm's offices are burgled and their computers stolen, the lost productivity and value of information will far exceed the value of the computers themselves. In this case, that value can be estimated and multiplied by the percentage change in the likelihood of a burglary due to the project's implementation. (If the project is estimated to decrease the likelihood of a burglary in a given year from 5% to 1%, and a burglary could cost the law firm $100,000, then the annual savings would be 0.04 times $100,000, or $4000 per year.) In true risk management terms, each security breach is termed a Single Loss Exposure

(SLE), and is multiplied by the number of times it occurs per year, the Annual Rate of Exposure (ARO), to yield a yearly total called the Annual Loss Exposure (ALE).

Wise security professionals never fail to consider the cost of settlements and jury awards resulting from lawsuits for inadequate security. Even one unfavorable jury award can have severe repercussions to an organization. The cost of security related litigation may not directly appear in the security department budget, but ultimately the organization's executive management holds security directors accountable for the fault even if insurance pays the settlement costs.

A final factor that goes into an ROI calculation is the timeframe of the return. Projects typically have an initial cost, with the benefits recurring year after year. Most finance organizations will have a standard timeframe (often three to five years) over which project benefits are considered. Thus, the return would include all of the benefits that occur in those years, adjusted for any costs associated with those benefits.[3]

As has been stated, an ROI analysis usually involves a fair amount of estimation. The security project manager should expect the organization's management to challenge his or her estimates. The best defense to these challenges is to have conservative estimates that are based on a consistent methodology, and backed up by documented facts (such as before and after insurance quotations) whenever possible. The organization's management should see that estimates are not "padded," but rather are reasonable and that they err on the side of lower ROI. This will result in better credibility for the project and for the project manager.

After the project has completed, the security project manager has a unique opportunity to provide senior management with an analysis of the true return on the security analysis. The analysis not only allows the calculation of realized savings from the project but also allows the security project manager to showcase their commitment to the security budget for current and future projects. For security consultants, conducting an ROI analysis after the project is a way to remind the organization of the good work they did, and of the credibility of their proforma analysis.

PROJECT MANAGEMENT ACTIVITIES

Project management in its most basic form consists of four distinct sets of activities: development, planning, execution, and closure.[4] Often these are thought of as phases, although they can overlap (particularly in large projects). For example, in a project to implement physical security at a new facility, the perimeter fence portion of the work may be concluded while camera installation is still underway.

DEVELOPMENT

For the security project manager, development is the process of obtaining the requisite approval to undertake the security project; delineating the scope, overall budget, and timeframe of the project; establishing an overall solution approach; and deciding whether to use internal resources, external resources, or both.

The leadership team of the enterprise's security function typically has an idea of the implementation strategy and other elements of the development process. The solution approach and the initial pass at scope, time, and cost will be refined in later planning activities. If the refinement shows that the initial estimates were far off, then the scope, cost, and time constraints of the project—or whether to even conduct the project—may be revisited.

Development can look very different depending upon whether the security project manager works within the organization conducting the project, or whether they are a security consultant. The security project manager who is embedded in an organization often manages projects as an added activity to another role, often on the security leadership team. For this security project manager, development entails making a business case[5] that clearly communicates the benefits and costs of the project to the enterprise's management. This business case typically contains all of the elements of the development process.

For the security project manager who is a security consultant hired by an organization, development is the contracting process. Typically, this consists of a scope of work that may have been developed by the client or may be developed collaboratively with the client, and a contract to formalize the engagement. Collaboratively developed scopes of work are better than client or consultant developed scopes of work in almost all instances, as the security consultant can inject expertise learned from other engagements. For example, a client may not be aware of alternate technical or administrative approaches to similar problems that have proved successful in other companies or industries with which the consultant has worked. A consultant who develops a statement of work without the benefit of client input will likely be unaware of internal initiatives or constraints that could support or hamper the proposal.

PLANNING

Depending upon the nature of the project, planning may be an extensive, time consuming process, or it may be simple. The output of the process is a project plan, which in its most basic form includes a schedule, a budget, and identification of the resources required for the project. The project schedule identifies the tasks to be performed, the resources needed to perform them, the time period over which each task will be performed, and the dependencies of each task.[6] Other outputs of the planning process for larger projects can include a formal work breakdown structure, communication plans, quality plans, and a host of other artifacts. Experienced security decision makers, project managers, and consultants know how to streamline this process so that a project has the right amount of planning. Plans that are too detailed will require unnecessary effort to manage during execution, while those that are not detailed enough increase the risk of a project's failure to meet its objectives.

Some team members may be identified in the definition activities. These are often the organization's personnel, and their selection is beyond the control of the security project manager. Generally, however, it is during the planning process that most project resources are identified and the project team is built. When selecting project team members, it is important to consider the relevant experience of the people, their financial cost to the project, their availability to execute the project, and the fact that they are people who will usually have to work with one another. The security project manager who is a consultant often has more latitude in selecting team members than the security project manager who works for the organization sponsoring the project, since s/he does not need to account for (and is often unaware of) organizational goals that are outside the defined scope of the project.[7]

Including the project team members in the development of the project plan is always a good idea where practical. Team members bring domain knowledge and can identify dependencies that the security project manager may not have seen. They can generate or validate effort estimates of tasks that are within their domain. Importantly, having their agreement to the estimates of the specific tasks they will later execute results in their commitment to the schedule. While this does not guarantee that the project will be executed on time, it greatly increases the likelihood of on time delivery.

Development of the project plan starts with the end goals in mind and an implementation strategy. Using domain expertise of the security project manager, project team members, and others when required, the strategy is broken down into more refined steps, over and over in a process called progressive elaboration. The process stops when the steps are small enough to be considered well-defined, manageable tasks. At this point, the work is well understood, and costs, dependencies, and durations can be seen. The total cost and duration estimates can be calculated and checked against the estimates from the development stage. If the cost or timeline exceed the project's authorization, corrective action should be taken before actual project work proceeds.[8]

One of the critical planning processes involves identification of project stakeholders. Some stakeholders will be known from the definition stage, such as the project's sponsor within the organization. During planning, the security project manager and the project team should ask themselves for each work item, "who in the organization is affected by this?" The answers will constitute the stakeholders. Different stakeholders will have different needs, and those must be understood in order for the project to ultimately be successful. The different needs will also impact how those stakeholders are engaged by the team during the project's execution. For example, the project's executive sponsor might only need to know if the project is on schedule and on budget, and of any major issues. End users of the project's deliverable, on the other hand, need to understand how this project will affect their day-to-day jobs.

During the planning stage, the project team should identify realistic risks to the project's success. A risk is an event that may or may not happen, and which will significantly impact the project if it does happen. Examples include availability of resources[9] who are critical to the project and also in high demand elsewhere, delayed delivery of equipment that is not readily available from multiple suppliers, and construction delays if a project is to outfit a new facility with security technology. Not everything that might happen is an appropriate risk to be identified and tracked. Good questions to identify appropriate risks are:

- What is the likelihood of the event happening?
- If the event happens, how severe will its impact be to the project?

These questions can be rated on a numerical scale (1 to 5, for example) and the results multiplied, to come up with a numerical score for each possible risk. Contingency and mitigation plans for each of the highest scoring potential risks should be developed, and they should be tracked as risks during the project's execution. Stakeholders should be updated on these risks regularly during execution, so that they will not be blind-sided if any of the risks turn into actual events.

Contingency plans are sometimes referred to as "Plan B," and are developed in the hope that they will not need to be executed. Their value is that if a risk indeed materializes, the response plan has already been formulated and just needs to be executed. Contingency plans do not reduce the likelihood of a risk occurring, they only improve the response if the risk occurs. Mitigation plans are actions taken to reduce the likelihood of a risk impacting the project's success. These actions typically increase the project cost but reduce the overall project risk. For example, consider a project to implement remote surveillance that uses a new, unproven technology. A contingency plan may be that if the testing of the installed technology shows it is inadequate, then the new equipment will be uninstalled and replaced by older, proven technology. This is likely to delay the project significantly. A mitigation plan for the same risk may be to pay for design work for both technologies up front, and work with a vendor to purchase the older technology with the understanding that if it is unused, it will be returned and refunded (probably for a restocking fee). Although the design work for the older technology and the restocking fee will be "wasted money" if the new technology is successful, these costs are not truly wasted for they have bought insurance that the project would not be significantly delayed if the new technology were unsuccessful. Contingency plans and mitigation plans are only appropriate for risks whose likelihood and impact are high enough to seriously jeopardize a project's success.

When forming the schedule and budget, it is important that the project manager has a realistic view of what might not happen, ideally during execution. Budgets should have a bit of padding, preferably in a "management reserve" category that can become a surplus if everything goes well. Similarly, the plan should have some slack to account for delays.

Finally, it is important to revisit the project's justification during the planning stage and ask whether the project still makes business sense. In the planning phase, assumptions from the development phase are validated, and the project team becomes far more knowledgeable about the activities needed to successfully execute the project. If the projected cost or timeframe is well beyond the initial expectations, the security project manager has a duty to inform the project sponsor, who will likely appreciate knowing bad news earlier rather than later. A decision can be made to terminate the project during planning (before much of the project's budget has been spent) or to adjust the budget and timeline to account for new knowledge.

EXECUTION

Execution activities encompass building the actual deliverables of the project, and managing the activities to ensure that budget, schedule, quality, and delivered scope are all within the project's authorization from the development stage. It is during the execution activities that equipment is ordered, delivered, installed, and tested. If the end result of a project is a report, it is during the execution phase that data is gathered and the report is written. The specific execution activities depend upon the defined scope of the project.

Projects will often fail during the execution phase if adequate oversight is not in place. The successful security project manager will obtain regular, frequent, fact-based progress updates from their project team members. The frequency of required updates can vary, but the security project manager must receive updates often enough so that corrective action can be taken to remedy off-track tasks without putting the project in jeopardy. In practice, this is usually between one day and one week intervals. The progress updates should be fact based, as human nature is to estimate that a job is half done when the time allotted to it is half used. Instead of accepting an update that a task is X% complete, progress should be in terms of delivered units (such as "34 out of 59 planned cameras have been installed"). This kind of quantification of work is not always possible, but should be attempted whenever possible.

Monitoring must be done against schedule, budget, and scope. The project schedule from the planning stage is rarely executed exactly as written, so it is important for the security project manager to update the schedule with actual dates, and to monitor actual expenditures against budget throughout the project. On longer, more elaborate projects, Earned Value analysis may be appropriate.[10]

During a project's execution, it is critically important to keep stakeholders appropriately engaged. Engaged stakeholders keep the project sponsored by the organization in the face of competing demand for the project's budget and resources. Engaged stakeholders can also keep the project manager informed of changing needs that might require changes to the project's plan or budget. A list of stakeholders will have been made during the planning stages but may be updated during execution as additional stakeholders are identified or if the organization changes. Engagement typically takes the form of regular, written summary updates for executives, project review meetings for management who are more actively engaged with the project's details, and other means for individuals who may be affected by the project. Those other means can include newsletters, question-and-answer sessions, or other forms of engagement as appropriate.

Large projects may have other management processes defined in the overall project plan, such as quality reviews, stage gates, and scope reviews. Ensuring that these activities are executed is the responsibility of the project manager, although actual execution may be done by other people. These processes are all part of the project's overhead. Some amount of overhead is necessary for a successful project: It serves to strengthen the organization's support for the project, and to ensure that the project remains aligned to the organization's goals. The right amount of overhead will vary depending on the project's size and risk, and the organization's maturity and comfort level with the project team. The best way for a project manager to reduce this monitoring is to build a solid record of meeting their commitments.

CLOSURE

Closure is the process of ending work in an organized manner. It involves confirming in written form that the work is in fact done, that billing is complete, that all parties have been paid, and that final documentation is completed and entered into the organization's files. Closure should be a formal process, so that there is no confusion about whether work or financial obligations remain. For the security project manager who is a consultant external to the organization, closure is an opportunity to recommend future work based on what was learned during the project.

THE SECURITY PROJECT MANAGER

The security project manager is an integral factor in the project's success. S/he is ultimately charged with managing, directing, and coordinating the project team's efforts; planning and organizing the project; defining the scope of work; overseeing the project's technical aspects; negotiating project terms with the project's sponsoring organization; ensuring efficient performance of all project related work; and financial management of the project's expenses. The role of security project manager is a challenging job that requires a high degree of organization, relationship management skills, communication skills, and knowledge of security principles. Generally, technical proficiency is less important than management and administrative competence for the security project manager role.

Domain knowledge is key to being an effective project manager in any industry, and the security industry is no exception. A keen understanding of security principles, best practices, and security industry standards promulgated by industry associations such as ASIS-International, the International Association of Professional Security

Consultants (IAPSC), the International Association for Healthcare Security and Safety (IAHSS), and the Security Industry Association (SIA) can set the bar for expertise in this industry. Additionally, knowledge of best practices and standards from organizations outside of the security industry, such as the National Fire Protection Association (NFPA), can round out the domain knowledge needed to be a top project manager in the security industry.

Domain knowledge is gained from experience and education. Those with experience working on projects for different companies and in different industries often bring the most useful background to a project. This is why so many companies turn to outside, independent security consultants to lead projects: Their exposure to best practices from other organizations is a source of new, better ideas for the company. Formal education is another source of knowledge. Today, security management degrees are becoming more common in colleges and universities around the world. Those with graduate degrees in security management or criminal justice can bring necessary philosophical knowledge to advanced security projects.

While domain knowledge is useful and necessary, the ability to discern the stakeholders' needs and find solutions that meet those needs is at the core of a successful project management effort. In other industries, this function is sometimes performed by a business analyst, but in the security industry it is most often performed by the security project manager.

Transforming a client's needs into solutions starts with the security project manager being an excellent active listener. S/he can then:

- Lead the project's stakeholders through a flexible, interactive, and iterative process to obtain a thorough understanding of their needs.
- Succinctly document those needs in terms that bar misinterpretation, and allow the stakeholders to validate that their needs are captured correctly.
- Develop multiple solution options and validate with the client how the solution options meet their needs, and describe holistic tradeoffs.
- Achieve consensus on the approach, process, and communication strategy to achieve the project's desired results as efficiently as possible.

Beyond skills and knowledge, other characteristics set top security project managers apart from the rest. Great security project managers must be strong decision makers and have the ability to quickly solve problems. The role requires the ability to multitask, to delegate, and to communicate effectively in both written and verbal forms. S/he must perform under pressure and ensure that the project team also performs under pressure that inevitably rises at times during the project. As the leader of the project team, the security project manager must be responsive to the team's needs and manage the team's interpersonal dynamics. Completion of a project on time and on budget are key indicators of project success, so time management, fiscal management, and performance management skills are critical for the security project manager.

Because of the nature of the security industry, two other characteristics are of great importance for security project managers, especially among security consultants. These two characteristics are ethical behavior and discretion. Most independent security consultants live by a code of ethics that outlines how they will respond in various scenarios. The International Association of Professional Security Consultants has a Code of Ethics for Certified Security Consultants (CSCs) that is included among the appendices of this book. Discretion involves treating the client's information as confidential. All security systems and operations have vulnerabilities, and the effectiveness of the systems and operations are reduced if those vulnerabilities are widely known. Understandably, an organization will be reluctant to fully share its knowledge if it does not trust that the information will be held in strict confidence.

THE SECURITY PROJECT TEAM

The security project team, under the direction and control of the security project manager, is charged with executing the project plan. Depending on the nature, scope, and size of the security project, the project team might consist of only a few people or it might be an extensive team with specialists, consultants, and subcontractors. Team members usually perform multiple tasks, although on larger teams, some specialists might be brought onto the team to perform single tasks.

The independent security consultant working in the role of project manager may benefit from including some of the client's own employees on the project team. These people bring institutional knowledge and can retain project knowledge long after the project is complete.[11] Additionally, they can provide the security escort that many client organizations require for outsiders.

Most security project teams are unique and are organized for a particular project. Some team members may have worked together before, but typically, the entire team has not worked on past projects together such that they can start the current project as a cohesive unit. Beyond ensuring that team members bring the skills needed by the project, the project manager is responsible for developing an environment conducive to teamwork, and an accelerated learning curve that will increase team performance. To create this environment, it is important for the project manager to understand how a project team matures into a high performing team.

When the team starts, team members are generally getting to know each other, to understand each other's strengths and weaknesses, and to understand what knowledge and skills each team member brings to the project. The project member can accelerate team maturity by establishing specific expectations of each team member, including identification of individual objectives and delegation of tasks. Not unlike a young sports team, conflicts and alliances may develop as the team members form relationships and jockey for position within the team. The project manager may need to step in and resolve power struggles to enhance the strength of the team as a whole. A climate that reinforces open communication between project team members expedites the transition from this rough phase into one where the team becomes a coherent, internally supportive organization. The project manager will find that, through ample support and intervention early in the team's life, less intervention will be necessary as the team matures. The desired end stage of team formation is that of a high performing work team, in which members support each other, work out their own problems, hopefully challenge each other to learn and grow, and display a great deal of synergy.[12]

In spite of a project manager's best efforts, team members sometimes will have difficulty working with each other. The experienced project manager is sensitive to the work styles and personal motivations of their team members and aims to use this knowledge to help the team function as a cohesive unit. Sometimes that means discreetly explaining a team member's role to another team member who feels their own role is being infringed. Sometimes it means strategically pairing team members who are compatible, or making work assignments to place distance between team members who are at odds with each other. In the best case, team members learn to value each other even if they do not personally agree with or even like each other. In the worst case, it may be necessary to remove a person from the project team.

PROJECT SUCCESS CRITERIA

Project success will be indicated by both objective and subjective measures. Objective measures are those that can be factually verified and usually come down to whether the project was delivered at the promised time, whether the project was delivered on budget, and whether the full scope of the project was delivered. Some mature organizations are able to measure the actual return on investment of a project after it has been completed, and compare that number to the planned return on investment. This would also be an objective measure of project success.

Beyond these high-level measures of the project's overall success, individual stakeholders may have their own objective success criteria. For some, it may be less work on their task lists, or fewer process steps to improve efficiency. For the security consultant who manages projects, as an outsider to the organization, it is important for both business relationship and development reasons to be sure that each stakeholder is satisfied with the results of the project. It is fair to ask how the project fits into a client stakeholder's career objectives, and how the project's outcome will cause the client to be judged within his or her own organization. If the project's outcome requires major changes to the way that stakeholders do their jobs, the project manager should prepare them for an easy and smooth transition.

Subjective criteria are those that cannot be directly measured and are based more on perception than on fact. Subjective criteria are often not written into contracts or project charters, but are nonetheless important. They include questions like: "Were my suggestions seriously considered?," "Does the proposed solution seem robust?," "As a project sponsor, does this project make me look good to my organization?," "Was the project team thorough in their work?," and even very nebulous criteria like "Do I feel good about this?"

An example might better illustrate the subjective ways in which the project and its manager can be judged. The security director of an organization was coming under increased scrutiny to ensure that appropriate security was in place at the organization's facilities. An off-the-shelf security risk assessment methodology did not exist in their industry. After careful consideration, the security director decided to hire an independent security consultant to develop the risk assessment methodology and assess his operation. The consultant learned that the security director's staff had the necessary expertise to create the assessment, but lacked the time to do so. They also understood that they were hired in order to keep the assessment at arm's length from the department, so that the results would not be perceived as biased.

The consultant, understanding the subjective terms by which the project would be judged, scheduled extra time with individual stakeholders to better understand their needs. Thus, the risk assessment they developed was not only judged objectively (being on time and on budget), but subjectively wherein stakeholders felt their needs were understood and reflected in the final product.

One member of the security staff was responsible for the organization's internal security reporting mechanism. He had spent considerable time and resources to build an accurate database of security incidents based on his organization's incident reports.

Policies, procedures, and organizational training all supported the maintenance of the database, but a proper system to analyze the data was lacking. Since the risk assessment methodology contained a threat identification component that included analysis of the internal security report information, the security consultant also developed a streamlined approach to analyzing the internal security report data. This extra effort on the part of the security consultant not only improved the risk assessment methodology but also saved the member of the security staff significant time and effort. While this extra step was outside the scope of services that the security consultant was hired to perform, it served to further develop the relationship between the consultant and the organization and resulted in higher client satisfaction. For security consultants, such extra steps often yield more future business. The end result in this case is that the security consultant and the project were judged as being successful.

REFERENCES

1 The definition of "acceptable quality" should be established during the project's initial development. People often desire "high quality," but that can come at a high price. Depending upon the organization's need and the specific project, a lower level of quality may provide the best value and thus be acceptable.

2 Such projects may be justified to meet regulatory, industry accreditation, or other de facto market requirements.

3 For example, the cost of maintaining a new system that resulted from the project.

4 Many project managers use a framework from the Project Management Institute (PMI), to which these activity sets align. The PMI refers to Initiation, Planning, Executing, Monitoring and Control, and Closing. The Executing and Monitoring and Control process groups from the PMI's framework are grouped here in the execution set of activities.

5 Organizations use different names for this document. It might be called a business case, project charter, or some other name unique to the organization. In some organizations it is quite formal, while in others it may be very informal.

6 Dependencies may be considered either mandatory or preferred. Mandatory dependencies cannot be broken; for example, one cannot install a security system until it has been received. Preferred dependencies can be broken; for example, a decision to install a security system in one building before installing a system in another building. It is important to know the differences, because breaking preferred dependencies is a popular technique used to bring a late project back on track.

7 For example, training and career development of employees.

8 Typical corrective actions include revisiting the project approach, breaking preferred dependencies, and proposing adjustments to the authorized scope, budget, and/or timeline.

9 Resources can include people as well as objects. For example, technicians and equipment are both considered resources in the context of project management. Critical resources would be those people or objects that are specialized, and for which acceptable substitutes are not readily available.

10 Earned Value analysis involves project performance metrics to measure whether a project is on schedule and on budget..

11 While project deliverables should always be documented, with the documentation handed over to the sponsoring organization at the end of the project, questions may arise later. Often these questions are why certain decisions were made, when the decisions themselves are documented but the documented rationale may be difficult to understand years later, when the context of the project is not remembered well.

12 For a more structured explanation of team formation, see Bruce Tuckman's seminal 1965 paper, "Development sequence in small groups." This paper introduces the popular model of team development phases of Forming, Storming, Norming and Performing. Tuckman, B. W. (1965). Developmental sequence in small groups. *Psychological Bulletin, 63*(6), 384–399.

CHAPTER **12**

Gaining Support for Security Programs

Robert J. Emery

Vice President for Safety, Health, Environment & Risk Management
The University of Texas Health Science Center at Houston Professor of Occupational
Health The University of Texas School of Public Health

CONTENTS

INTRODUCTION

An inevitable finding of any review of a security program is the need for "improved communications." The recurrent commentary provided by groups ranging from front line workers to executive management is that they often don't really understand what security programs do and may not know how the program's efforts actually contribute to the organizational mission or the bottom line. When presented with such findings, the natural response on the part of the security professional is to explore ways to improve the transmission of information orally or in writing. While efforts to enhance oral and written communication are always laudable, there is another means of communication that also warrants close examination. The way in which important security related data is displayed is an equally important means of communication, and it is ironic that in an era when security professionals are implored to develop and collect key performance measures and metrics, little attention is provided to the way the data is actually displayed and communicated. This is a crucial shortcoming within our profession, and one that serves as a major barrier to achieving full management support. This impression is based on five years of intensive field research, where an examination of the existing literature on the science and art of effective data displays was performed, and then data displays from literally hundreds of actual safety and security programs were reviewed. From this effort, it became apparent that when data is displayed in a manner that is compelling, desired decision making often ensues.

BARRIERS TO EFFECTIVE COMMUNICATIONS

Successful security programs function largely in the realm of prevention, so on a - good day, "nothing happens." Therefore the challenge for security programs is to be able to articulate what resources are needed to "make nothing happen." In order to do this, data is needed to justify assertions and claims. The old adage among administrators is "what gets measured gets managed," so it is crucial that security programs establish mechanisms to collect data and also focus on how the information is communicated to others.

Security programs typically communicate via the following means:

- Person to person meetings
- Memos or emails
- Presentations to classes or decision makers
- Newsletters of websites
- Publications, reports.

In the communication sciences, the "fidelity" of the communication mechanism is the amount and quality of information that is transmitted in a communications sequence. Typically with the smaller the audience (e.g., one on one meetings, small groups), the fidelity is high. But as the population being communicated to grows (e.g., classroom auditoriums, newsletters, etc.), the fidelity is reduced. So a constant challenge in communications is this loss of fidelity and is something security programs should be cognizant of. When possible, person-to-person meetings are most effective, particularly during difficult situations. But this may not always be feasible or practical, so security professionals should keep in mind the loss of fidelity as the number of information recipients grows. As the audience grows, the message needs to be simplified and perhaps restated several times to ensure that the main idea or concept is conveyed. Communications can become diminished when technical jargon is overused, communications are too lengthy, or communications that don't link back to the overall objective of the organization.

EVOLUTION OF SECURITY MEASURES AND METRICS

In basic management theory there are two main categories of measures for any operational program. "Systemic measures" consist of data that describes the ultimate outcome of a program. For example, a security program might be measured by the number of reported thefts or assaults recording in a given time frame. The other main category of measures is "organic measures," which are data describing efforts undertaken prior to a systemic outcome. Examples might include the number of workplace site security inspections that were conducted, the number of lighting and emergency phone system tests performed, or the number of persons trained in basic security techniques. In theory, the systemic measures should drive the organic measures, such that preventive activities are focused on reducing or eliminating negative systemic outcomes.

As security programs mature, more advanced measures related to key organizational parameters can be developed, commonly referred to as "metrics." A metric typically has a denominator and is used to gauge improvement over time. For example, a typical security program may be examining the number of thefts that have been reported (a systemic outcome). To address the issue a number of preventive and educational activities may be undertaken (an organic measure). As part of this intervention, a metric may be developed that speaks to the number of thefts per 100 employees or visitors as it is assumed that with a growing population the risk of theft may increase. The metric of reported thefts per 100 employees or visitors can then be tracked over time to see if the interventions are working and the desired outcome is being achieved.

A word of advice regarding metrics: sometimes programs develop metrics that may be meaningless to persons outside the department. It is suggested that any metrics that are going to be communicated to persons outside the department be linked to a meaningful denominator. For example, in the healthcare setting a very common measure of size is number of in-patient beds. This is a measure every healthcare administrator understands and resonates to. So if wishing to communicate efforts regarding improved security in a hospital, linking performance data to the number of beds greatly enhances your ability to convey your story effectively.

HOW AND WHY TO COMMUNICATE SECURITY MEASURES AND METRICS

The collection of measures and metrics allows the security program to tell its story. The data describes what the program does and the ultimate outcomes. But with this the collection of such data comes the inevitable comparisons, as it is often said "comparison is the mother of insight." This is particularly true in the realm of prevention, where many administrators may not fully understand what security programs do each day. It is important for security programs to ensure that any comparisons that are being made are reasonable. For example, comparisons across different industry types may not be valid. The number of security personnel supporting a hospital may be very different from the number needed to protect a nuclear power facility. And even within specific industries there can be significant differences that can impact comparisons. Returning to the hospital example for a moment, some risk factors such as local crime rate, presence of an emergency room, and the presence of pharmaceuticals can all impact security program resources. So as programs develop their performance measures and metrics they should keep in mind that the next logical step is comparisons, but these need to be performed judiciously, and usually with the insight of a seasoned professional.

KEY DATA DISPLAY ASPECTS

Once data is collected, the next major step is to present it in a way that others can readily understand what is being said. Although there are many techniques that can be considered when displaying data, we have encountered a list of very basic precepts that are better described by Tufte and others, but can at least help get people started on improving the way in which information is conveyed:

- Do not blindly rely upon the automatic formatting provided by standard graphing tools imbedded in software. The programs provide useful a basis upon which to create a good data display, but rarely do compelling data displays automatically spew out upon hitting a button.

- Eliminate the unnecessary – in other words, most of the ink on the data display should be employed to show data, and not all of the superfluous stuff around it. For example, in some graphic programs, the automatic graphs produced carry with it a gray background which only serves to diminish the importance of the actual data being displayed.
- Use clear and thorough labeling. Make sure each axis is labeled, and add text and lines to help the reader understand other aspects. Be sure to include a clear descriptive title too.
- And don't forget to include comparison data, as this will help tell the story as well.

DATA DISPLAY EXAMPLE

To drive home some of the points described above, let's take a very simple, but fun example. For this example, we'll use a real world data set from a sixth grader's science experiment.

The first step is to determine what we're trying to say. This sixth grader would like to perform an experiment to estimate what the optimal thickness of blubber is of a penguin that lives in Antarctica. To do this, cooking lard will be used to simulate penguin lard. An ice chest filled with water and ice will be used to simulate the water conditions in the Antarctic. The lard will be formed into spheres and allowed to equilibrate to room temperature. Then each sized ball will be immersed in the ice water for 10 minutes, at which time a thermometer will be inserted into the ball's center and the temperature recorded. The idea is that at some point in lard thickness, the insulating quality will become self-limiting, e.g., no significant additional insulating value is obtained by the added thickness (and weight) of the lard. The theory is that this would be the point likely where actually penguin blubber thickness falls.

Based on this experimental design, the following data shown in Figure 12.1 is obtained.

TABLE 12.1   Data Set Example

Lard Ball Radius (cm)	Recorded Temp (Degrees C)
0	2
1	15
2	14
3	22
4	22
5	22
6	22
7	23
8	24

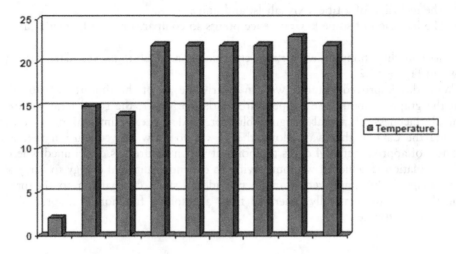

FIGURE 12.1   Example of basic graph.

If we then take this data and place it into the spreadsheet cells of a widely used computer graphics display package, Figure 12.1 shows what the automatic formatting would provide (except it would likely be in blue).

Now let's see what we can do to improve this data display. Some key steps include:

- Elimination of the unnecessary three-dimensional effect shown on the bars.
- The elimination of the text box labeled "temperature" as this will be the variable specifically mentioned in the title.

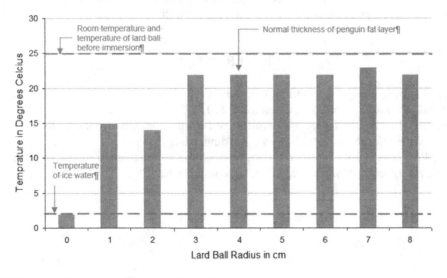

FIGURE 12.2   Example of improved graph.

- The inclusion of a title, axis labels, and units.
- The inclusion of some key reference points so comparisons can be made easily.

These modifications allow for the creation of a much-improved data display, as shown in Figure 12.2.

With this improved graphic, we can clearly see all of the important information: what the graph is about, the temperature of the ice water, the room temperature, the nominal thickness of actual penguin blubber, and the experimental data collected. Showing the data in this way allows the viewer to draw the conclusion that a lard thickness of approximately 4 cm is the point at which nature has determined where sufficient insulation is achieved without having to expend additional energy to carry about excess weight. This improved example provides a stark comparison to the previous graph that was automatically generated from a graphing function in a spreadsheet or presentation software.

SUMMARY

From our intensive review of the data display literature and the examination of hundreds of real world safety and security data displays, we have become convinced that the key to desired decision making on the part of executive leadership (and other key stakeholders) is the ability to display data compellingly. If we can take the time to think about what it is we're trying to say, and then refine the way our data is displayed to clearly make this point, we are more likely to achieve desired decision making. In our experience, most of these data display adjustments require the removal of unnecessary graphical features and the inclusion of clear and through labeling. The creation of graphics for paper distribution rather than temporary projection onto a screen also improves the way in which information is conveyed and comprehended.

Those wishing to learn more about the science and art of effective data displays are encouraged to examine the works listed in the bibliography by Tukey and Tufte. By taking the time to digest and reflect upon their messages, you will be able to improve the way in which you can convey your message as well.

REFERENCES

Tufte, ER, *Envisioning Information*, Cheshire, CT, 1990.
Tufte, ER, *Visual Explanations*, Cheshire, CT, 1997.
Tufte, ER, *The Visual Display of Quantitative Information*, Cheshire, CT, 2001.
Tukey, JW, *Exploratory Data Analysis*, Reading, MA, 1977.
Tukey, PA, Tukey, JW. Summarization: Smoothing; supplemented views, in V. Barnett, ed. *Interpreting Multivariate Data*, Chichester, UK, 1982.

CHAPTER 13

Forensic Security Consultants and Security Liability

Norman Bates

CONTENTS

PREMISES SECURITY LAW: BASIC PRINCIPLES

Premises security liability is the application of principles in the civil tort of negligence. It arises when a business is sued by an individual who was the victim of a violent crime on the property of the business and is claiming that the lack of security was a factor in allowing the crime to occur.

A common example of when a premises security liability claim could be made involves a situation where the resident of an apartment complex or the guest of a hotel is sexually assaulted by a criminal who was able to gain access to the victim via a defective door lock. The fact that the intruder actually committed the sexual assault is not overlooked. If that intruder was caught, he too could be liable civilly (and criminally, of course) but under different legal principles. A claim, if made, against the assailant would be brought in the tort of battery.

A claim for *inadequate security* is a claim that the property owner failed to provide a reasonable level of security, given the risk of crime at the property during the time of the attack. What constitutes "risk" will be discussed in the *foreseeability* section of this chapter.

The claim against the property owner is made pursuant to the laws of negligence for the particular state where the incident occurred. The laws of each state may vary somewhat and, as such, businesses and other private institutions that operate in more than one state will need to know each of those state's rules if negligent security liability is to be avoided. Be mindful that this area of law continues to evolve and can change drastically with any new appellate decision addressing this area of law.

The tort of negligence, as with all other tort claims, contains a number of elements or components that plaintiffs (the party bringing the lawsuit) must prove by the preponderance of the evidence to prove their case. The basic elements of the tort of negligence are duty, breach of duty, injury, and causation.

DUTY

"Duty" is the legal responsibility requiring a property owner to maintain reasonably safe premises. The extent of the duty, or what is required of the property owner, is directly tied to the level of risk (foreseeability) of crime. Absent a legal duty imposed by operation of a statute, ordinance, or code, the responsibility on the property owner is to provide reasonably safe premises proportionate to the level of risk at the property at any given point in time. This means that the extent of the responsibility can change over time as the level or risk of crime increases or decreases.

The legal duty of a property owner to provide reasonable security can be imposed in several different ways. A duty may arise by operation of a statute, ordinance, or code, through case law, under the terms of a contract, where a special relationship between the plaintiff and defendant exists (e.g., student and university), or where the defendant has voluntarily undertaken the responsibility.

A duty created by statute or code is one where the property owner is required by legislative action or regulations of a state or federal agency to provide certain measures. As examples, in South Carolina the state law requires hotel and motel rooms to be equipped with certain specified locking devices; and in Pittsburgh, Pennsylvania, public garages are required to be outfitted with panic alarms and minimum stated lighting levels.

A duty arising from case law tends to be more general in nature in that one or more appellate opinions of a jurisdiction will state that certain types of property owners (e.g., hotels, office buildings, residential landlords, etc.) have a legal duty to provide reasonable levels of security. Case law that imposes a legal duty often fails to provide clear details of what specific actions are required in contrast to a building code or regulation that usually states the specific requirement (e.g., type of locking device to be used).

When a contract exists between the parties (e.g., landlord-tenant) that includes terms that the landlord will provide specified security measures, the duty exists by operation of that agreement and may be enforced in contract law as well as in tort law.

Occasionally, a special relationship is found to exist between the plaintiff and defendant giving rise to a special duty of care. In some cases, a student in a college may be found to have a special relationship with the college due to the former's dependency on the latter to provide security measures.

A common situation of where a duty will be found occurs when the defendant has voluntarily undertaken the responsibility to provide certain security measures. If a hospital's security staff provides additional protection to a patient/victim of domestic violence to prevent a subsequent attack by the offending spouse in the hospital, a duty voluntarily assumed is likely to be found. Generally, the rule of law states that a duty undertaken voluntarily must be performed with the same care as if that duty were imposed by law.

BREACH OF DUTY

Breach of duty is typically the easiest element in the tort of negligence to understand. Breach simply means *failure*. It is the *failure* of a defendant in a civil action to perform the duty that was imposed either by law or when assumed voluntarily. For example, a hotel may either be required by law or voluntarily decides to provide dead bolt locks on all guest rooms. The innkeeper who fails to keep these locks working properly has breached the duty of care.

In another example, a hospital's administration has decided to employ a security staff to provide protection to the hospital facility. The security department, however, is poorly trained and understaffed to handle the problems of the institution. Poor training and insufficient staffing levels may also be "breaches" in the hospital's duty to provide reasonable security measures.

INJURY

Injury in the legal context includes the more obvious physical injuries one may suffer as a crime victim, as well as less obvious mental trauma frequently resulting from an attack. Injuries also include financial losses sustained from the damage to property and lost income.

CAUSATION

Causation or proximate cause is probably the most difficult concept to understand. Simply stated, in order for a defendant to be found negligent, there must be a causal connection or link between the failure of the defendant property owner to meet the duty of care and the ultimate harm suffered by the plaintiff. The law of negligence requires that the failure or deficiency (breach) be a *cause* or *substantial contributing factor* leading to the plaintiff's injuries. However, there may be more than one cause of an injury. This is where the law of negligence can be confusing.

Examples of which failures are *causally* related to an injury and which are not may help illustrate the concept.

Example – A man is assaulted and robbed in a parking lot. Investigation reveals that the parking lot was poorly lit. In fact, in the area of the assault, there was no measurable (with a light meter) light. A local municipal ordinance requires all parking lots to have illumination of at least 1.0 foot candles.

The deficiency in the parking lot lighting would constitute a breach in the duty of care imposed upon the defendant property owner by the local ordinance. However, if this assault occurred during daylight hours, artificial lighting meant for night-time use would be irrelevant or not *causally related* to the plaintiff's case. Should the incident have occurred at night, the lack of lighting may be related to the assault if, for example, the assailant used the cover of darkness to hide and wait for the victim.

Example – A woman is raped in her apartment by an intruder who gains access to her unit via the ground floor window. The lock on the window was broken, and the victim had complained previously to the management company. The defendant management company would most likely have a duty to provide reasonably operating locking devices on unit windows as a matter of law (e.g., building code). The failure to repair the lock in a timely manner would arguably constitute a breach of duty.

The question is whether the broken lock is causally related to the plaintiff's injuries. If the intruder was able to enter the window because the plaintiff could not lock it, then the answer most likely is yes. If the plaintiff left the window open for ventilation, would the broken lock have been a contributing factor? Maybe.

Some might argue that the broken lock is irrelevant or not causally related to the assault. The analysis does not stop here, however. The plaintiff's response to the defendant's argument might be that other secondary locks (i.e., ventilation locks) should have been provided to accommodate the resident's need for fresh air without someone being able to access their unit.

Ultimately, the question is had the deficiencies complained of by the plaintiff been corrected, would they have prevented the assault? Under the law of negligence, the plaintiff does not have to prove that correcting a deficiency would have *absolutely* prevented the crime, only that the deficiencies, more likely than not, contributed to the crime.

FORESEEABILITY: THE RISK OF CRIME

The element of *foreseeability* is essentially a question of whether the criminal act was one that a reasonable person would have foreseen or reasonably anticipated, given the history of crime that existed at the time of the assault at the property in question. Ultimately whether a crime is considered legally *foreseeable* will depend on the court, the jury, and the laws of that state.

Property owners are not expected to predict with absolute certainty when someone may be victimized, by whom, or exactly how the crime will occur. However, owners are expected to take into consideration the various factors that constitute risk at their properties according to the law of premises security liability (negligence) in their jurisdiction. This risk factor is referred to as "foreseeability." As a matter of law, a property owner is not usually held responsible for those events that could not have been reasonably foreseen.

In contrast, the higher the risk of crime, the more foreseeable it is and, hence, the greater the duty imposed upon the owner. What constitutes a foreseeable criminal event, legally, varies from state to state. There are two basic approaches to this concept followed by the states with some minor variations. There are some states, however, that have yet to adopt a position due to a lack of sufficient case law on the subject in their jurisdiction.

The two most common rules followed by most states are the "prior similar crime" rule and the "totality of circumstances" rule. The "prior similar crime" rule is the older, more conservative approach and requires that there be some evidence of prior crimes that are similar in nature to the one complained of in the plaintiff's case. Under this rule a plaintiff who was robbed and physically assaulted in the parking lot of a shopping center must provide evidence of some type of prior robbery before the case can reach a jury. If there were no prior robberies, the defendant may be able to get the case dismissed before trial.

The major problems with the *prior similar crime* rule is the lack of clear direction on what constitutes "similar," how far back in time the prior crime occurred, or how close/far geographically the prior crime must be to make the current crime foreseeable. Currently, no state law requires evidence of absolutely identical prior crimes.

The legal effect of the prior similar crime rule is to take a black and white position on the issue, that either there was a risk of a certain type of crime or not. However, the risk of crime is not black and white.

The more contemporary approach to analyzing foreseeability is the "totality of circumstances" rule. Many courts throughout the country have adopted the rule that property owners should consider other factors, beyond prior crimes, to determine the level of risk. Under this rule, evidence is typically allowed to show the existence of prior dissimilar crime, crime in the neighborhood, and other risk factors (see below) to determine whether a crime was foreseeable.

By using the "totality of circumstances" approach to evaluating the level of risk, owners and managers will be better able to assess the risk of crime at their properties than if they restricted their analysis to only prior crime at that site.

OTHER RISK FACTORS

Practitioners may consider a number of factors or sources of information that may affect the risk of crime at a property. The following factors are representative of the most common sources of crime risk data; however, one should be aware that additional sources may be identified, especially as new risks are developed (e.g., domestic terrorism).

Prior Crime at the Site

Both property and violent crime may be considered when evaluating risk. It is commonly accepted by both security and police practitioners that an environment conducive to criminal activity in the form of some property crimes (e.g., burglary) may create a higher risk of more serious crime. The rationale for this approach is straight forward. Some property crimes can be a "threshold" offense for the violent crime (e.g., a burglar enters a hotel room and subsequently rapes the guest). In this example, the burglary would have to occur before the subsequent assault/rape.

Crime History of Neighborhood/Immediate Vicinity

Defining what constitutes the "neighborhood" or "immediate vicinity" is difficult because of differences in geographical terrain, economic status, or other demographic factors. In fact, there is no single definition of what constitutes a "neighborhood" or "immediate vicinity."

The local law enforcement agency may be helpful in defining the "neighborhood" or "immediate vicinity" or geographical area where the subject property is located, based upon their experience and knowledge of the area. Once the geographical boundaries are defined, crime data for that area can be obtained and analyzed for type and frequency of criminal activity.

For more information, see Chapter 4, which addresses Crime Analysis in detail.

Crimes Inherent to Certain Business Establishments

It is well known that certain types of establishment are prone to the same kinds of criminal activity. For example, nightclubs frequently have problems with assaultive behavior and disorderly conduct; parking lots and garages frequently have car theft problems; convenience stores and fast-food restaurants generally experience higher rates of robbery; and apartment complexes, along with hotels, have to address the risk of burglary.

This area of risk analysis requires managers to keep current on crime trends affecting their type of business. By reviewing reported cases and trade journals and through interaction with their peers in professional associations, managers can learn about developing crime problems as well as potential security solutions.

Prior Complaints

Prior complaints made to a property owner about problematic residents, unsafe conditions, suspicious activity, and others are examples that may indicate the propensity for a security problem or crime to occur. For example, a resident in an apartment community complains to the security decision maker about high levels of foot traffic in and out of an adjacent apartment at all hours of the day and night. The resident also adds that these "visitors" appear to stay for only a short period of time. There may be a legitimate reason for the activity at the apartment; however, a property owner may want to investigate the circumstances, seeking out the aid of the police to help determine whether or not drug dealing or other criminal activity is occurring.

Knowledge of Crime and Acknowledgment of the Risk

Frequently in negligent security lawsuits, defendants will claim that they were unaware of the existence of certain criminal activity or other significant problems that could establish the "foreseeability component" of the plaintiff's case. Where it can be shown, however, that the defendant had actual knowledge of a particular risk and took no action to address it, that evidence can have a significant impact on the case.

"Acknowledgment" of the risk may be more subtle than just a history of prior crimes. It could include evidence of the defendant's awareness of the potential for problems when the security program was designed.

The following examples illustrates this point:

In a Massachusetts case, *Roe v. The Marriott Hotel*, the plaintiff, who was raped in the defendant's parking lot, sought to introduce evidence of the foreseeability of the crime through the hotel's own security manual. A portion of the manual outlined the responsibility of the security staff for external patrol and, most significantly, the reasons for such patrol. Among the reasons for patrol cited were the prevention of crime such as auto theft or "rape." While the hotel's documented history of crimes in their parking lot was limited to property crimes, such as theft and vandalism, the hotel's patrol guide acknowledged the risk of rape in the parking lot.

PLAINTIFF'S THEORIES

Most inadequate security cases fall into three categories: defective equipment/devices, crime deterrence theory, and operational failures.

Defective equipment/devices are fairly self-evident. They include issues such as defective locks, inoperative alarms, or broken entry doors.

"Deterrence theory" cases are those where the plaintiff asserts that the assailant would have been deterred from committing the crime had certain security measures been in place at the time of the incident. Under this theory, a claim is asserted when, for example, the plaintiff is assaulted in a parking lot in an area where security has not been patrolling regularly. The "deterrence theory" argument in this instance would likely claim that had the defendant's security staff been patrolling as it should, then the assailant would have been deterred from committing the crime. The plaintiff may seek to introduce evidence of the assailant's behavior prior to, during, or after the assault that demonstrates his deterrability. Efforts to plan the crime in advance, conceal one's identity (e.g., wearing a mask or using a condom in a rape to avoid DNA detection), or trying to evade capture may be evidence to be considered by the jury when deciding whether the assailant was deterrable and whether the defendant property owner's failure to provide security patrols amounts to negligence.

The third category of plaintiff theories is "operational failure." This is a fairly broad category and can include several different deficiencies in an organization's security program alleged simultaneously. Operational failures include such issues as failure to train, failure to supervise, inadequate pre-employment screening (negligent hiring), lack of specific policies and procedures or violation of one's own policies, and inadequate staffing levels.

Example – Policies and Procedures – The defendant has a policy and procedure that requires regular accounting of master keys and distribution of such keys on a controlled basis. If the evidence in the plaintiff's case indicates that an intruder gained access to the plaintiff's apartment using an unauthorized master key, the failure to comply with one's own key control procedures becomes a central argument in the plaintiff's case.

SECURITY OFFICER MISCONDUCT

While most civil claims of inadequate security stem from the failure to provide reasonable security measures (e.g., lack of locking devices, insufficient number of security officers on patrol, etc.), there is the potential for liability claims arising from the misconduct of security personnel. These claims typically occur when the officer has either used too much force, has unlawfully detained someone, or has conducted an unlawful search of the person.

Most often, the allegations for misconduct are based on the arguments that the security officer was overzealous, used too much force, and caused an injury as a result. The allegations may claim that the officer lacked sufficient basis to detain and/or search a person who was suspected of a crime. These allegations commonly cite a lack of sufficient training, the improper selection of a candidate who lacked the appropriate experience, a failure to supervise, or that the officer had previously demonstrated a propensity for excessive force/violence but was still retained by the employer.

Example – Failure to Train – A security officer uses force during a detention of a shoplifting suspect. The plaintiff incurs injuries during the detention process. In this situation, the plaintiff will often argue that the officer was not adequately trained for the position. However, the alleged failure to train must be shown to be the cause of the injury. Further, the actions or behavior of the injured person will also be considered during the liability analysis.

NEGLIGENT HIRING LIABILITY

Negligent hiring is a claim which asserts that the defendant business failed to exercise reasonable care in the selection and hiring of an employee through proper pre-employment screening to avoid hiring an individual with an unsuitable background and where that employee subsequently injures the plaintiff.

Traditionally, employers have been held responsible for the actions of their employees under the legal doctrine of *respondeat superior*, which operates on the principle that employers are responsible for the acts of their employees when tasks are performed on behalf of the employer's interests. If, through the carelessness or negligence of the employee, a member of the public is injured, the employer is held financially and, occasionally, criminally responsible vicariously (e.g., a moving van driver causes an accident and injures others).

However, this doctrine has its limitations. If the employee committed a harmful act outside the scope of her or his employment and not in the interests of the employer, the company would not likely be held responsible. If the harmful conduct clearly falls outside the scope of her or his employment, then the doctrine of *respondeat superior* does not apply, and no recovery can usually be made against the employer under that legal theory.

Negligent hiring liability, however, is the failure of an employer to exercise reasonable care in selecting an applicant in light of the risk created by the position to be filled. This means employers must screen individuals adequately *before* they are hired.

Employers are not always exposed to liability just because they failed to check an applicant's background. Liability usually results only when an inadequate screening effort is logically connected to the wrongful conduct. If a reasonably conducted investigation would have revealed facts indicating the applicant was undesirable, the failure to obtain the information may be considered negligence.

The legal cases emphasize that the amount of screening to be conducted on an applicant should be proportionate to the degree of risk presented by the position to be filled. Hence, the greater the risk, the greater the effort to investigate a potential employee's background.

The case law is also helpful in identifying what constitutes risk. It suggests the risk posed by a particular position depends on *access*. If employees are able to subject others to harm as a result of having *unsupervised access* to them, then risk exists. *Access* is the focal point. To determine risk factors in employment, the focus must be on the position to be filled, not the applicant, the job title, or the wage rate. When conducting background checks, employers should consider an employee's unsupervised *access* to vulnerable people or dangerous instrumentalities such as:

- Children
- Elderly persons
- Persons who are disabled (mentally or physically)
- Patients
- Private homes
- Master keys
- Narcotics (licit or illicit)
- Explosives
- Dangerous chemicals
- Weapons/ammunition.

Security employees who exercise arrest power, use force, or carry weapons should also be included. Although generally employees who misuse their authority or force subject their companies to *respondeat superior* liability as well. The concept of negligent hiring also encompasses incompetent conduct that causes harm, as illustrated by the overzealous security officer, bouncer, or doorman.

Documentation and consistency are the keys to avoiding negligent hiring liability. Whatever options an employer chooses to use for screening, *all* information gathered from legitimate sources should be well documented. Since most litigation is not resolved for years after the employee has been hired, the written word becomes invaluable. Consistency in pre-employment screening practices is also important because of the evidentiary effect a company's practices can have at trial. For example, if a decision was made to obtain criminal history data on all positions of risk, be sure to conduct such a search for each and every applicant who becomes an employee.

Evaluating a Security Program

The adequacy of a security program is evaluated in one of two scenarios, either in the context of a negligent security lawsuit or in a general assessment for planning purposes. The analysis of a security program in a lawsuit is conducted using the specific set of facts about the crime and an identified risk level, compared to actual security measures employed by the property owner. In a civil suit, only a portion of the defendant's security program is usually examined as it relates to the criminal event. For example, if the assault occurred outdoors during daylight hours, exterior lighting would not be evaluated.

SECURITY STANDARDS: THE ROLE OF STATUTES, ORDINANCES AND REGULATIONS

Throughout the United States, there are numerous examples of laws in the form of statutes, ordinances, and codes that require specific security measures. In some municipalities, minimum measurable lighting levels are required. In others, certain types of locking devices may be required.

One of the most important questions security decision makers should ask is whether any portion of their security program is subject to any statutes, codes, ordinances, or regulations. If so, they should seek to satisfy the criteria of the applicable law.

Unfortunately, laws are frequently written with a degree of ambiguity. An ordinance may require "reasonably secured windows and doors" without specific indication on what constitutes "reasonable." Interpretation may be required by counsel and/or an experienced consultant. In addition to codes and regulations, most states have case law which may help explain or specify the nature of the legal responsibility (i.e., duty) of the property owner with respect to these security measures.

The failure to meet the minimum requirements of a law can be strong evidence of negligence in a lawsuit and may subject the business to civil fines as well.

NATIONAL SECURITY STANDARDS

Historically, the private security industry has been poorly regulated. Frequently, such regulation has only taken the form of limited state statutes that set forth licensing requirements and on rare occasions, minimum training standards for contract security agencies. Proprietary security staff, individuals who are the direct employees of, for example, a hotel, shopping center, or office building, traditionally had not been regulated by states or municipalities. This has changed in recent years.

Since the early 1970s, when the Connie Francis rape case against a motel in New York received widespread publicity, there has been a multitude of civil litigation alleging inadequate security against privately owned businesses. With many verdicts of more than a million dollars and increased public awareness of this alternative remedy for victims of crime, business owners have become motivated to improve the quality of their security services to guests, tenants, visitors, and employees. Unfortunately, with a lack of standards guiding property owners on how much or what type of security to provide, many of them failed to take the appropriate steps to properly analyze the risks of crime associated with their businesses. As a consequence, these businesses have failed to provide adequate protection for the public despite their legal duty to do so.

After decades of claims against property owners for poor security, a public outcry for nationwide security standards requiring some minimal measures to prevent crime would seem inevitable. In fact, during those years, only a handful of technical standards were developed by standard-setting organizations. However, these standards typically have been limited to technical items such as locks, fencing, safe construction, or lighting levels. There were no standards or guidelines for the management of security services or the use of security devices in any given application. This means that the landlord of an urban apartment building or the general manager of a downtown hotel would not be able to refer to a written standard regarding what type of locks should be installed on sliding glass doors. The liability of the motel in the Connie Francis case was predicated on the poor quality locks that were provided for the singer. She was raped in her room by an unknown intruder who gained access via a defective locking device on a sliding glass door.

As recently as the early 1990s, there was still opposition by three major industries to the development of any type of security standard or guideline. The apartment, hotel, and shopping-center industries, through their respective trade groups, fought an effort by ASTM (American Society for Testing and Materials) to develop minimum guidelines for security measures in all types of privately owned businesses open to the public. A three-year effort to develop the guidelines dissolved with threats to the non-profit

ASTM that it was working outside its charter. Although it is doubtful that there was any charter violation, the organization could not afford the cost of litigation and, consequently, disbanded the committee.

In 2001, two national organizations started the process of developing national security standards. The American Society of Industrial Security, now known as ASIS International, and the National Fire Protection Association (NFPA) both established committees that were charged with the task of identifying the types of security standards needed and writing them. Subsequently, ASIS International has published several guidelines, including the General Security Risk Assessment Guideline, Private Security Officer Selection and Training Guideline, and numerous others. The NFPA published two guidelines, NFPA 730 and 731, which recommend a variety of minimal security measures in a number of business settings and guidelines for the installation of security equipment, respectively.

"STANDARDS" VERSUS "GUIDELINES"

The difference between standards and guidelines is to some degree a matter of semantics, and yet, there are important distinctions. A standard usually refers to an adopted standard of practice for the construction, design, use, or application of a product or service. For example, there are national standards for the manufacturing of certain types of locking devices. An adopted standard usually goes through a time-consuming consensus-setting process where all interested parties have input on the content. Words such as "shall" are frequently used. Standards can be and are often adopted by municipalities as codes or ordinances, such as a building code, and as such become law.

Guidelines are generally less restrictive than standards, using language such as "it is recommended" or "courses of action may include." By definition, guidelines are meant to provide guidance to the end user, the private business owner or manager, who needs help in identifying options that may be available for a certain type of application.

The legal implications of a standard versus a guideline can be somewhat blurry. While a standard is developed over a longer period of time and goes through a more rigorous process, the effect in the courtroom of invoking standards or guidelines is not likely to be very different. For the plaintiff who is introducing a guideline, the objective is to show a jury that there was a business practice that, arguably, the defendant company should have followed in this case. The alleged failure to adhere to that practice or guideline becomes evidence of negligence in most jurisdictions.

Standards are a measure of a security program but should not be taken alone as proof of a program's adequacy. And conversely, the failure to comply with a standard does not necessarily translate into liability. Standards need to allow for variation not previously anticipated such as an emerging threat or crime trend.

SECURITY CONSULTANTS AND EXPERT WITNESSES: THEIR UNIQUE ROLES

Types of Security Consultants

The following descriptions discuss the various types of security consultants and the roles they fulfill in assessing the adequacy of a facility's security program.

Security Technology Consultants

Generally, there are three basic types of security consultants in practice in the United States. They include the technical "design/build" professionals who can design and specify security equipment and technology systems that may encompass closed-circuit television systems, access control devices, fire alarm systems, computer-based information technology, and the integration of some or all of these technologies. For example, the owners of an older urban hotel want to upgrade their closed-circuit television system and use more current technology. One of the owners' options is to reach out to a manufacturer's representative who can design, install, and sell their products. This approach can be hazardous to the hotel owner though, as the installer inherently wants to install as many cameras and related technology as possible. This is not to suggest that everyone in the installation business is unethical, but there is an inherent self-serving interest that can create a conflict of interest. The better alternative is for the property owner to hire an independent security technology consultant who can design and specify the system needed, without having a financial stake in the ultimate project cost.

Management Consultants

The second category of security consultant is the individual who is retained to evaluate an existing security program with a focus on the current and future needs of the organization. This type of consultant will usually conduct a general security risk assessment when the property owner wants to determine whether the current security program is adequate for the overall needs of the facility, in light of the types of crime risks and nature of the business existing at that time.

While there are some parallels to the case analysis approach, a security program evaluation looks at broader issues and is not limited to a single criminal event or set of circumstances. General security risk assessments, in this broader approach, usually consider the four basic components of a program. Those basic components include crime risk analysis, management practices, security equipment, and security staffing.

Conducting a security risk assessment of a facility is a common practice that helps managers identify crime risks and other threats (e.g., natural disasters) to the organization and the various options available to address those risks. These evaluations typically include physical surveys of the property and a review of the practices and procedures followed at the management level.

ASIS International developed the General Security Risk Assessment Guideline to establish a standardized approach to conducting security risk assessments. Regardless of the application or the business or organization type, there is a long recognized, logical method of analyzing security risks and identifying the options that are available to manage security related problems.

The Guideline is described as being: "applicable in any environment where people and/or assets are at risk for a security-related incident or event that may result in human death, injury, or loss of an asset." The phrase "a security-related incident or event" is not limited to criminal activity. It also includes natural disasters, war, and other activities that could result in a loss of life or property.

The Guideline is a "seven step process that creates a methodology for security professionals by which security risks at a specific location can be identified and communicated, along with appropriate solutions." It also includes definitions, a flow chart, appendices, and a bibliography.

The Forensic Security Expert

The third type of consultant is known as a forensic security expert. This type of consultant acts as an expert witness in litigation where they are called upon to provide testimony in the form of expert opinions about the adequacy of security measures in relation to a crime that has occurred. Most often the crimes involve incidences where someone has been a victim of a violent crime, such as a rape, shooting, robbery, homicide, etc. The function of the forensic expert is to analyze a security program after such an incident has occurred and to determine whether there were any deficiencies in the security measures that had a causal relationship with the occurrence of the crime.

Generally, expert witnesses are individuals who through their education, training, and/or experience have special knowledge or skill in a particular field and are determined by the court (i.e., judge) whether they will be permitted to testify about issues that the average juror (lay person) would not have enough knowledge or understanding about. The expert's role is, in part, to educate the jury about the issues in the case and assist that jury in arriving at a decision in the case.

Forensic security experts are most commonly retained by law firms who represent either the victim bringing the lawsuit against the property owner and/or the property manager where the crime occurred, or by the attorneys representing the defendant organization being sued. The ultimate task of the security expert is to testify at trial in front of the jury.

There are occasions when the opposing counsel in a lawsuit will challenge the other side's expert and whether he or she is adequately qualified to offer opinions to the jury. Through a procedural motion, the opposing counsel can ask the judge to either limit the scope of the testimony or prohibit it outright.

The basis for excluding or limiting an expert's testimony could include one or more of the following reasons:

- The expert's background doesn't "fit" the type of case at hand. For example, the case involves security measures at a hotel and the expert has no experience, training, or education in the operation of a security program in a hotel environment.
- The expert's opinions are considered too speculative in nature and are not supported by the appropriate research, data, or evidence of applicable standards of care.
- The expert failed to follow an accepted and reliable methodology in the evaluation of the facts and circumstances of the case.

To address the last category as a basis for excluding a security expert's testimony, in 2000 the International Association of Professional Security Consultants developed a best practice called "Forensic Methodology." In its position statement, the Association states:

> The International Association of Professional Security Consultants does hereby recognize that its members will be called upon to perform as "Forensic Consultants" and serve as Expert Witnesses in a court of law or other legal proceeding. The purpose of these guidelines is to meet the need for a standardized methodology used in the evaluation of premises security cases.

The Forensic Methodology was initially adopted by the full membership of the Association in 2000 and has been updated several times through 2017. It has also been accepted as reflective of what activities a forensic security expert would commonly undertake when evaluating a premises security case by two Federal District Courts in Kentucky and Puerto Rico.

It is a common practice for the forensic security expert to use examples of standards, best practices, guidelines, and other information of what may be considered good and accepted security practices for all types of organizations. Such evidence seeks to establish the applicable standard of care for the organization being evaluated by the expert, who will either attempt to show that the organization failed to comply with the standards of care or did comply with the standards and should not be found negligent.

Some examples of guidelines/standards include: the design of a daycare center to protect against the risk of child sexual abuse; national lighting standards published by the Illuminating Engineering Society of North America that set forth minimum lighting levels for a range of locations, such as walkways, garages, parking lots, and elsewhere. Other examples include: standards for electronic locking systems, fencing heights, landscape control for crime prevention, robbery prevention guidelines for convenience stores, locks for hotel guest room doors, and so on.

CONCLUSION

There is an acute public awareness of the right to seek civil recovery for injuries sustained as a result of a criminal act committed by a third party or as a result of the misconduct of an employee. However, the right to sue does not necessarily automatically translate into the fault of the property owner.

Effective security planning goes beyond the establishment of a security program to protect employees, customers, and others from crime. Effective planning to reduce the risk of liability of an organization includes consideration of the issues discussed in this chapter. Furthermore, documentation, consistency, and follow through are essential to ensure that a liability prevention program works.

REFERENCES

ASIS International (2003). *General Risk Security Assessment*. ASIS International Guidelines Commission.

Bates, N. D. (1990). "Understanding the Liability of Negligent Hiring," *Security Management*, 34(7), pp. 7A–9A.

Bates, N. D. (1997). "Forseeability of Crime and Adequacy of Security," in R. W. Lack (ed.), *Accident Prevention Manual for Business & Industry*. National Safety Council, pp. 137–138.

Bates, N. D. (2003). "Recent Developments in Nationwide Security Standards: The General Security Risk Assessment Guideline." *Victim Advocate*, 4(2), pp. 7–10.

Bates, N. D. (2004). *Major Developments in Premises Security Liability III*. Liability Consultants, Inc.

IAPSC Forensic Methodology (2017). IASPC. 34(7), https://iaspc.org

CHAPTER 14

Workplace Violence Prevention

Steve Kaufer

CONTENTS

INTRODUCTION

Say the words *workplace violence*, and for most people what comes to mind immediately is a rampage shooting; a disgruntled current or former employee comes to work armed with multiple firearms and kills indiscriminately. It is what seems to be a common news story, and high-profile active shooter incidents help to reinforce that common perception of homicide and violence where we work.

While such deadly acts certainly pose a threat to the US worker, of the average of 450 homicides that occur in the workplace each year,[1] the majority were the result of a robbery in the workplace. Fully two-thirds of victims had no prior known relationship with their assailant.[2] The angry worker accounts for a very small percentage of occupational deaths.

This disparity between reality and perception can at times make it difficult for the Security or Human Resources professional tasked with creating and maintaining a safer work environment to accomplish that mission. Management and staff may think that active shooter training will address workplace violence, when the most effective solution is far more encompassing and nuanced.

The public or lay person often has a different perception of the workplace, one perpetuated by stories that appear in newspapers or on television:

MEDIA DEFINITION: A disgruntled employee or client enters the workplace armed with multiple weapons and shoots selectively or indiscriminately at employees, supervisors, and managers.

The more accurate threat faced by workers is described as:

OCCUPATIONAL SAFETY AND HEALTH ADMINISTRATION (OSHA) DEFINITION: Any act or threat of physical violence, harassment, intimidation, or other threatening disruptive behavior that occurs at the work site.[3]

Reducing the likelihood of workplace violence isn't just watching out for Bob, the disgruntled former loading dock worker, who might return to the workplace armed with a couple of semi-automatic weapons to get revenge for being fired. A truly effective workplace violence prevention program includes a well thought out policy, a multidisciplinary Threat Assessment Team, physical security, pre-employment screening, legal and compassionate termination practices, Employment Assistance Programs, outplacement, and a host of other ingredients.

JUST HOW SERIOUS IS THE PROBLEM?

Each day thousands of US workers face threats, harassment, intimidation, and physical and verbal attacks. This is the true and very serious exposure to workplace violence that most employers will deal with routinely. An estimated 2 million US workers are victims of occupational violence each year.[4] Every workday, there are more than 5500 acts of physical and verbal violence, threats, harassment, and intimidation reported in the workplace.

Many more incidents take place but are not reported. This under reporting is due to a lack of a known method of reporting either an incident or concerning behavior, lack of knowledge among employees about what is acceptable and unacceptable behavior, and employees that haven't been trained on the importance of their role in preventing workplace violence.

While the fatalities in the workplace attributable to violence are a tragedy, more workers suffer serious effects from the other elements of workplace violence.

The National Institute for Occupational Safety and Health estimates the economic cost of workplace violence to be approximately $121 billion a year.[5] Non-fatal workplace assaults alone result in more than 876,000 lost workdays and $16 million in lost wages, on average, annually.

In addition to those hard costs, employers often experience hidden costs following a serious act of violence in the workplace. Lost productivity; low morale; security concerns of employees, customers and visitors; employees leaving the team due to fear and concern; business interruption; added security costs; and the fear of another incident all have the potential to add initial and on-going costs.

As an example, Minneapolis Police Department Detective Duane Frederickson reported that for six to eight weeks following a serious incident, on average, productivity is cut in half.[6]

WHAT ARE THE THREATS?

Going back to the definition of workplace violence, we know the types of incidents that can be faced in the work environment, but where do threats come from?

Early research was done by CAL-OSHA, the State of California's equivalent organization to the Federal Occupational Safety and Health Agency. CAL-OSHA's typology of workplace threats, shown in Table 14-1, has been relied on for decades in helping to understand the threats that organizations must work to reduce.

While Type III is the most common threat, each work environment will be different. Your organization should consider a prevention program, determining the most likely source of the threats and planning countermeasures and training to address the greatest potential risks.

OTHER THREATS IN THE WORKPLACE

Aside from the danger of violence from workers, former workers, and outside factors such as robbery, another significant workplace threat is domestic violence. Research by the U.S. Bureau of Labor Statistics shows that relatives or domestic partners were the most frequent assailant in work related homicides of woman – 40 percent compared to just 2 percent for males.[7]

In the case of domestic violence, often what starts at home is completed at work. Assaults by abusers or spouses in the workplace are common. For those being stalked by a former spouse or other unwanted interest, the workplace is the one location where the victim can usually be found; the abused employee can change their phone number and move, but most can't switch jobs to avoid the threatening abuser or stalker.

While legal definitions of stalking vary from one jurisdiction to another, a good working definition of stalking is *a course of conduct directed at a specific person that would cause a reasonable person to feel fear.*

Like domestic violence, stalking can wind up in the workplace because it is the easiest, and perhaps the only way the stalker can located his or her victim. Sometimes stalking originates at work; a co-worker develops an unhealthy and unwanted attachment to a co-worker.

TABLE 14.1   CAL-OSHA Typology of Workplace Threats

Type	Source of Threat
I	Offender has no relationship with the victim or the workplace; the person is there to commit a crime. Most often a robbery or other crime committed at the workplace.
II	The person committing the violent act is a recipient of service from the workplace, often a patient, customer, public support recipient, student, or similar individual.
III	The offender is a current or former employee who is acting out against co-workers, managers, supervisors, or others connected with work.
IV	The person committing the violence has a personal relationship with an employee. The offender is likely a current or former suppose or intimate partner or stalker who came to the workplace to carry out the act of violence because that is where he or she could locate the victim.

Stalking is a crime under the laws of all 50 states, the District of Columbia, the U.S. Territories, and the Federal Government.[8]

In the case of domestic violence or stalking, the company is often unaware of the conflict between the employee and the person intent on revenge. Once on notice, the employer must take reasonable precautions based on the threat to protect the employee and co-workers.

In the last decade, the number of states that either allow open carry of a weapon or concealed carry with a permit has increased.

The availability of a handgun in or near the workplace increases the potential for a conflict to escalate to a more serious and potentially fatal incident. Employers are encouraged to review the impact of having employees with concealed weapons on their property and develop a written policy on weapons. Most companies are adopting the stance that firearms are prohibited on the firm's property, with a violation resulting in termination.

Most laws require entrances to company property and buildings must be clearly posted with a warning message prohibiting guns on the property if that is the company's policy. The vexing question facing employers is how to deal with guns kept in a vehicle parked on company property. Firms often find it best to review this complex subject with legal counsel before implementing a written policy.

LEGAL ISSUES OF WORKPLACE VIOLENCE

Aside from existing legal and regulatory obligations that employers must follow to provide a safe and secure work environment, the potential for costly civil litigation often factors into the plan that companies follow to reduce the likelihood of workplace violence.

There is no Federal law that specifically addresses prevention of workplace violence against employees. But employers do have a requirement under The General Duty Clause of OSHA regulations. This requires the employer to provide a workplace free from recognized hazards that are causing or are likely to cause death or serious injury to its employees.

Some states, like California, Connecticut, Washington, and Florida, have enacted laws that govern security countermeasures or training specific to an occupation that may have a higher rate of violence. These jobs typically are in healthcare, or convenience stores and other retail establishments with late hours of operation.

Civil litigation commonly follows a serious incident of workplace violence involving physical or mental trauma or death. Examples of jury awards include $5.2 million paid to a supervisor who was shot and permanently disabled by a disgruntled fired employee; $5.49 million against a temporary employment agency who failed to adequately screen an employee provided to a client, after that employee fatally stabbed a worker at the client company; $4.25 million against the U.S. Postal Service stemming from a shooting.

In legal action following an incident of workplace violence, issues often involve:

Negligent Hiring: failing to properly screen employees can result in a person being hired that the courts can judge had a history that should have caused the employee not to be hired.

Negligent Retention: keeping an employee after the employer has become aware of the employee's unsuitability and failing to act on that knowledge.

Negligent Supervision: failing to provide the necessary monitoring to ensure that employees perform their duties properly.

Inadequate Security: if security measures provided to safeguard employees, Customers, and members of the public at a business or place of employment are not consistent with the potential threat, and an injury results from the omission of proper security precautions, then a case can be made for this type of action.

While these are the most common elements of civil suits filed on behalf of those injured by an incident of workplace violence, many other factors can be drawn into a case.

With the average out-of-court settlement of $500,000 and an average $3 million jury award, it makes sound business sense to reduce the potential for workplace violence and avoid exposure to litigation.

DEVELOPING A WORKPLACE VIOLENCE PREVENTION PROGRAM

The critical component in reducing the potential for workplace violence is a well thought out and executed prevention program. The program can be developed and customized using available and credible resources. You don't have to start from scratch, but it must be refined to fit your organization's culture, environment, and risks.

ASIS International is the largest organization of security professionals in the world; its 37,000 members work in almost every conceivable security specialty and location. They teamed up with the Society of Human Resource Managers (SHRM) to develop a standard recognized by the American National Standards Institute, Inc. (ANSI) which is an excellent blueprint on which to base an effective program.[9]

The Association of Threat Assessment Professionals (ATAP), a well-respected professional organization of legal, law enforcement, medical, and threat assessment experts that have specialized skills in violence prevention and mitigation, conducted a study on prevention programs.[10] The ATAP survey found that approximately 71 percent of the respondents reported that their organization had a workplace violence prevention program that used the ASIS/SRHM Standard as a resource to develop the program. Using a recognized and widely adopted Standard allows your organization show adherence to an accepted standard of care.

Programs should be customized for each employer, and not all businesses need every element; the ideal program development process includes common elements:

- Form a multi-disciplinary threat assessment team.
- Assess current risks and needed enhancements.
- Prepare written workplace violence prevention policies.
- Establish a reporting mechanism.
- Develop and deliver a training program.
- Review hiring practices (including pre-employment screening).
- Review the termination process.
- Prepare a crisis response plan.
- Test and periodically review the program.

This list may make developing a program seem like a daunting task, but companies often have some of the components of an effective program already in place. These include access control, physical security, security policies and procedures, sexual harassment policies, standards of acceptable conduct, and Employee Assistance Programs.

A strong and resourceful partner in the program development should be the Employee Assistance Program or EAP. An effective EAP program can deliver the help needed by many workers to face and resolve stressors or behavioral health issues that affect work and create the potential for violence. Within established guidelines, EAPs can be an excellent source of information to help reduce the opportunity for violence.

Forty-seven percent of employees say that problems in the home or their personal lives spill over into the workplace and impact their performance. The survey of more than 24,000 employees conducted by Bensinger, DuPont & Associates also found that 50 percent indicated that non-work issues caused them to be unable to concentrate while on the job, and 16 percent said that they call out from work in response to these stressful personal issues.[11] The volume and significant impact of personal stress on the workplace is the reason many large and mid-sized employers have EAP services and benefits available.

If your organization has an EAP, information on its benefits should be clearly and frequently communicated to employees, and not just to employees that are exhibiting concerning behavior.

Smaller firms, without a formalized EAP, can provide information on local mental health, substance abuse, credit counseling, domestic violence, and other resources to address the needs of employees experiencing these issues. Often these services are provided by non-profit organizations at little or no cost.

THE THREAT ASSESSMENT TEAM

When developing a workplace violence prevention program, the first step is often setting up the Threat Assessment Team (TAT). This multi-disciplinary team is known by other names, such as the Threat Management Team or Workplace Violence Prevention Committee. The function is the same, so pick a moniker that melds with your culture.

In the beginning, the TAT is charged with assessing the organization's needs, developing the program, and then implanting it. They may bring in outside resources, such as consultants, with specialized skills. Once the program is in place, the TAT assumes the operational role of its maintenance and responding to incidents.

The TAT is typically composed of ranking representatives from human resources, employee assistance, legal, risk management, security, facility management, public relations, and, if applicable, sometimes unions. While smaller companies may not have distinct representatives for each area of responsibility, these functions, if they exist, each should be included. It is important that upper level representatives actively participate on the TAT, since they are accustomed to interfacing with other department heads and have the authority to make policy decisions. For the TAT to be effective in developing the program and for it to be ultimately successful, senior company management must endorse the program and telegraph their support clearly to all employees.

An important initial step is to assess any current programs, physical security, any policy related to threats, harassment, or unwanted behavior. The current resources that can be used as part of the program need to be identified. Some existing policies or procedures may need to be modified to enhance the workplace violence program. The results of this evaluation will provide a baseline and allow the committee to identify existing strengths and potential vulnerabilities.

Often this step poses the greatest challenge to the TAT. While its members have the best and most intimate knowledge of their company, they lack the benchmark to judge how their firm measures up to accepted standards. The solution for many companies is the use of a specialized consultant who can provide, with company input, an independent evaluation of exposures and vulnerability. The consultant can also assist in guiding the process as a facilitator of the planning committee.

POLICIES, TRAINING, AND INFORMATION COLLECTION

The next three steps in the process are intertwined. Policies must be written to clearly define what is not acceptable behavior related to workplace violence, the employees must be trained on these policies and how to recognize potential violence, and finally a point of contact for employees must be established to allow workers to report behavior that may be symptomatic of potentially violent acts. Look to the ASIS/SHRM Standard and other guides for ideas and suggested language.

One of the most important elements in any prevention program is a written policy against threats, harassment, intimidation, and possession of weapons. Such a policy will help employees understand the elements of unacceptable behavior, the consequences of exhibiting such behavior, and provide legal support for termination, should that become necessary.

With a written policy drafted, the next step is the establishment of a mechanism to allow employees to report threats and other concerning behavior. Without an easy to use reporting system, this significant information may not make it to the TAT, creating a missed opportunity to address unwanted behavior before it escalates to something more visible and serious. This part of the program establishes a place within your company that employees can, anonymously and without fear of retribution, report abnormal behavior or dramatic behavior changes by a co-worker, or violations of the company's workplace violence policy. In some organizations this reporting process is managed the Human Resources Department, in others it might be a Security Department function, and others contract it out to a third-party that operates a tip line on behalf of the organization.

Once this information is received, it is evaluated and a response plan determined. Unless there is the possibility of immediate harm to an employee, the initial response ideally should be supportive if appropriate for the behavior reported. If employees see their co-worker receiving help for the stress or other problems they are facing, they will continue to provide information; a punitive response to every report will quickly dry up the information pipeline. Of course, there are some behaviors or threats of violence which must be handled quickly and decisively, including potential termination of the employee.

The reporting mechanism is particularly effective since the employee working alongside a co-worker will sense changes in behavior that could signal the build-up of stress that could lead to a violent episode. This behavior may not be noticed by a manager, human resources, or security person who does not have daily contact with the employee.

Employee reports and tips also serve as a conduit for information about weapons in the workplace, or employees that are harassing fellow workers. If there is no easy opportunity for employees to report what they observe without having to become closely involved, this information may not surface until after an incident.

The most effective prevention programs incorporate all employees in the solution. Employees trained to recognize the symptoms exhibited by a fellow employee who could potentially commit an act of violence, greatly increase the odds that this behavior can be spotted, proper action taken to evaluate the threat of violence, and assistance provided to the employee in dealing with issues that could be causing the suspect behavior.

Experience has shown that training at three levels is most effective. An orientation session is recommended for senior company executives, providing an overview of the issues of workplace violence, and detailing the financial and legal consequences of not having an effective prevention program in place, to gain their support for the program.

Next to receive training are department managers and supervisors. This training should include conflict resolution, background on workplace violence and how it effects the workforce, communicating with workers, stress reduction, and effective communications. These employees should be trained in the company's policies on workplace violence. Experience has shown that four to eight hours provides sufficient training for managers and supervisors.

A shorter training session, about two to four hours in length, should be given to all other employees. This training should include discussion of the company's workplace violence prevention policy, what constitutes threats, harassment, and intimidation, and the warning signs that could be exhibited by potentially violent co-workers. Reporting this behavior and learning of the help that the worker who is displaying these behavioral flags will receive should also be a part of this session.

Another important element in employee training programs is conflict resolution. Providing employees with the skills needed to work through and resolve workplace conflicts will dramatically reduce the incidence of more serious violence. An incident of unresolved conflict does not simply go away; it escalates and often leads to physical violence.

HIRING AND TERMINATION ... TWO OPPORTUNITIES FOR PREVENTION

Human resources has an important role in reducing the potential for workplace violence. The hiring and termination processes are two prime examples of the vital human resources link in the prevention program.

Hiring the right person is a critical part of a workplace violence prevention program. With the potential for overstating qualifications, inflating education, adding phantom job experience to the resumé, and forgetting to list jobs the prospective employee would rather you not know about, the potential for hiring the wrong person is great if the application is taken at face value. In fact, studies have shown that up to 42 percent of applications contain material misstatements of facts.

How do you increase the odds in your favor when hiring new workers? First, verify everything on the employment application. Some firms undertake this investigation themselves; others use a professional service. This step will, at the least, ensure the person you interview possesses the skills, qualifications, and job history claimed and meets the job's requirements.

Anyone who has tried to verify past employment likely encountered a military-like response: *name, rank and serial number*. To shield themselves from potential civil litigation, most employers give little or no meaningful information to prospective employers. Most will only verify that the applicant worked at the firm and the dates of employment. Using methods similar to those employed by professional investigators, you can develop additional sources of information from the references supplied by the applicant.

An employment screening benchmark report produced by HireRight found that 85 percent of employers caught applicants misstating information on their applications.[12] It is important to carefully review the application, verify the information provided about work history, education, and verify references. Having a structured process for this is even more important for smaller organizations without an HR department.

Equally important is the interview. Even for entry level jobs, potential employees should be interviewed twice, at different times, and in-person by a company employee skilled in the process. These two face-to-face meetings provide the opportunity to verify the information provided on the application. Often those who lie have trouble remembering the fictional tale they have woven. To be most effective, ask open ended questions to verify dates, job history, and other information provided.

Another part of the screening process should involve, as an element of the background investigation, verification of any prior criminal convictions. In most states you may ask if the applicant has been convicted of felony or misdemeanor charges. You may not, in most instances, ask if there have been any arrests that did not lead to conviction.

It may not be a reasonable policy to automatically exclude all applicants with convictions. The best course of action may be a system to fairly and consistently evaluate each case individually and weigh the potential liability. The best advice on this issue will come from your legal counsel.

Many companies are tempted to lessen the screening and background investigation requirements for lower level, entry positions. This decision, often based on expense and expediency, could well be a costly mistake. Not fully screening a certain class of applicant could expose the firm to a bad hiring decision and result in a tragic incident. Only with an effective program can the likelihood of hiring the potentially violent employee be reduced.

TERMINATIONS

How to best handle employee terminations can make the difference between a routine separation and one that leads to threatening behavior or worse. The separations typically fall into three broad categories: routine terminations, terminations due to violent or menacing behavior, and downsizing. We'll review how to structure routine terminations to avoid escalation; how to conduct company downsizing while mitigating potential violence; and how to minimize risk when the termination itself is due to violent behavior. It is vital to evaluate your options to handle a difficult, potentially violent situation in advance. Part of the process involves determining if you need outside professional to help minimize the potential for violence when the situation falls outside your level of comfort or you want to ensure your process meets the legal standard of care.

It is common that people equate their identity and worth with work; it's typically a matter of degree. A job and a career are not only an affirmation of status but also a measure of individual achievement. In the case of long-term and loyal employees, the sense of self and perception of identity are even more ingrained. Evidence shows this belief system is more prevalent with males than females. If an employee feels blindsided by a termination, males are more predisposed to become agitated and act out.

Underscoring this dynamic is the need to feel appreciated and recognized. Human Resource professionals can attest that employees want to feel valued for their contribution. When an employee gets derailed, or experiences personal or performance problems, and compounds that with the prospect of termination, the situation can spiral out of control quickly. Losing a salary, job security, and the very endeavor that may have shaped someone's identity can cause stress and depression, and sometimes lead to violence. Call it the makings of a perfect storm.

Stay ahead of the curve. Begin working with the employee at the first indication of a challenge; this enables you to resolve issues before they become intractable. Think of a well-documented plan as taking preemptive action.

Beginning job counseling or instituting a performance improvement plan, as appropriate, may not only help to reduce or resolve the unwanted behavior but also provide a written record of your efforts and actions. Employing genuine concern and compassion while motivating and empowering people goes a long way. And while your actions may not get the intended result, you'll have a clear record of your efforts.

If problems continue to escalate, diligently comply with your organization's employment policies and procedures, taking all necessary steps for discipline and resolution leading up to – and through – termination. Ideally, these actions provide you with the tools to effect change, as well as the ability to monitor the behavior, while the individual is still employed with your company.

It's important to demonstrate that you've assisted the employee to elevate his or her situation. Document every detail; if civil litigation results from the situation, following your organization's protocols and documenting this process will prove invaluable.

Adhere to all applicable employment laws. Both legal and practical in nature, this strategic approach can help your organization avoid future litigation. Consult with in-house counsel or an employment law specialist.

If the employee is considered to be in a protected class due to age, race, gender, or disability, it is all the more imperative to invest in legal advice. If the employee claims that the unwanted behavior is caused by a disability, referring to protection under the Americans with Disabilities Act (ADA), a labor law attorney can help you navigate this complex issue. And if your sense is that the employee could act out when the separation occurs or later, consult a professional who specializes in workplace violence threat assessment.

Once the decision has been made to terminate the employee, set up the employee termination meeting with foresight and a plan. Decide who will conduct the meeting and who should be a witness if necessary. Showcase during the meeting the many benefits available to the separated employee and provide all relevant takeaway materials. Written information is essential; the employee will likely not retain much of the dialogue once he or she hears and begins to process the termination decision.

When an employee has acted out and made threats, it is sometimes difficult to deal with them in a polite and productive manner. Keep in mind that the way in which the termination is conducted will likely influence future behavior toward the organization by the separated employee. If you are conducting the meeting, say something positive and encouraging. Be kind and remain focused on the future. Promote the idea of finding another opportunity, ensuring a life beyond your organization at a company with a better fit. Consider providing outplacement counseling to help the terminated employee quickly begin the successful hunt for a new position. The intention is that optimism will prevail and produce a better outcome for everyone.

While it might seem counterintuitive to provide additional funds to someone who, in some cases, does not appear to deserve them, consider this: from a strategic standpoint, offering a severance package or other bridge compensation to provide stability through the transition can be a low-cost and effective way to reduce the potential for continuing or even escalating unwanted behavior against the organization or specific employees. You are, in effect, helping to augment the employee's ability to be reasonable while reducing the financial stress of losing a job. Financial worries can exacerbate the upheaval of losing a job, and stress can be pivotal in whether an individual decides to act out. Look at compensation as an investment in your firm's safety and well-being, reducing the chance of a violent reaction.

HR professionals know it is standard operating procedure to provide limited information to a potential employer seeking a reference. Yet the separated employee might think that your organization will share all the details, warts and all. Make it clear that you will neither give the former employee a bad reference nor provide details regarding the behavior that precipitated the termination. It will provide solace, help defuse the angst that a bad reference will sabotage their job hunt, and, no doubt, ease the person's mind.

HR and security professionals often know from experience that seemingly routine terminations can still take a turn for the worse. The watchword is to practice precaution, ensuring you've documented all interactions and observations through the evolution of events. Even though an employee has not previously demonstrated a tendency toward violence, any termination has the inherent chance to activate strong emotions, in turn igniting a desire to act out.

As an example, employee Sakyra Ellis acted violently toward the HR professional with whom she was putting in her resignation from a Troy, Michigan company. Ellis put the staff member in a chokehold, stabbing her with a pen during the meeting. What happened? When Ellis was told she would have to pay for the broken computer tablet she turned in, she became angry. Misplaced or misdirected anger is just as volatile as any other. Protect yourself and your company.

To begin with, set up the separation meeting in a conference room with more than one exit. Make sure you or another HR person can sit near the exit, especially if there is only one. Make certain the employee cannot block the exit. If the meeting must be conducted in an office, do not sit behind a desk with the employee between you and the exit. This could prevent your ability to leave the room if the individual makes threats or becomes violent. Ensure that whomever conducts the meeting has a "script" prepared ahead of time that covers precisely what – and what not – to say. Keep it brief.

To ensure safety, arrange to have a neutral second person in the room as a witness. The individual should not have been involved in the matter. If the supervisor or manager had a conflict or difficult relationship with the soon to be former employee, don't have that person involved in the meeting; it could encourage a heated discussion and aggravate the exchange. Have all prepared documentation ready prior to the termination including wages due in accordance with your state's employment regulations. On a separate front, have the employee's computer access deleted and access control card deactivated *during the termination meeting*. Do not handle this before the meeting, which could give premature notice of the separation. Remove any potentially dangerous items on the desk that could hurt you if thrown or used to strike; this includes staplers, letter openers, heavy mugs, or paper weights.

After the meeting, do not allow the employee to return to his or her work area. If personal items are required immediately, such as a cellphone, car keys, handbag, or briefcase, send a manager to retrieve them. Do not have the separated employee pack belongings, especially in front of others. Simply have their personal items boxed up and delivered to their home via courier the same or following business day. Have the individual escorted out of the facility after the meeting; if he or she relies on a ride share to get home, provide transportation such as a taxi or Uber at no cost. Planning and common sense can help defuse potential issues that could cause conflict during the meeting.

Once a termination decision has been made, remember that the purpose of the meeting is to act on that decision. Minimize explanations of "why" and avoid deep discussion of past performance or an employee's effort to get more chances. Communicate clearly and firmly that the employee is not permitted to return to the premises. If another on-site meeting is necessary, the employee must schedule it in advance, only through a predetermined HR single point of contact. The HR person is the only one whom the separated employee may contact with questions. If conflict was present, the contact should not be the supervisor or manager. Staying ahead of the curve keeps you prepared and proactive.

Managing Potentially Violent Terminations

Previous behavior is a bellwether for an upcoming termination. When an employee has demonstrated a propensity for violence or aggressive behavior, implement increased safeguards to navigate the process. In addition to the measures outlined for routine terminations, it is critical to fortify your protection and security when faced with this kind of termination. Consult with a threat management professional for support and recommendations to mitigate the situation. Err on the side of caution.

When there's substantial concerns about the individual's behavior, consider conducting the termination by phone. While on the surface it may appear to be cold, it increases security and safety by not having the separated employee come to the workplace and interact with people he or she may have significant animosity toward. Follow up right away with a letter that confirms in writing not only the termination but also the company point of contact going forward, and instruct the employee not to return to your company's premises. The letter should document that the employee's personal items are being delivered, and both the letter and personal items should in fact be couriered to the employee's residence as soon as possible.

If you must opt for an in-person meeting, be vigilant. Have qualified security personnel discretely standing by to lessen the likelihood of a violent outcome. With a heightened level of concern, you'll want to have the professionals who can act if required. Consider an off-duty police officer or highly trained, armed private security officer. The building's lobby security officer is probably not the right choice for this assignment. The safeguard of a trained professional can protect the HR person and nearby employees from a violent response.

Do not provide advance warning to the employee about the meeting. Rather, use an acceptable, plausible reason to bring the employee to the location. Take further precautions by ensuring that handbags, backpacks, briefcases, or other bags are not permitted into the room. Further, do not allow a break, even a short restroom break; interrupting the meeting could provide the opportunity for an angry employee to retrieve a weapon.

To reiterate, if the employee has shown indications he or she could act out, get help. People that may be on an escalation course to violence exhibit some common signs of impending rage include clenched fists, a face that becomes flushed, banging on a table, rising from a sitting position for no apparent reason, or verbal threats. If the employee makes threats, ascertain right away what he or she plans to do, whether the anger is directed toward a specific co-worker or supervisor identified by name, or toward the organization in general.

DOWNSIZING

In our climate of perpetual uncertainty and shifting organizational needs, the volatility of downsizing is real. As with all change, the possibility of negative reaction is amplified when a situation is not in someone's control. Employees who feel they've been treated unfairly or fired due to circumstances not related to their performance can harbor deep resentment. From poor management to underperforming products or over expansion, a multitude of factors can create a division between expectation and reality. Employees who may bear the brunt of these scenarios could react with indignation or worse.

When not handled correctly, the result of downsizing can be angry employees intent on retaliation. Once your management team decides what can reasonably be shared with employees, communicate in earnest. Be open and transparent with employees such that the management team communicates, as much as possible, the company's financial and organizational challenges. Being honest about the need for budget and staff reductions – and providing time for employees to weigh options and make choices – will help encourage civility with, and trust for, your organization.

While the most volatile reactions are related to the terminated employee, remaining employees can also be affected. Survivor guilt, feeling undeserving of being retained in the face of another's misfortune, is conceivable. Employees could also wonder if they're next or what to expect from the management perceived as having betrayed a colleague.

Of genuine concern is the burden of additional work from those who've been let go, and the fear of not having the skill set for a different job in the company. Historical statistics point to increases in vandalism and sabotage. Provide and promote additional counseling services as a valuable resource to existing employees.

As with all terminations, plan ahead. Assemble a team of senior leaders to evaluate the needed budget cutbacks, and develop a viable, strategic plan for workforce reductions. As part of this process, evaluate the key positions and budget amounts that must be cut.

When to Call for Reinforcements

Know that, unless your organization is very large, you may never have had to deal with an employee that is making threats or exhibiting behavior that makes co-workers fearful. Despite your professional knowledge and best attempts, some situations escalate and require highly specialized skills. When an employee's behavior intensifies toward aggression, it poses a threat. If the situation makes you or others uncomfortable or you believe another approach might produce better results, consult a threat assessment professional. With specific skills, training, and credentials in the area of workplace violence prevention, the threat assessment professional can provide much-needed backup to reduce a potentially dangerous situation.

PHYSICAL SECURITY AND HARDWARE

Although a significant portion of serious workplace violence incidents are internal, it still makes sense to include security systems and physical security measures as part of the complete, integrated approach to combating workplace violence.

The myriad of technologies available have driven an approach to system design commonly known as integration. Integration allows distinct systems such as access control, alarms, video surveillance, and other security related sub-systems to function as a cohesive whole.

For example, an employee who has been terminated but failed to surrender his or her ID badge might pose a threat to the workplace. The badge might allow this person to gain access to sensitive areas or into the building, posing a danger to workers.

With an integrated system, if the worker presents his or her card to an electronic reader, the card that was canceled when the employee was terminated will generate an alarm, indicating that an unauthorized person attempted to gain access. The system could also display a stored photo image of the employee to the on-site guard and even print out a copy for distribution. In addition, when the alarm is registered, a nearby video surveillance camera is automatically positioned to view the door, giving further information to security personnel.

The control of workplace vulnerabilities, risks, and potential losses requires sound and efficient integration of both electronic and physical security elements with an effective program of prevention and employee-care programs.

The first step in including technological improvements to the security program is an assessment of threats, risks, and needs. The major shortfall of ineffective programs is poor planning and failure to define the system parameters.

In addition to electronic and physical boundaries, many companies rely on security personnel, either proprietary or contract security officers. Again, failure to define the goals to be accomplished by the use of security personnel is the major reason for security inadequacies.

In planning to include electronic systems and security personnel, it is vital that a cohesive group representing the primary areas within the company be involved in determining the best combination of devices and people. This ensures that the program design meets the security needs in a cost-effective way, in a manner that blends with the corporate culture of the company.

PLANNING FOR THE CRISIS TO REDUCE ITS IMPACT

Despite all the best planning, use of policies, and practices, dealing fairly with all employees and otherwise having a model prevention program, an incident could happen. What do you do now? The answer is to have planned for it.

Another element of the program is a crisis response plan that details the steps that will be followed should the unthinkable happen. Not only is this plan effective for workplace violence but also for other manmade or natural disasters. The same plan can minimize damage following a chemical spill at a company facility or an earthquake that affects the workplace.

The plan should detail the positions responsible for the many duties required to properly respond to a crisis. An effective plan involves most departments within a company.

If a serious incident of workplace violence occurs, particularly if there are injuries and fatalities, reporters and camera crews from media outlets will descend on the company's facility. Planning for who speaks for the company is critical to ensure a consistent voice. Just as important, is who is not authorized to speak with the media – and that would be all personnel except the designated spokesperson.

Only plans that are exercised, revised, and remain fluid are effective. A plan that is written, put in a binder, and never removed from the shelf until an incident happens is dangerous because it creates a false sense of protection. Write the plan, test it, and then continue to test it.

BUT IT *COULD* HAPPEN HERE...

While some industries and occupations seem more predisposed to workplace violence, no work environment is immune. Incidents have occurred in three-person businesses as well as those employing thousands of workers.

No one can absolutely prevent workplace violence, but with proper planning and an effective program, the chances of it occurring can be reduced dramatically.

REFERENCES

1 "National Census of Fatal Occupational Injuries in 2017," U.S. Department of Labor, Bureau of Labor Statistics, December 18, 2018.
2 "Workplace Homicides from Shootings," U.S. Department of Labor, Bureau of Labor Statistics, September 16, 2015.
3 U.S. Occupational Safety and Health Administration (OSHA).
4 "Workplace Violence OSHA Factsheet," U.S. Department of Labor, Occupational Safety and Health Administration, 2002.
5 Centers for Disease Control, National Institute for Occupational Safety and Health (NIOSH).
6 "The Financial Impart of Workplace Violence," Workplaceviolence911.com, June 22, 2005.
7 "The Economics Daily – There Were 500 Workplace Homicides in the United States in 2016," U.S. Department of Labor, Bureau of Labor Statistics, January 23, 2018.
8 "Stalking Fact Sheet," The National Center for Victims of Crime, Stalking Resource Center, January 2015.
9 "Workplace Violence Prevention and Intervention – American National Standard ASIS/ SHRM WVPI.1–2011," ASIS and SHRM, September 2, 2011. www.asisonline.org or www .shrm.org.
10 "Workplace Violence Prevention Survey Findings," Association of Threat Assessment Professionals, December 3, 2014.
11 "When Trouble at Homes Becomes Trouble in the Office," Minda Zetlin, INC. Magazine, July 2013.
12 "85 Percent of Job Applicants Lie on Resumes – Here's How to Spot a Dishonest Candidate," J.T. O'Donnell, *INC Magazine*, August 15, 2017.

CHAPTER 15

Security Risk Modeling

Jack Leonard Follis

CONTENTS

Background
The Project Goal
Data
Explore the Data

Think about data ... like a statistician.

A statistical analysis can be thought of as a story. Every story has a theme, characters, and a plot that ties everything together. For an analysis project, the goal of the project is the theme, the data being used are the characters in the story, and the analysis is the plot. For a story, understanding the characters in a story can help clear up the plot, and one of the keys to a sound statistical analysis is understanding the data. The focus of this chapter will be on understanding data, or thinking about data like a statistician, but will also include sections on other aspects of the analysis process, including the project goal and data analysis.

BACKGROUND

If randomly selected individuals were asked what comes to mind when they hear the word statistics, a variety of answers such as 'I don't understand statistics,' 'I don't like statistics,' or 'statistics is great' might be given. What might explain the various responses? One possible explanation would be an individual's past experience with statistics. Providing an explanation(s) for the variation in the responses is the basic idea behind a statistical analysis. Statistical analyses depend on data to explain variation.

When someone hears the word 'data' the first thought that comes to mind is a collection of numbers. When using the term data, this is often referring to a dataset, which is a collection of records and variables. A record (or subjects) for a study is who data is collected from, and variables are characteristics that have been recorded or measured for each record (subject). Part of a dataset may look like Table 15.1.

The records for a dataset are from whom the data was obtained, be it individuals, businesses, cities, etc. Many times, especially if data is being recorded from people, records are assigned an identification code to protect confidentiality. The terms 'subjects' or 'observations' are often used instead of 'records.'

TABLE 15.1   A Sample Data Set

Record #	Distance	Smoke	Stress	Steps
11110	233.5	Yes	Low	2
11111	234.8	No	High	4
11112	230.6	No	Medium	1
11113	240.1	No	High	4

Variables may be either categorical, where each record belongs to a particular cat-egory, or quantitative, where values represent different magnitudes of the variable. In Table 15.1, smoke and stress are all categorical variables since each record can only be classified in one of the categories. For smoke, a subject may be classified as a smoker (yes) or a non-smoker (no), and for stress a subject may be classified as low, medium, or high. Distance and steps are quantitative since they have magnitudes for each sub-ject. Categorical variables with only two categories, such as if an individual is a smoker (yes or no), are referred to as dichotomous. The variables correspond to the characters in the statistical analysis story.

The main character in an analysis story is the outcome variable(s). This is the variable that is the focus of any analysis and may be categorical or quantitative. Examples of an outcome variable may be the number of crimes, the average number of crimes per year, the type of crime, etc. Although it may not be expli-citly stated, the statistical analysis is designed to explain the variation in this vari-able through effect estimation, comparisons of groups, or models. The other variables in the dataset may be used as explanatory variables, that is, variables that explain some of the variation in the outcome variable. Variables such as prop-erty location, type of property, or type of business may be explanatory variables for an outcome variable such as type of crime. Other common terms used for the outcome variable are dependent variable or effect, and other common terms used for explanatory variables are independent variables, exposures, or predictors.

All of the records in a dataset represent a sample from a population of interest. A population is a collection of all records/subjects. The population could be all restaur-ants in Houston, Texas, or all individuals between the ages 18–24 who work in

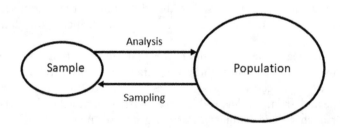

FIGURE 15.1   Using sample data to draw conclusions.

restaurants in Houston, Texas. Since it may not be possible to gather information for all records in a population, samples are taken from the population. Samples are subsets of the population of interest from which data is collected. Ideally, the sample is representative of the population. The sample data are used in an analysis to draw conclusions about the population. Figure 15.1 shows the process.

THE PROJECT GOAL

While a story may not directly state its theme, a statistical analysis always should state its theme, that is, it must have a clearly defined goal and/or hypothesis/hypothesis. The project goal should include the study population and the outcome variable(s). The goal is used to determine what data needs to be collected and what type of statistical methods are needed to analyze the data. Examples of goals could be:

1. Determining what physical characteristics of shopping centers are related to property crimes in City X:
   a. Study population – shopping centers in City X;
   b. Outcome variable – property crime;
   c. Data to be collected – property crimes, shopping center physical characteristics, neighborhood characteristics, business characteristics, etc.
2. Estimating the risk of violent crime on retail properties between midnight and 5 a.m. in Houston, Texas during the month of June:
   a. Study population – retail properties in Houston, Texas;
   b. Outcome variable – violent crime;
   c. Data to be collected – violent crimes during June, physical characteristics of properties, neighborhood characteristics, business characteristics, etc.
3. The amount spent on security is related to the square footage of the retail property:
   a. Study population – retail properties;
   b. Outcome variable – amount spent on security;
   c. Data to be collected – amount spent on security, square footage, crime rates, physical characteristics of properties, etc.

Project goals may also involve prediction. For example:

4. Predict the risk of crime for neighborhoods in City X based on variables found to be related to crime
   a. Study population – neighborhoods in City X;
   b. Outcome variable – risk of crime;
   c. Data to be collected – property crimes, neighborhood characteristics, etc.

Whenever confronted with a project goal, try to identify the study population, the outcome variable, and, if possible, what data was or needs to be collected.

DATA

Much like a story revolves around the characters, statistical analyses revolve around data. Not knowing or understanding the data being used in an analysis can lead to invalid analyses, spurious conclusions, or the inability to explain the results of an analysis. When it comes to data, always be a skeptic – always ask questions about the data.

Get to Know the Data

In the example dataset above with the four variables, there are entries for each record and variable, but what does any of that information mean? If the data were analyzed and there appeared to be a relationship between distance and smoke, how would this be interpreted? In this case the data lacks context. Without any context to the data, there is no meaning to the results. The context of the data can be found by answering the questions who, what, why, where, when, and how. Always answer these questions before using data.

Who

The 'who' of the data revolves around the records/subjects. When answering the question of 'who' for the data, it is important to know the criteria that was used to select the records/subjects for the analysis. Records/subjects could be included or excluded for various reasons. If the study population is restaurants/bars, then possible inclusion criteria may be that a restaurant has been in operation for at least one year and the restaurant is not located in an office building. Knowing who the data was collected from gives the context for generalizing the results of the analysis.

What

The 'what' of the data is about the variables. Each of the variables needs to be identified as to what type of variable it is, whether it is categorical or quantitative. If a variable is categorical, knowing what the categories are and what the categories mean is essential. For quantitative variables, it is important to know what each variable measures and the units of measure. Usually categorical and quantitative variables are straightforward to identify, such as whether someone has been convicted of a felony (yes or no), or the day of the week a crime was committed, or the length of time between crimes, but there may be cases where it isn't as clear.

Suppose there is a variable where each entry is either 1, 2, 3, 4, or 5. Since these are numbers, it may just be easy to think of it as a quantitative variable. However, if this variable represents perceived safety ratings, then is it a quantitative variable? The values could be averaged together so the average ratings could be compared between different locations, with a higher average indicating feeling safer. On the other hand, the percentage of the highest rating of 5 a location has received may be of interest, in which case each of the ratings could be considered a category. To determine whether a variable such as this one should be a categorical or quantitative variable, it is important to know the project goal, that is, why the data was needed.

Why

The 'why' of the data comes from the project goal and can help answer other questions about the data. As mentioned in the previous section, knowing why data was collected can help determine if certain variables should be considered categorical or quantitative. If the project goal is comparing changes in perceived safety over time, then the variable can be treated as a quantitative variable, since differences in ratings can be used. On the other hand, it may be treated as a categorical variable if the project goal is to determine the percent of locations that fall into each category. Knowing the purpose of the data can also help answer who the data should be collected from, where the data should be collected, when the data was/will be collected, and how the data will be collected.

Where and When

The 'where' and 'when' of the data is related to both the records and the variables. The way in which data is measured and recorded could differ between cities, states, or countries as well as different time periods. The location may also restrict the availability of records and different variables. Similarly, data may not be available for different time periods. Values for variables may also naturally vary between different locations and change over time. Knowing where and when the data is collected can help with explaining the results of an analysis.

How

The 'how' of data is about how the data was collected. Was the data obtained by interviews, surveys, from publicly available data sources, or all, or some? Knowing how the data was collected can determine whether the data is useful or worthless.

Every dataset is different, so answering the questions of who, what, why, when, where, and how should always be done before exploring the data or conducting any data analysis.

EXPLORE THE DATA

After gaining an understanding of the context of the data, it is important to examine each of the individual variables that will be used in the analysis (univariate), as well as explore possible relationships between variables (multivariate). Conducting univariate examinations allow for seeing what a variable looks like, namely the distributions of values for quantitative variables and the frequencies for each category of a categorical variable. Seeing the distributions and frequencies for the different variables also allows for identifying missing values, data errors, and outliers. Multivariate examinations may be used to see if two variables are related and if a third variable may be influencing that relationship. Explorations of data can be done using analytic and/or visualization methods.

Univariate

The first step in examining each variable is to determine whether a variable is a quantitative or categorical variable. Once each variable type has been determined, the next step is to look at the distributions for each variable.

Suppose a categorical variable in the dataset is 'Type of Crime' that lists three categories of crime: Property, Violent or Type 2 (Disorder) crimes. What is of interest for this variable is how many of each type of crime occurred, to see the distribution of the types of crime. For a categorical variable, a frequency table can be used to see the distribution. A frequency table lists the categories for the variable with the count, or frequency, for how often that category occurred. In addition to the frequencies, the relative frequency should also be calculated. The relative frequency is the percent of the total that fall into each category. The relative frequency is used since many times it is easier to look at percentages than counts.

For the 'Type of Crime' variable, a frequency table might look Figure 15.2.

Looking at this table, it can be seen that Type 2 crimes are the most common, with 225 of the 400 total crimes, or 56.3% of the crimes, followed by Property crimes and then Violent crimes. When examining the percentages, one thing to look at is if this distribution of crimes is similar to national, state, or local (county, city, etc.) distributions. The distribution also allows one to see if there are any categories that have small counts. If the count (or percentage) for a variable is low compared to the other categories, then that category may be combined with a similar category, or it may excluded from the analysis (e.g., if there was a singular occurrence and all other categories had at least 50). Frequency tables may be done by hand for smaller datasets, but software, such as Excel, may be used to generate the frequency table. Software generated frequency tables make it easier to identify errors in the data. If Property was misspelled as 'Prperty,' then 'Prperty' would be listed as a separate category, and that error would need to be corrected.

Using a bar plot to visualize a distribution may be helpful, especially for variables with a large number of categories. A standard bar plot usually has categories of the variable on the horizontal axis. For the vertical axis, either the frequency or the relative frequency may be used; however, much like the frequency table, it is easier to look at percentages rather than counts. The bar plot for the 'Types of Crime' variable is shown in Figure 15.2.

Suppose 'Amount Spent on Security Last Year' is a quantitative variable in a dataset. To examine the distribution of a quantitative variable, a histogram is the most commonly used. A histogram is a bar plot that shows frequencies for classes created from a quantitative variable. A histogram for the variable 'Amount Spent on Security Last Year' may look like Figure 15.3.

In this histogram, each of the bars, or classes, represents a range of $1000 (the width of the class); so, the first bar represents the number of values between $5000 and $6000, the second represents the number of values between $6000 and $7000, etc. The

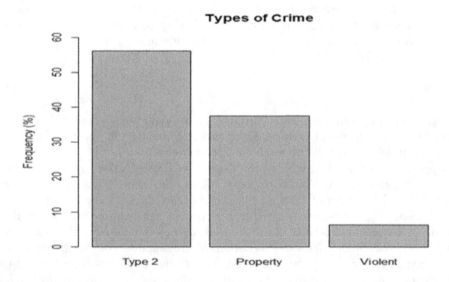

FIGURE 15.2   Bar plot for types of crime.

TABLE 15.2 An Example of a Frequency Table

Type of Crime	Frequency	Relative Frequency (%)
Type 2	225	56.3
Property	150	37.5
Violent	25	6.2
Total	400	100.0

width of the classes may be selected manually, or one may have software determine the width of each class. The height of each bar represents the frequency for each of the classes. Thus, there was only one observation between $15,000 and $16,000, while there were approximately forty-five between $10,000 and $11,000.

When examining a histogram, look to see if there are peaks in the distribution, if the distribution is symmetric, and the spread of the values. In Figure 15.3, the Amount Spent on Security has a peak around $9000–$11,000, indicating that the most common amount spent was in this range. The distribution is also approximately symmetric and bell-shaped, indicating a clear center value for the variable and the values decrease at roughly the same rate the further the values are from the center. The values range from a minimum of approximately $5000 to a maximum of approximately $16,000, for a maximum range of $11,000 spend on security. Based on knowledge of spending on security, one could determine if the distribution is similar to what has been observed previously or is in agreement with what was expected. The key features to look for when examining a histogram are the shape and the spread of the values.

The shape of a distribution for variables will vary from dataset to set. Some common shapes of distributions are in Figure 15.4.

Distributions with one peak are referred to as unimodal distributions. As mentioned earlier, symmetric, bell-shaped distributions have one peak and an identifiable center value. Symmetric distributions may also have more than one peak or they may not have a peak. If

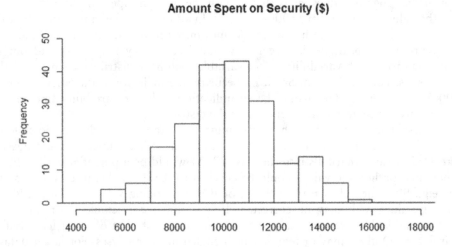

FIGURE 15.3 An example of a histogram.

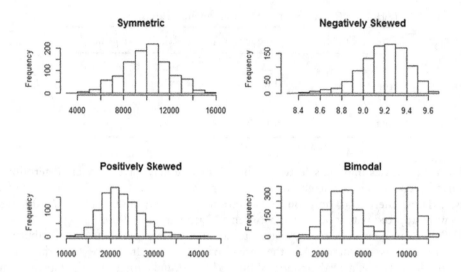

FIGURE 15.4   Common shapes of distributions of data sets.

there is no peak in the distribution, then all values are equally likely, or are uniformly distributed. Most of the values above or below the center of a symmetric distribution will be approximately the same distance from the center, but this is not the case for negatively skewed or positively skewed distributions. These distributions are asymmetric, extending more in one direction or the other. These distributions have one prominent peak, but it is not as easy to identify a center value. Examples of positively skewed data are housing prices and income, and examples of negatively skewed data are ages at death and distances in long jump competitions. If the data has more than one peak (multimodal), this indicates that the values come from different groups. In the case of Figure 15.4, one group has values centered around 4000 and the other group has values centered around 10,000.

The shape of the distribution also shows the spread of the data. The classes of the histogram give an indication of the minimum and maximum values, thus giving an indication of the range of values, as is shown with the Amount Spent on Security example where the values ranged from $5000–$16,000. In addition to the range, how the values vary can also be seen in the histogram. Values may be concentrated in one particular class (a prominent peak) indicating low variability, or they may be spread out uniformly, indicating high variability. Most variables will have distributions between these two extremes. For the Amount Spent on Security, the majority of the values are in the $8000–$12,000 range. This would be an indication of lower variability since most of the values are concentrated in the middle of the distribution.

One last item to look for when examining histograms is to identify possible outliers. Outliers are values that are far away from the other values in the dataset. In Figure 15.5, a value that falls into the class 22–24 would be a potential outlier. If there is a potential outlier, the value should be checked to see if it is because of a data entry error (e.g., 99.1 entered instead of 9.91), or if it is a coding value (e.g., using 999 for a missing value) so it may be corrected. If it is not a correctable error, the outlier should be checked to see if it is a plausible value (e.g., a height of seven feet), but one that it is rare. Outliers may or may not be included in the analyses. For larger datasets, the outlier may be removed, but for smaller datasets analyses should be conducted with and without the outlier to see its effect. If the nature of the outlier cannot be deter-mined, then it should not be included in analyses.

Multivariate

Much as the relationships between characters in a story are important for the plot of the story, knowing the relationships between variables in a dataset are important to the analysis. As with the univariate analysis, variables need to be determined if they are cat-egorical or quantitative variables. Multivariate relationships between two categorical variables, two quantitative variables, and a categorical and a quantitative variable may be examined using graphical methods. Finding relationships between variables should not be misinterpreted as finding that one variable causes the other.

Suppose 'Amount Spent on Security' and 'Total Number of Crimes' are two quanti-tative variables in a dataset. To examine the relationship between these variables, a scatterplot is employed. A scatterplot is a graph with value for one variable on the horizontal axis and value for the other variable on the vertical axis (usually the out-come variable). A point is placed on the graph for each record that has information for both quantitative variables. After each point has been plotted, the scatterplot can be examined for any apparent patterns. If there appears to be a pattern, then the variables are related; otherwise the variables are not related. The plots in Figure 15.6 are examples of some possible patterns/relationships that a scatterplot may reveal.

Each of the scatterplots gives an idea of what type of relationship may exist between 'Total Crimes' and 'Amount Spent on Security.' The linear scatterplot in the upper left indicates a negative linear relationship, which may be interpreted as when less is spent on security, the number of crimes is higher. If the points on the scatterplot moved from the bottom left corner to the top right corner, it would indicate that increases in spending are related to increases in crime. The linear relationship suggested by this scatterplot implies a constant relationship between the variables. If it is assumed that lower levels of spending predict higher crime rates, then a constant relationship means that if spending is decreased by $1000 the increase in crimes will be a fixed value, whether that decrease in spending is from $10,000 to $9000 or from $5000 to $4000.

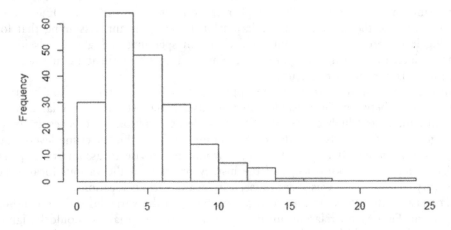

FIGURE 15.5 Values should be checked and verified as potential outliers, or not.

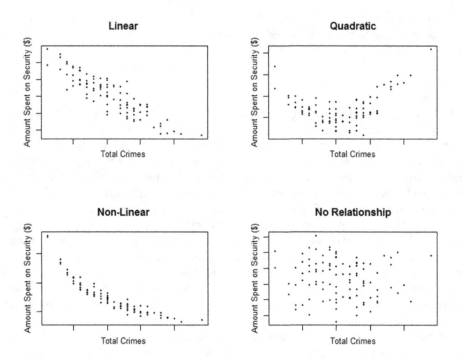

FIGURE 15.6   Possible relationships and patterns from scatterplots.

When two variables are linearly related, the strength of the linear relationship may be quantified using the Pearson linear correlation coefficient, which is denoted by r and is commonly referred to as the correlation between two variables. The value for the correlation falls between –1 and 1, with –1 indicating a perfect negative linear relationship and 1 indicating a perfect positive linear relationship. The closer correlation values are to the extremes of –1 and 1 the stronger the linear relationship, and the closer a correlation value is to 0, the weaker the linear relationship.

The non-linear scatterplot in the lower left shows a similar relationship as the linear scatterplot. However, in this case, the amount spent decreases more rapidly with lower crime rates and less rapidly at higher crime rates compared to the linear scatterplot. In this case the change in the relationship is not constant. Assuming that lower spending levels predict higher crime, a decrease in spending at higher levels indicates a smaller increase in crime compared to a similar decrease in spending at lower levels indicating a larger increase in crime.

In the quadratic scatterplot in the upper right, a different type of non-linear relationship exists between the variables. In this case, higher spending is related to both low crime totals and high crime totals. A possible explanation for this result could be that higher spending leads to a decrease in crime, and that higher crime levels lead to increases in spending. If this is the case, it would be unwise to assume that spending predicts crime without knowledge of the history of crime at the various locations and the history of how much was spent on security at the various locations.

The last scatterplot shows no relationship between the variables – there is no obvious pattern. Finding no relationship does not mean these variables should be ignored. These variables should be further examined to see if a third variable, such as location, may be obscuring a relationship between the variables. There may be a relationship between spending and crime at different locations, but the relationships may be different – some may be linear, some may be quadratic, some may be non-linear.

Even though there are different patterns that may be seen in scatterplots, when examining scatterplots, always check to see if there are any outlier points. A value may not be an outlier when looking at an individual variable, but may be when looking at a scatterplot. In the quadratic scatterplot, the point in the upper right of plot and the points at the far left of the graph may be potential outliers.

The examples of relationships covered here are a small sample of patterns that may be seen in the data. When examining scatterplots, knowledge of the variables will always help to make sense of the patterns (or lack of a pattern). The patterns in the data will help with building statistical models.

Suppose that 'Most Common Type of Crime' and 'Location' are two categorical variables in the dataset, where the types of crime are Property and Type 2 and there are four different locations (location 1, 2, 3, and 4). To see if there is a relationship between categorical variables, contingency tables and bar plots may be utilized. A contingency table is a table that has the categories for one variable as the rows and the categories for the other variable as the columns. The cells of the table will contain the frequencies for each combination of categories (e.g., property crime and location 1). In addition to the frequency, each cell also has the percent of the column or row total. Table 15.3 is an example of a frequency table for 'Type of Crime' and 'Location.'

In this table, the percentage is the percent of the column total. For Location 1, there were a total of 47 records, and of these 47 records, Property Crimes were the most common for 38 of them, or 80.9%.

The percent of column total or percent of row total are calculated since the counts for the categories of variables are usually different. Because of these unequal counts, it would be inappropriate to compare the counts for each cell. Categories with larger frequencies will more than likely have larger frequencies for the categories of the other variable compared to categories with smaller frequencies. For example, in the table, comparing Location 1 and Location 2, Type 2 crimes at Location 1 are a smaller percentage than Type 2 crimes at Location 2, even though there are more (9 vs. 2) at Location 1. The number of Type 2 crimes at Location 1 is higher since there are more records for Location 1 than Location 2 (47 vs. 7).

When examining contingency tables, what is of interest is if the distribution of the outcome (Crime) differs between categories of the predictor variable (Location). In this case it appears that the distributions for Location 1 and Location 3 are similar, but the distributions for Locations 2 and 4 differ from the others. This indicates a possible

TABLE 15.3 An Example of a Frequency Table

	Location				
Most Common Type of Crime	**1**	**2**	**3**	**4**	**Total**
Property	38, 80.9%	5, 71.4%	31, 79.5%	4, 57.1%	78
Type 2	9, 19.2%	2, 28.6%	8, 20.5%	3, 42.9%	22
Total	47	7	39	7	100

relationship between location and crime. If the distributions were similar, then it would indicate there is no relationship between the two variables.

In addition to examining the percentages, it is also important to pay attention to the frequencies to make sure that categories don't have low frequencies. In the table, Locations 2 and 4 have a total 7 records each, which is a small number. This small number may explain why the percentages are different compared to Locations 1 and 3 and to each other.

Bar plots may also be used to see if there is a relationship between categorical variables, especially if there are a large number of categories. Figure 15.7 shows two different versions of bar plots. The one on the left has the categories next to each other to show the differences, and the one on the right is a stacked bar plot, where the bars are stacked on top of each other. Either type of bar play may be utilized when there are a small number of categories, but the one on the left is recommended for variables with a large number of categories.

A contingency table should always be done with a bar plot since bar plots may not show the counts for each category.

Suppose 'Number of Crimes' and 'Type of Property' are a continuous and categorical variable in the dataset, with the categories for 'Type of Property' being Retail and Industrial. To see if there is a relationship between these variables, histograms may be utilized. In this case, histograms should be created using only the data for each category of the categorical variable, and the distributions for each compared to see if there are differences. When creating histograms for categories, the vertical scale should be

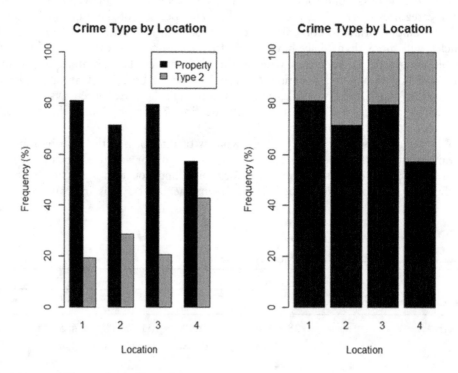

FIGURE 15.7   Illustration of bar plots.

density, instead of frequency, and similar classes should be used. Figure 15.8 illustrates histograms for 'Number of Crimes' for Retail and Industrial properties.

The histograms do appear to be slightly different. The main peak is in the 20–25 class for Retail and a steady decline after the peak. For Industrial, it appears to be the opposite with a build to a peak in the 25–30 class and then a sharp drop-off. In examining these histograms, it does appear that there may be a relationship to Property Type and the Number of Crimes. However, similar to the contingency tables, it is always important to know how many are in each category. Smaller categories may not approximate the true distribution accurately.

Statistical Analysis

Understanding the individual variables and the relationships between the variables assists in making inferences from the data. To make inferences, statistical tests are conducted. This is the plot of the story where the variables are the characters; this plot ties the variables together. These statistical tests may involve direct comparisons between groups, or they can be conducted with a model framework – a statistical model, known as a regression model, accounts for the relationships between variables and takes multiple variables into account to predict an outcome. A full explanation of these methods is beyond the scope of this chapter, so a brief overview of statistical tests will be given.

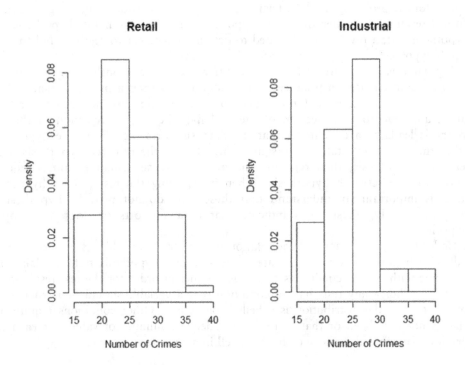

FIGURE 15.8   Example histograms.

Statistical Tests

A statistical test, usually referred to as a hypothesis test or test of significance, is a set of procedures used to test research hypotheses. A hypothesis test begins with a research hypothesis. The research hypothesis is based on the project goal and is used to determine the null and alternative hypotheses. The null hypothesis is a statement indicating no difference or no relationship between variables, and the alternative hypothesis is a statement indicating a difference or that there is some type of relationship between variables. The research hypothesis may be either the null or alternative hypothesis. In practice, it is best to state the research hypothesis so that it becomes the alternative hypothesis, that is, it should be a statement that there is a difference between groups, or that variables are related. Below are two examples:

1. *Research hypothesis* – the crime rate in city A is higher than the crime rate in city B;
   Null hypothesis – there is no difference in crime rates between city A and city B;
   Alternative hypothesis – the crime rate in city A is higher than the crime rate in city B.
2. *Research hypothesis* – the type of crime is related to the type of property;
   Null hypothesis – there is no relationship between type of crime and type of property;
   Alternative hypothesis – type of crime is related to the type of property.

Hypothesis tests are conducted assuming the null hypothesis is true.

A hypothesis test can be thought of as a court trial, where the null hypothesis is the defendant is innocent and the alternative hypothesis is that the defendant is guilty. In the trial, it is assumed that the defendant is innocent, and evidence must be presented to show that the defendant is guilty. For a hypothesis test, the evidence that is used is the data for the project. Just like a trial, the strength of the evidence must be considered before determining whether the data supports the null or alternative hypothesis. For a hypothesis test, a p-value is calculated to determine whether to reject or fail to reject the null hypothesis.

A p-value is a measure of how likely differences or relationships in the data are due to random chance. In practice, if a p-value is less than a preset threshold (usually 0.05), this indicates that differences or relationships are not due to random chance, and lead to the rejection of the null hypothesis. The rejection of the null hypothesis leads to a conclusion that the data supports the alternative hypothesis, or that the results are statistically significant. Thus, if the research hypothesis is the alternative hypothesis, then rejecting the null hypothesis (small p-value) indicates support for the research hypothesis. When interpreting the results of a hypothesis test, it is important to understand that these tests do not prove a hypothesis is true or false. Hypothesis tests indicate that data supports or does not support a hypothesis.

Understanding the data and the relationships between variables is important when conducting hypothesis tests. There are many different hypothesis tests available and most come with certain conditions that must be met in order for the test results to be considered valid. Many tests have a condition that a variable should be normally distributed, that is, the distribution is a bell-shaped curve. Other conditions require that variables not be related or that there are an adequate number of values for each category for a categorical variable or for each cell in a contingency table.

CONCLUSION

Much as characters are important to a story, data is fundamental for any statistical analysis. Thinking about data as a statistician thinks about data (without much math) can give a smoother flow to the data analysis process. Knowing the background of the variables in a dataset and understanding each variable individually and how the variables may be related to one another will help lead to a sound statistical analysis.

CHAPTER 16

Security Program Leadership

Ken Wheatley

CONTENTS

> There is No Silver Bullet to Save the Union.
>
> Abraham Lincoln

THE "WHY" OF SECURITY: INTEGRATION OF GOVERNANCE, PHYSICAL SECURITY, AND SECURITY PERSONNEL

In August 1862, Abraham Lincoln wrote a letter to Horace Greeley, the editor of the *New York Tribune*, in which he addressed the complexities of trying to both save the Union and deal with slavery. The letter also commented on the needs, or demands, of the various constituents that had to be taken into account as he attempted to forge a solution to the problems.

The paraphrased Lincoln quote also applies to business and the issues, limitations, and competing agendas that you deal with on a regular basis while attempting to safeguard your employees, customers, intellectual property, inventory, brand, profits, and assets. You're not just responsible for physical assets. In many instances you're responsible for people's lives. Unfortunately, there are too many examples where weak "leadership" and misplaced or misguided priorities resulted in the loss of life – like BP's Deep Water Horizon event in the Gulf of Mexico in 2010 or the Space Shuttle Challenger explosion in 1986.

We live in a world where some in an organization want to protect everything, the minority viewpoint; and others, the vast majority, either couldn't care less or they're somewhere in the middle. Protecting everything, as we know, is not possible, practical, or even business savvy. And one of your jobs as the security leader, or the person tasked with security as part of your responsibilities, is to help the organization determine where along that spectrum the organization should fall. What really should and shouldn't be protected?

One of the obvious key limitations to protecting everything is … money. Money to pay for staff, training, auditing, technical systems, maintenance, enforcement, creation of policies and procedures, etc.

But there are other equally impactful things that affect your ability to safeguard your company assets, such as the fact that you're not running a dictatorship, and you have to work across the aisle, or in bigger organizations, in a matrixed environment. And sometimes with a consensus-driven decision-making culture. Or with competing priorities.

So, as the leader … the person tagged with the responsibility for safeguarding everyone and "everything," you have some big challenges to deal with and big decisions to make.

The good news, hopefully, is that your position within the company provides you with the organizational access you need to find out how the security group can contribute to the objectives of the company; what REALLY needs to be protected; what it needs to be protected from; and the best way(s) to save the Union.

Let's briefly review the difference between a threat and a vulnerability.

A threat can be the expression of an intent to harm someone or something. It can also be a natural occurrence, like a hurricane, earthquake, flood, pandemic, etc.

A vulnerability is a known or unknown weakness in operations, an individual, a process, the supply chain, etc.

A great example of a supply chain vulnerability, and one that impacts a good number of companies, is the reliance on only four bridges between Canada and the United States to handle one-third of all the cargo trucks that enter the United States.[1]

It's possible that the decision makers in your company aren't aware of this potential weakness and the impact it would have on their just-in-time manufacturing operations; their ability to run lab tests; or their ability to deliver goods in time for the holidays. If at all. It's this type of information that company leadership should be hearing from the security group.

The security department is a business unit, the same as finance, sales, marketing, design, engineering, logistics, retail, R&D, etc. Each business unit will have its own unique goals and objectives, but what they all should share is the need to contribute, successfully, to the goals and objectives of the organization as a whole.

The foundation of your security management program is four pronged:

1. The organizational and value goals of the company.
2. The external and internal assessments (threat, risk, and vulnerability).
3. The metrics and analysis of your program.
4. The budget.

But it's also more than that.

CORPORATE CULTURE

There are lots of articles, seminars, books, and consultants who talk about corporate culture. What that comes down to is a corporate ecosystem that all the constituents live and operate in. The success of a security program, or any department that's trying to affect compliance or a change in behavior, is alignment – from the top to the bottom of an organization.

But a big challenge is, how do you instill that in adults from disparate backgrounds and ideologies? This is one of the challenges that the training department or any function that's tasked with delivering results where humans are a key driver struggles with at times. If the habitat is toxic, the interdependencies are dysfunctional, or the "nutrients" are insufficient, then the system collapses.

So, the successful, secure, and profitable organizations have a relational alchemy (the leaders, the teams, and eco-system (internally and externally) that are in sync).

Part of your organizational assessment as the leader in this area is ... what's the organization's risk tolerance level? If you look at it from a personal financial planning perspective, are you/the organization (very) conservative, moderate, or aggressive when it comes to defining the organization's acceptance of loss?

The meaning of physical security and security personnel are clearly and easily understood. But what is "governance?"

Investopedia defines corporate governance as: "the system of rules, practices and processes by which a firm is directed and controlled." Those rules, practices, and processes provide the lattice for achieving the company's objectives, in a legal and ethical manner.

Good, effective, and desirable corporate governance takes place at the intersection of stakeholder interests (employees, management, shareholders, suppliers, government, community, customers) and transparent (and enforced) rules and controls.

The lattice work for achieving the strategic plans and objectives of a company therefore greatly influences how the company is managed; the creation of department-level business plans, and policies and procedures.

Recent examples of bad corporate governance are Wells Fargo Bank and Volkswagen.

Wells Fargo created 3.5 million unauthorized bank and credit card accounts to meet unrealistic sales goals; charged inappropriate mortgage fees; charged people for car insurance they didn't need; and the list goes on.

Volkswagen installed software in 11 million diesel cars that allowed the company to cheat on emissions tests, all in its efforts to become the world's largest automaker.

Bad governance is reflected in perceptions of a company's integrity and reliability, which can have ramifications on the company's financial performance. In both cases, the stock value of Wells Fargo and Volkswagen dropped and, as of this writing, didn't fully recover, especially compared to their competitors.

WHAT IS THE ROLE OF A SECURITY LEADER TODAY?

The person responsible to lead the security function of a company should know the following things:

- Why is the company in business?
- What drives the company?
- What motivates the leadership?
- What motivates the security team?

- What is the company's stated value proposition?
- What does it not value?
- Where does it draw the line when it comes to ethical decision making?
- What does it stand for in the community at large?
- What does it promise to deliver to its customers, beyond the product or service it produces?
- How does it purport to operate?
- How are decisions made (unilaterally or consensus)?
- How is the company organized (hierarchy or matrixed)?

If you work for a publicly traded company, some of this information can be found in the company's 10K Securities and Exchange Commission (SEC) annual filing, or 20F if it's a foreign entity.

LEADERSHIP VERSUS MANAGEMENT

When you search on Amazon.com, you'll find that there are over 60,000 books on "leadership" and over 80,000 on "management." So clearly, there are a lot of views and definitions of what leadership is and what management is.

In simple terms, Warren Bennis said, "Leaders do the right thing; managers do things right."

Vineet Nayar wrote in *Harvard Business Review* that there are three differences between managers and leaders:

1. Creating value versus counting value: A leader focuses on adding value, above and beyond what her team does. She is a value generator. A manager on the other hand counts value.
2. Circles of influence versus circles of power: A leader has followers, managers have subordinates. Leaders create circles of influence while managers create circles of power. A quick way of determining your leadership "effect" is by looking at how many people outside of your reporting structure come to you for advice.
3. Leading people versus leading work: Leaders influence and motivate people to achieve organizational success. Management consists of controlling a group or set of entities to accomplish a goal.

To gain those followers a leader is also a teacher, mentor, and fortune teller. Hmmm ... a fortune teller?

> I never predict. I simply look out the window and see what is visible but not yet seen.
>
> *Peter Drucker*

Part of what separates a good business leader from a great business leader is foresight. Being able to look over the horizon and divine trends, opportunities, threats, or vulnerabilities. A good starting point for you as the leader, if you work for a publicly traded company, is to read the "Cautionary Statement" section in the company's 10K or 20F SEC filing. As you do with a lot of the information you take in, you're passing it through your SWOT (Strengths, Weaknesses, Opportunities, and Threats) filter to determine, is this relevant to the achievement of the strategic plan? And if so, what is my role and my team's role in addressing it?

To be clear, a manager can also be a leader, but that's not always a given. As Stephen R. Covey, author of *The 7 Habits of Highly Successful People*, stated, "Leadership ... it's a choice, not a position." And it's one that you must prepare for.

Leadership, or management, is like snow and ice climbing, or dancing.

Early on, back in the 1970s, there were two climbing techniques – flat-footed or on the front points of your crampons. It was certainly possible to complete a climb using one technique or the other, but, depending on the conditions, sticking to only one was not always the most efficient or effective.

And when it comes to dancing, if you only know one or two dances, you'll be out of sync when the DJ changes the style of music.

So, all of this is to say that there's clearly no one specific way or style of leadership or management. There are many, many different ways to lead and manage, successfully. And there are also many (many) ways to lead, unsuccessfully. Success can be situational ... largely dependent on the team you're leading. Including yourself. There are examples of highly successful leaders who left GE only to do poorly at another company. Success in one environment doesn't guarantee success in another.

For years, many security leaders have said that they're business people first, security people second. That skillset and mindset is more needed today than ever.

The security department should, as best they can, align their goals and objectives with those of the business. As Stephen Covey once famously said, "As you climb the ladder of success, be sure it's leaning against the right building."

Training, proficiency, preparedness. When a situation requires a response from Delta Force, Navy SEALS, Army Rangers, or Air Force Pararescue, their competence and ability to handle the situation isn't a consideration. At all. The ability to successfully execute the mission is never called into question because of the intense preparation and training they undertake. They are trained up, tested, and PREPARED.

You wouldn't choose a surgeon or dentist who was unsure of their abilities to treat you, or who projected insecurity. So why would an executive management team entrust you with the safety and security of the employees, the brand, and millions (or billions) of dollars in assets?

SECURITY METRICS: CONNECTING THE DOTS VERSUS COLLECTING THE DOTS

Imagine you're driving down an interstate freeway at 70 miles an hour, and you are directly behind a large delivery truck. The truck is taking up a good part of your field of vision. You can see that the traffic on either side of you is moving along, but you can't see anything that's up ahead of them. Or what's in front of the truck. You've probably found yourself in this exact situation.

Well, that's what a poorly designed and managed metrics program is like:

- Your field of view to your external environment is so restricted that you can't foresee any on-coming threats to your operation(s).
- You have very limited information on which to make decisions.

- The warning signs – vehicles braking very suddenly for example – doesn't provide you with enough time to react appropriately.

Metrics, in general, are used to inform decision making, influence behavior, and to evaluate performance. Security metrics are used for those same purposes, but they also highlight how the security program is contributing to the achievement of the company's goals and objectives.

Many security groups go to great lengths to collect and store data (collecting the dots), with much of it focused on counting discrete, and in many cases, historical events, i.e., the number of _____ (fill in the blank).

And then when it comes to connecting the dots, the analysis and reporting aren't always done in a manner that's relevant, applicable, interesting, or actionable to operational business units.

So obviously, the security program shouldn't be set up to collect massive amounts of dots, also known as "just in case" data, but rather data that can ultimately lead to better decision making, budgeting, etc. This can be viewed as "just in time" data.

For a much deeper treatment of the field of measures and security metrics, two excellent resources are George Campbell's book, *Measures and Metrics in Corporate Security: Communicating Business Value*, and ASIS Foundation's *Persuading Senior Management with Effective, Evaluated Security Metrics*.

An excellent article on the subject of metrics was done by Anil Markose, "Metrics that Matter: How to Measure the Effective of Corporate Security Programs (www.securitymagazine.com/articles/89625-metrics-that-matter-how-to-measure-the-effectiveness-of-corporate-security-programs). In that article Markose talked about the three stages of measurement: Foundational, Intermediate, and Advanced.

1. Foundational – Measuring Security's Capabilities and Maturity

   This phase is for companies that have no idea about the state or capabilities of their security program. So they need to build out the framework of the organization's threats and vulnerabilities, determine what the security department's capabilities are for addressing those threats and vulnerabilities, and how their program compares to those within their industry, so that they can develop a plan to upgrade the controls and fundamental capabilities they have at their disposal.

2. Intermediate – Measuring the Return on Security Investment (ROSI)

   The senior management of a company will want to know if the investments they're making in security have any impact on their strategic plan, company profitability, and safety of employees.So, this is the stage that the security department, in concert with key stakeholder business units, would determine, what are the key performance indicators (KPI) or metrics that need to be collected and analyzed? A KPI is determined by identifying what the desired performance level should be during the measurement window and assessing how your department actually performed. As mentioned previously, the objective of collecting data and performing an analysis on those data is to identify what's going well and the areas that need improvement.Two examples of this, given in the Markose article, are:

   - If there's low security awareness among the employees, then the metrics and analysis must measure the training program and a material increase in test scores.
   - If the threat assessment process identified certain threat vectors, then the metrics and analysis should show an increased level of detection capabilities.

3. Advanced – Measuring Readiness to Respond
   This stage presumes that you have a mature, well-functioning security program and, much like Maslow's hierarchy of needs, your program has reached the Self-Fulfillment stage where you can evaluate your readiness to respond to whatever is thrown at the organization and determine if you have the right mix of trained people, resources, processes, and policies.

A few common ways to determine your department's readiness are: table-top exercises (also known as simulations or war-gaming), or the use of a red team, in which people physically test the porosity of the facility, physically or through cyber means.

SECURITY PROGRAM MONITORING/METRICS FOR SUCCESS

Let's use business accounting to illustrate collecting dots (metrics) and connecting the dots (analysis). In an overarching way, a business needs to monitor its performance on a regular basis, and from an accounting perspective there are some core metrics and analysis to monitor:

- Profit and Loss (P&L) or Income statement
  - Probably the most important report for any business. It tells you how much money you're making, where that money is coming from, and how you're spending it. If you're running a consulting business the categories can be broken down into revenue sources (or accounts) such as writing, consulting, teaching, etc.
  - The analysis of that data is looking at trends, comparisons to last month, last quarter, last year, etc.
- Balance Sheet
  - This tells us what we have in regard to assets and liabilities. Assets can be physical (computers, buildings, vehicles, production equipment, tool dies, fixtures, etc.) or intangible, like checking, savings and investment accounts. The balance sheet also tells us what we owe, or what liabilities we have. Ultimately you want to have your equity number (the difference between what you have and what you owe) to be a positive number.
  - The ongoing analysis of that data is certainly to determine if your equity number is increasing or decreasing, whether you have enough short-term liquid assets to cover your short-term liabilities, or how much of your assets are illiquid and determining how quickly you can convert them to a liquid asset if the need arose.
- Accounts Receivable (A/R) Aging
  - After you send out an invoice, you want/need to get paid, so this report shows how much money is outstanding or unpaid and for how long. So basically, this report tells you how you're doing when it comes to collecting what's owed to you.
  - The analysis is identifying customers who pay early, on time, or are habitually late in making their payment. Or maybe you have a customer who normally pays promptly and you start seeing a trend where the payments are later and later. That might be an early detection of financial problems at the client company.

- Revenue by Customer
  - Pretty self-explanatory. This gives you data on which customers give you the most revenue.
  - The analysis can be whether the business is dependent on one or two customers (not good); whether your business is generating repeat business; or if you're having to spend more time and money on marketing and client acquisition because most of your business is based on one-offs.
- Accounts Payable Aging
  - Who you owe and how much.
  - Analysis is determining how much you're paying in late fees and other costs, or ... the loss in savings if you're not taking advantage of early payment discounts.

Before we get into a discussion about what to monitor or measure when it comes to security, let's talk about a couple of foundational issues first – why to do it in the first place, and second, the analysis aspect.

As we've talked throughout this book, one of the key responsibilities of any business leader and their team is to support and contribute to their company's strategic objectives.

Regardless of industry, a company succeeds by delivering on their differentiated products or services. Their ability to consistently do that over the long term is based on the core competencies, skills, tools, resources, methods, processes, relationships, values, ethics, etc. that they've developed.

When a company does all of that well, they (and if they're a publicly traded company, their shareholders) are rewarded with a level of profitability that helps them and their employees prosper. So, as we proceed, a key question is, how does the security business unit contribute to the company's competitive advantage?

One of the critical paths to success in any business is organizational alignment. And alignment is primarily achieved by the development of a strategic plan. Many organizations have broadly defined goals and expect the business units to establish goals that are tied to both the broadly defined corporate goals and their specific business unit activities.

That's why it's important for any business unit leader to ask the senior management for a copy of the strategic plan ... so that you can align your departmental and personal goals and objectives to those of the company.

The flow chart in Figure 16.1 outlines a general process flow for strategic, tactical, and operational decisions with a feedback loop.

In assessing the external environment you have to take into account where the company is operating (Domestic? International? East Coast? West Coast?), who their clients are, and who is the competition.

Strategic decisions are borne from the analysis of the external, competitive environment and an internal assessment of the company's capabilities and resources. Those decisions set the tone and direction of the company for the coming year(s).

Tactical decisions involve the development of policies and programs that will guide the functions of individual business units, such as security, engineering, sales, marketing, HR, finance, procurement, etc.

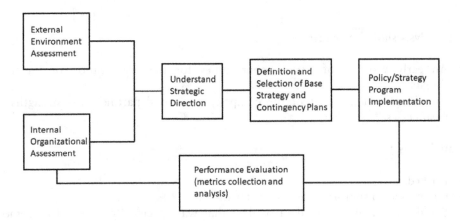

FIGURE 16.1 Process flow for strategic, tactical, and operational decisions with a feedback loop.

Operational decisions affect the day-to-day running of a company and are generally reactive in nature, versus the more deliberative tactical or strategic processes.

Under the best of circumstances, corporate security should operate in all three decision cycles. But all too often, security departments are consumed with day-to-day fire-fighting (operational level) issues, and only at certain times of the year do you have the pleasure of dwelling at the tactical level. You, as the leader, should be striving to have security valued at the same level as the finance or marketing group, for example, to be involved in the strategic planning level.

Once the first two decision cycles are complete, the part of the feedback loop that's very important is the Performance Evaluation phase, which should be done on a regular, ongoing basis. Sort of like balancing your checkbook. Doing that once or twice a year can lead to some rather ugly surprises. The same in a business. Without constant input, monitoring, and evaluation, you may not know until it's either too late or too costly, that you have a problem.

A manufacturing plant was having severe product quality and staffing issues. A consultant was called in to get to the bottom of the problems and propose solutions. While waiting in the main conference room he noticed the following on the white board:

If We Don't Know, We Cannot Act
If We Cannot Act, The Risk of "Loss" is High
If We Do Know and Act, The Risk is Managed
*If We Do **Know** and **Don't Act**, We Invite The "Loss"*

At the end of his analysis he determined that middle management was aware of the problems, didn't seek help to address those problems (for fear of negative consequences from HQ), and therefore took no action, in hopes the problems would fix themselves. The plant went out of business.

Analysis

Good analysis should provide:

- An early warning of either opportunities for the organization or impending threats.
- An objective assessment of the company's – and department's – strengths and weaknesses.

Bad analysis is:

- Rushed.
- Often used to support a decision after the fact.
- Based on a faulty set of data or data that was specifically collected to come up with a pre-determined outcome.
- Crafted to either tell the senior staff what it wants to hear or read, versus what's truly important to fulfill true corporate governance.

"Metrics" are a funny thing. It requires data collection and hopefully the correct analysis and interpretation of what that universe of data means. And the process of doing all of that implies that something (positive?) will be done with the results. That change will occur. Or a decision will be made, such as a project being funded. Or a jury finding in favor of a defendant or plaintiff. But of course, those eventualities don't always materialize (perhaps because of flawed data collection and interpretation), and more importantly, not all metrics matter.

If you look at football, or any sport for that matter, there are LOTS of metrics that are collected and analyzed, but what really matters is … performance. You may remember the story of Billy Beane and the Oakland Athletics back in 2002 that was memorialized in the book, *MoneyBall, The Art of Winning an Unfair Game* written by Michael Lewis and published in 2003.

The basic premise of *Moneyball* is that despite the overwhelming amount of data that was being collected and analyzed in scouting reports, a player's on base percentage was the primary and key statistic to be considered when putting together a winning team. Prior to Beane, that data point was an asterisk at best for most scouts and teams.

In football, time of possession is tallied, often cited, and comparisons are drawn between teams during a game with the inference being that, the longer a team possesses the ball, the more likely they will win the game. But in reality, it's a completely meaningless metric if the possession doesn't result in putting points on the board!

So, in security management, what should be collected and analyzed are those things that reflect your performance against things that matter.

SECURITY DASHBOARDS

Given the operational and tactical tempo of most departments, it's important to establish a dashboard that displays regularly updated information to monitor the areas that are important to your boss (and your boss's boss) and you. There is no "one" dashboard that works for everyone or every situation of course. So you have to determine what areas are most critical and influential for you to monitor on a regular basis.

In Campbell's, *Measures and Metrics in Corporate Security*, he lists some examples of "meters or dials" that you can consider: security costs, info security, business conduct, security audits, pre-hire backgrounds, and business continuity.

Let's talk about three of these: security costs, business conduct, and pre-hire backgrounds.

SECURITY COSTS

You can start tracking the cost-per-business unit based on sq. footage or headcount. That cost structure could include tracking the "frequent fliers" – the people who are constantly flouting the rules, violating polices, causing numerous investigations, etc. Perhaps the analysis of those cases would expose a weakness in either the employment backgrounding process, or the lack of performance management efforts in that particular business unit.

BUSINESS CONDUCT

While the following scenario applies to a retail setting, it could also apply to disparate business units.

You probably track the frequency and costs of investigations by location, which would be a routine activity. But the analysis and application of that data could come into play when a decision is being made by senior management on what locations to close.

There was a situation where the head of domestic retail needed to close stores because overall sales in the system had been trending downward. He made the decision based on which stores had the highest sales volume, or sales per square foot. Even though he had been provided with a monthly inventory loss data report, the knowledge contained in the reports wasn't factored into the decision. What they failed to realize was that the stores they were closing had the lowest shrinkage rates, while the stores they were keeping open had the highest shrinkage rates.

So, this example illustrates some of the fallacies and pitfalls of data collection and analysis:

1. In this case, it seems apparent that what was considered the most important metric to base the store closure decision on (probably based on their performance bonus calculation) was sales revenue versus profitability, which may seem crazy, but it happens. You can't operate under the assumption that just because an important report is generated that it will be read, let alone factored into important decisions.In actuality, according to The Hackett Group, an Ohio-based business advisory company, "the average senior executive is inundated with 132 metrics (83 financial and 49 operational) every month." (http://ww2.cfo.com/strategy/ 2004/11/swamped/)It also highlights, again, the need to understand what the business unit's goals and objectives are and how the leadership team is measured and/ or incentivized. Remember Volkswagen and Wells Fargo? Knowing those things will give you the ability to float more important reports to the top of their reading pile.According to John McMahon, a Hackett senior business adviser, "The reality is that even the most complex businesses have only around 10 to 15 key elements

driving performance." You can score points by asking your CFO or other senior executives what those key elements are, and building your security program around them as much as possible.Another key point is building your shared dashboard and your metrics with more leading indicators – things that may signal a future risk or potentially harmful event – versus lagging indicators which are a look in the rear-view mirror.

2. There's also a presumption that if the stars are aligned you'll be at the table when such important decisions are being made, and you'll have the opportunity to constructively add to the conversation. Perhaps you aren't permanently assigned to the C-Suite meetings, but the data and analysis you provide should at least garner inclusion on senior management's agenda.

3. This example also highlights a common occurrence in business ... when times are good, there's less focus on monitoring or enforcing policies and procedures, and the problems don't quite seem so big or important in the grand scheme of things. As a leader, you're thinking about both the short and long term. Good economic times and bad ones. As we see in the stock market, the ebb and flow of fortunes can be an hourly affair.

PRE-HIRE BACKGROUNDS

All too often during an investigation, or for-cause terminations when you're reviewing the subject's HR file, you'll find the file is incomplete. Even though they had already been hired, important background information was still pending – such as educational verification, resolution on an alleged criminal record hit, conflicting names, different social security numbers, unsubstantiated prior work experiences, etc. and in haste, the employee was processed through without the necessary determinative information.

When business is booming there's a tendency to ramp up staffing quickly to meet production, sales, customer service, engineering, or other critical positions, and corners are invariably cut. If there's a recession and finding a job becomes very competitive, candidates can get "creative" on their resumés. In either situation – a booming economy or a recession – the need for attention to detail is critical to the sustainability of the organization.

Therefore, part of your dashboard may include the status of pre-hire background investigations with the ability to highlight differences among business units that may or may not be cutting corners, lowering hiring criteria, etc., so that you can partner with the HR department and business unit leaders to be sure you're screening out problem individuals before they become employees. You can impress upon them that, if their competitor wouldn't (or couldn't) hire them, why should yours?

There are other categories of metrics, such as compliance, threats, and value. Let's talk about security value for a moment.

DEMONSTRATING THE VALUE OF SECURITY

When either of these questions arise: "Does security provide a value to the organization?" or "What part of the security department provides value to the organization?", the presumption may be that security does provide value, but people aren't actually sure HOW it does, or by how much. So that question is followed by: "Well then, how does security demonstrate its value?" Many non-security people associate security with gates, guns, and guards.

The implication in both questions is that security stands apart somehow from the organization, like an appendage. Sort of like your appendix. What exactly does it do, and why do I have it?

It's fairly safe to assume that the value propositions of finance, audit, IT, sales, or engineering for example are rarely questioned. Security on the other hand is like insurance or a highly trained Navy SEAL unit. It operates in the background, for the most part, until a crisis arises and then it springs into action and (hopefully) saves the day.

Given that "value" is in the eye(s) of the stakeholders and the people who create the corporate strategy, the measures of value have to be in the terms that resonate with that group.

For example, as part of a larger project for Boeing, the Security Executive Council looked at the value metrics for the security group. One of the metrics that was being warehoused was the number of laptops that were either stolen or left unsecured and then found by security personnel.

The data collected originally fell into the "just in case" or "nice to know" categories and stayed there.

A study conducted by the Ponemon Institute for Intel determined that the average cost, in 2009, of a lost laptop was $49,246 (https://phys.org/news/2009-04-typical-lost-laptop-companies.html). At that valuation, the security group saved Boeing $6,894,400.

Some final thoughts:

On the finance side, be bold and strive for transparency with your numbers. It'll help you and it just might impress your leadership team.

If you have several areas that you oversee, meet with the finance or accounting department to find out how many cost centers you can have. Whenever possible, break down your budgets to as many cost centers as allowed. This will provide you with a more incremental, detailed view of each function and give you the ability to quickly catch trends when comparing actuals to budget.

The downside of course is that you have no place to hide expenses or play a shell game. It'll force you to be a better manager and leader.

The big upside is that you and your team will be in a better position to immediately spot problems, such as coding errors where an expense from another department got charged to your budget, for example.

Security is a multidisciplinary, cross-functional team sport, as is innovation. Innovation and problem-solving require collaboration, diversity of thought and experiences, and different skillsets.

When Walter Isaacson, author of *Steve Jobs*, interviewed Jobs for the book, he asked, "Which of your creations make you most proud." Contrary to what you think he responded, Jobs said, it was the teams he had produced.

We develop, as individuals and leaders, from the inside out, and from the outside in. Our education and meditations inform or greatly influence our internal development, the formation of how we think, how we process information, how we make decisions and our experiences and interactions with others. Our "street" knowledge further refines who we become.

So the more experiences and stimuli we can expose ourselves to, the better-rounded we'll be, the better emotional intelligence we'll have, and the better decision-making skills we'll develop.

"Trust" is a vital and integral part of effective team execution. Empowering your staff and pushing decision making to the lowest levels of the organization will benefit the growth and development of the staff and the organization as a whole.

ALIGNMENT WITH COMPANY OBJECTIVES: BAMBOO AND PLANT GROWTH

You've probably seen countless photos of bamboo being used in a variety of applications, most notably, as scaffolding. If you peel back the bark on a bamboo stalk you'll see a very tight and uniform vertical alignment of the strands. That alignment and density gives some species of bamboo a tensile strength of 28,000 psi. For comparison, the tensile strength of steel is ... 24,000 psi. Bamboo is often three times stronger than conventional construction grade timbers.

What gives bamboo this strength and durability is its uniform strand alignment and cohesion.

In your early science classes you probably experimented with altering the orientation of a plant to the sun. When you changed the plant's position from one day to the next you hopefully noticed that the plant always bent toward the sun.

So, your "sun" is the company's strategic plan, and your objective as the leader/manager is to get your part of the team always bending in the direction of the plan.

As the leader of the function – whether it's a department of one or many – your role is to provide the resources and environment for the team to prosper.

CHANGE

The secret of change is to focus all of your energy, not on fighting for the old, but building on the new.

Socrates

"Seek first to understand then to be understood." That's Habit 5 of *The 7 Habits of Effective People* by Dr. Steven Covey. Our nature in conversations is to start formulating our response to someone as they're still talking. Or to presuppose (interpret) a situation, or need, based on our own biases or subjective "read" of the situation or need. Those actions are the opposite of active listening traits.

To "understand" is to give your undivided attention to fully listen to what the other person is saying. It's also taking the time to really understand the process, culture, system(s), etc. that run your organization.

In Japanese management circles it's referred to as "front-line awareness." All too often management is not in touch with what's actually happening out in the field, on the manufacturing floor, in the supply chain, in the retail or hospitality setting, etc. and uninformed decisions are being made.

Similarly, Tom Peters and Robert Waterman used the term, "Management by Wandering Around" in their seminal book, *In Search of Excellence*, a complementary concept to front-line awareness, in which managers wander around the workplace interacting with all levels of employees to truly get an understanding of how things are REALLY working versus how management THINKS they are working.

UNINTENDED CONSEQUENCES

The dangers of sea ice were well known in the North Atlantic in the 1900s, but it wasn't a problem that had caused massive loss of life. It could damage a ship, but normally there was always time to rescue the passengers and crew. In the Titanic's case, the rescue obviously didn't happen fast enough and 1,503 of the 2,208 passengers perished on April 15, 1912.

The first lifeboats to leave the Titanic only carried 28 people, although they could have held 64 each. The ship needed a total of 2,208 lifeboat seats, but only 1,178 were carried aboard. That "lesson" resulted in new laws that required ships to have enough lifeboats and seats for everyone onboard.

In 1915, the Eastland capsized in the Chicago harbor and killed 841 people. The reason it capsized, in part, was because of the extra lifeboats that were added that made the already unstable ship even more unstable.

So it's not easy to know which lessons or data to draw from and the danger of generalizing a "solution" without factoring in as much of the totality of the systems as possible.

As you devise your plans and solutions to aid in the achievement of your company's strategic objectives, do try to think over the horizon about any unintended consequences to your decisions.

CONSTANT IMPROVEMENT

Not all readers are leaders, but all leaders are readers.

Harry S. Truman

Maya Hu-Chan is an international management consultant and executive coach with clients in Europe, the Americas, and the Asia-Pacific region. She is a co-author and contributing author to 11 books, including *Global Leadership: The Next Generation* with Dr. Marshal Goldsmith, the world-renowned business educator and coach. The book is recommended by Harvard Business School. She's a columnist for Inc.com and her work has appeared in *BusinessWeek, Harvard Business Online,* Bloomberg, etc. She's been selected as one of the World's Top 30 Global Leadership Gurus, Top 100 Thought Leaders in Management & Leadership, Top Leadership Guru from Asia, and a member of the President's Leadership Advisory Council with the World Bank.

You would think that with all of these accomplishments and accolades that Maya is at the pinnacle of her career and she could very successfully "coast" at this point. Instead, Maya reads all manner of publications and journals, every day; she's hired a business coach; and she's pursing a very difficult master's in coaching program.

In talking with her she said,

If you want to be the very best in your field, and stay at the top of your field, you can never, ever, stop learning. And even the greats in sports, like Michael Jordon or Tiger Woods, benefited from having a coach, so I'm not above learning from a coach as well.

Never stop your efforts and preparations to be the very best at what you do.

NOTE

1 www.foreignaffairs.com/articles/2002-01-01/america-vulnerable.

Best Practices

FORENSIC METHODOLOGY

Table of Contents

The International Association of Professional Security Consultants has issued this consensus-based and peer-reviewed Best Practice for the guidance of and voluntary use by businesses and individuals who deal or may deal with the issues addressed in the context of third-party premises security litigation.

POSITION STATEMENT

The International Association of Professional Security Consultants does hereby recognize that its members will be called upon to perform as "Forensic Consultants" and serve as Expert Witnesses in a court of law or other legal proceeding. The purpose of these guidelines is to meet the need for a standardized methodology used in the evaluation of premises security cases.

It is recognized that the task of the Forensic Consultant is one of education. Forensic Consultants will provide their opinion(s) to the client, to opposing counsel during deposition, in response to written interrogatories, in reports, and to the judge and jury at trial or any other lawfully convened hearing. This is done with the goal of making others aware of the security issues and contributing to a just and proper conclusion on the litigation.

The responsibility of the Forensic Consultant lies within our system of justice and the ethics of the security profession. The opinions so offered are made as an objective expert witness/consultant, without any financial or other interest in the outcome of the litigation.

Forensic Consultants will, at all times, be forthright, honest and precise in evolving the ultimate conclusion(s) and opinion(s). The opinion(s) will be the result of a review of all available, applicable documentation and discovery material presented by all parties to the litigation. Site inspections and analytical procedures generally followed by the "Forensic Consultant" are described in these guidelines.

The following methodology is to be used in a typical premises security case, including crimes committed by employees. The Forensic Consultant is expected to exercise diligence in requesting and/or obtaining information that the Consultant reasonably believes is relevant to the facts and circumstances of the case. _It is reasonable to expect variations of the steps, with some steps deleted and others added as the facts and circumstances of the case being analyzed warrant._

EVIDENCE REVIEW— THE PROCESS

In the context of this Guideline, the Forensic Consultant will review and analyze various information, whether produced during the discovery process of the litigation or otherwise obtained through research, common knowledge, investigation, and/or the consultant/expert's experience which allows the Consultant to identify factors leading to an understanding of the crime risks present at the time of the criminal event.

Types of evidence generally available to the Forensic Consultant include, but are not limited, to the following:

1. Complaint/Petition

2. Police Report of the subject incident

3. Site and Immediate Vicinity Crime History, including police and security incident reports

4. Interrogatories and Responses

5. Requests for Production of Documents and Responses

6. Requests for Admissions and Responses

7. Affidavits, Witness Statements and Interviews

8. Depositions

9. Expert Witness Reports

10. Applicable Medical Records Relating to the Facts of the Incident

11. Photographs, Video and Audio Recordings, etc.

12. Other Related Evidence (e.g., prosecutors file, if available)

RISK ASSESSMENT

A risk assessment is the general process of identifying relevant risks, given the facts of the case. It is a qualitative, quantitative, or hybrid assessment that seeks to determine the likelihood that criminals could successfully exploit a vulnerability or compromise a security countermeasure.

There are two main components to a risk assessment: a threat assessment and a vulnerability assessment. The threat assessment is an evaluation of the various sources for crime threats. The vulnerability assessment, includes an evaluation of the physical aspects of the facility and an analysis of the overall security program as it relates to the specific facts of the case.

The security survey, along with documented evidence, is the means by which security measures utilized and/or available at the facility at the time of the incident that is the subject of the litigation are identified and analyzed.

A risk assessment provides the foundation for effectively determining the adequacy of countermeasures employed.

THREAT ASSESSMENT

A threat assessment is an evaluation of events that can adversely affect operations and/or specific assets. Historical information is a primary source for threat assessments, including past criminal and terrorist events. A threat assessment considers actual and inherent threats.

1. Actual Threats - The crime history at the subject property based on data reflecting actual crime data.[1] Actual threats are a quantitative element of a threat assessment. When assessing actual threats, the following may be considered *as deemed relevant by the security expert*:

   a. Relevant crimes on the subject property for a three to five year period prior to the date of the incident.[2]

   b. Relevant crimes in the immediate vicinity of the subject property for a three to five year period prior to the date of the incident. [Note: There is no single definition of what constitutes an "immediate vicinity" or "neighborhood" around a given property. Often what is available for evaluation from a law enforcement agency depends upon that agency's software programming and/or staff capabilities (e.g., the agency can only provide data for a set size of an area, such as a quarter mile radius).]

   c. The expert may consider the relationship between offenders and victims (e.g. interpersonal, domestic, targeted, etc.).

2. Inherent Threats – The crime risk at the subject property as determined by the expert based on the property's characteristics, the expert's research and/or experience in similar environments, information gathered through the discovery process, and/or a site inspection (if conducted).

VULNERABILITY ASSESSMENT/ SECURITY SURVEY

The vulnerability assessment is an analysis of security weaknesses and opportunities for criminal activity. A security survey is a method for collecting information used in the vulnerability assessment.

A security survey may include a physical survey of the scene of the incident and areas/functions that are applicable to the incident to achieve an understanding of information that has potential application to the matter in litigation.

The following areas of review are not meant to be all inclusive, nor all exclusive. The decision to review the material is at the judgment/discretion of the expert.

1. Incident Review

   a. Police incident and investigation report(s)

   b. Security incident report(s)

   c. Medical records (emergency room and/or autopsy as it relates to information about the occurrence of the incident)

   d. Other sources of information about how the incident occurred (e.g., witness statements, testimony, etc.)

---

1. Depending on the police jurisdiction that serves the subject property, different types of crime records may be available. The most common type of crime record used in a crime risk analysis is Calls for Service or dispatch logs. It is important to note that Calls for Service or dispatch log accuracy varies by jurisdiction. Further, changes to incident management and dispatch systems may also impact accuracy even within the same jurisdiction. When assessing relevant crimes, Calls for Service and dispatch logs should not be used alone. Offense/Incident Reports are necessary to validate the Calls for Service or dispatch logs, specifically the crime type, crime location, and whether a crime actually occurred. Calls for service or dispatch logs alone, in many jurisdictions, are insufficient for these three elements.

2. The IAPSC recognizes that criminology studies and related research have generally found that crime in the area may or may not be relevant to the subject property.

2. Site Inspection – Inspect site where the incident occurred and the surrounding area, if relevant. *(Note: Not all cases will require site inspections, nor is it always possible to conduct site views—e.g., if the site has been altered substantially or no longer exists.) Further, the facts of some cases and potential liability issues are not related to the site/property layout, design, or other physical attributes. As such, a site inspection may be unnecessary.*

   a. Determine layout of the premises

   b. Evaluate relevant factors (lighting, lines of sight, places of concealment, remoteness, accessibility, security measures, conditions, etc.)

   c. Review relevant documentation (lease, contract, diagram, map, etc.)

   d. Assess the characteristics of the surrounding area and what impact, if any, those characteristics may have had on the subject property

3. Security Personnel

   a. Review security officer(s) (including off-duty law enforcement officers) actions, staffing levels, post orders, duty hours, equipment provided, tours, evaluations, training, hiring procedures and supervision

   b. Review law enforcement presence and actions (e.g., on-duty, police details, etc.)

   c. Review roles and actions of non-security related persons who may have participated in the security program and/or incident

   d. Assess the qualifications and performance of owner/management personnel overseeing the security program

4. Security Management Program

   a. Review management and security related policies, procedures, and practices

   b. Review any risk assessments performed prior to the date of the incident

   c. Review daily activity reports, job descriptions, incident reports and internal correspondence

   d. Review security services contract

   e. Review training manuals and materials

   f. Review depositions regarding employees' understanding of their duties, and all customs and undocumented practices

   g. Evaluate the qualifications, training, and experience of security management and supervisory personnel

5. Security Equipment

   a. Review building design and site plans

   b. Inspect all security devices related to the incident

   c. Inspect structural security features related to the incident

   d. Determine the position, function and maintenance status of the relevant security equipment and features in place at the time of the incident

   e. Determine levels of illumination, if relevant

ANALYSIS AND OPINIONS

The security expert will determine the level of adequacy of security at the location of the incident on the date and at the time the incident occurred. This will be based on the information obtained in the previous steps, and the application of a qualitative analysis based on the experience, education and training of the expert.

Based upon the analysis, the expert will reach conclusions on the issues of risk analysis, preventability and the adequacy of the security program at the subject property. At this point the expert has formed opinions and is prepared to provide a written report, be deposed and/or testify at trial. Those opinions will state the detailed basis for the findings, including evidence, standards, best practices and guidelines, where applicable.

BIBLIOGRAPHY/REFERENCES

The process of evaluating the risk of crime at a specific location or geographical area is widely recognized and has been adopted nationwide by private industry, public law enforcement, municipalities, and other governmental agencies. The following published sources reference the process used to perform a crime risk analysis. *This is not all-inclusive, but a representative sampling of available references.*

This bibliography is not to be construed in any way as an endorsement by the International Association of Professional Security Consultants of the publications or the respective authors.

ASIS International (2003). *General Security Risk Assessment Guideline.* Alexandria, VA.

Bates, Norman D. (1997). "Foreseeability of Crime and Adequacy of Security," Accident Prevention Manual for Business & Industry, Security Management, National Safety Council.

Broder, James F. and Tucker, Eugene (2012). Risk Analysis and the Security Survey, 4th Edition. Boston, MA: Butterworth-Heinemann.

Bureau of Justice Statistics http://www.bjs.gov/index.cfm?ty=tp&tid=941

Caplan, Joel M. and Leslie W. Kennedy (2016). Risk Terrain Modeling: Crime Prediction and Risk Reduction. Jackson, TN: University of California Press.

Clarke, R., & Eck, J. (2007). Understanding Risky Facilities. Problem Specific Guide Series. Washington, DC: Office of Community Oriented Policing, U.S. Department of Justice.

Crowe, Timothy D. and Fennelly, Lawrence (2013). Crime Prevention Through Environmental Design, 3rd Edition. National Crime Prevention Institute, Boston, MA: Butterworth-Heinemann.

Department of the Navy, Naval Facilities Engineering Command, (1983). *Physical Security Design Manual 13.1*, Washington, DC: Government Printing Office.

Eck, John E. and Weisburd, David (1995). Crime and Place. Monsey, NY: Criminal Justice Press (Police Executive Research Forum).

Eck, JE, Clarke, RV, and Guerette, RT (2007), "Risky Facilities: Crime Concentration in Homogeneous Sets of Establishments and Facilities" in Graham Farrell, Kate J. Bowers, Shane D. Johnson and Michael Townsley, ed. Imagination for Crime Prevention, Crime

Prevention Studies, Volume 21, Monsey, NY: Criminal Justice Press.

Eck, JE, & Weisburd, D. (Eds.). (1995). Crime and Place. Crime Prevention Studies 4. Monsey, NY: Criminal Justice Press.

Gottlieb, Stephen, Sheldon Arenberg, and Raj Singh (1998). Crime Analysis: From First Report to Final Arrest. Montclair, CA: Alpha Publishing.

International Association of Crime Analysts (2009). Exploring Crime Analysis. 2nd Edition. Overland Park, KS: BookSurge Publishing

Madensen, Tamara D. and John E. Eck (2013). "Crime Places and Place Management" in Cullen, F. T., & Wilcox, P.. The Oxford Handbook Of Criminological Theory. New York, NY: Oxford University Press.

Miethe, Terance D. and Richard McCorkle (2005). Crime Profiles: The Anatomy of Dangerous Persons, Places, and Situations. 3rd Edition. Los Angeles: Oxford University Press

National Crime Prevention Institute (2001). Understanding Crime Prevention, Boston, MA: Butterworth-Heinemann.

"Premises Security Experts and Admissibility Considerations Under Daubert and Kumho: A Revised Standard," Norman D. Bates and Danielle A. Frank, Suffolk Journal of Trial and Appellate Advocacy, June 2010

Sennewald, Charles A. (2015). Effective Security Management. 6th Edition. Woburn: Butterworth-Heinemann.

Sennewald, Charles A. (2012). Security Consulting. 4th Edition. Woburn: Butterworth-Heinemann.

U.S. Army Corps of Engineers (1990).

Security Engineering Manual, Missouri River Division/Omaha District.

U.S. Department of Justice, Federal Bureau of Investigation, "UCR: Uniform Crime Reporting Handbook" Revised 2004, U.S. Government Printing Office, Washington, DC.

U.S. Department of Justice (1995). Vulnerability Assessment of Federal Facilities, Washington, DC: Government Printing Office

Vellani, Karim H. (2006). Strategic Security Management: A Risk Assessment Guide for Decision Makers. Woburn: Butterworth-Heinemann.

Weisburd, David, Elizabeth Groff and Sue-Ming Yang. (2012), The Criminology of Place: Street Segments And Our Understanding of the Crime Problem. Oxford: Oxford University Press.

Weisburd, David, et al. (2016), Place Matters: Criminology for the Twenty-First Century. Cambridge: Cambridge University Press.

FORENSIC SECURITY COMMITTEE MEMBERS

Norman D. Bates, Esq.,
Committee Chairman;
President, Liability Consultants, Inc.

Chad Callaghan, CPP, CSC, CLSD,
Premises Liability Experts, LLC

James H. Clark, CPP,
Managing Partner,
Clark Security Group, LLC

Lance Foster, CPP, CSC
Security Associates, Inc.

Karim Vellani, CPP, CSC,
Threat Analysis Group, LLC

Alan W. Zajic, CPP, CSP,
AWZ Consulting

CASES CITING METHODOLOGY

Childress v Kentucky Oaks Mall, 2007 WL
2772299 (W.D. KY) 2007

Reinaldo Robles Del Valle, et al v Vornado
Realty Trust, 06-1818 US Dist. Crt., Puerto
Rico, 2009

DOCUMENT REVISION HISTORY

Initial Release: June 2000 approved by the
IAPSC membership in attendance at the
annual meeting.

Revised: May 2, 2005 with approval by the
IAPSC membership in attendance at the
annual meeting.

Revised: November 2008 with approval of
the Board of Directors

Revised: November 2011 by Forensic
Security Committee – minor formatting
changes and addition of "Premises Security
Experts…" article to bibliography.

Revised: April 28, 2014 with approval of
IAPSC Forensic Security Committee – addition of language to Actual Crime section:
"Relevant crimes in the immediate vicinity
of the facility (three to five years prior to
the date of the incident) *as defined by and
deemed relevant by the security expert.*"

Revised: January 19, 2018 with approval by
the Board of Directors

*Founded in 1984, the International Associ-
ation of Professional Security Consultants
(IAPSC) is a widely recognized and respect-
ed association committed to establishing
and maintaining the highest standards for
security consultants in the industry. IAPSC
members are independent, non-product
affiliated consultants who are required to
meet strict educational, experience, and
practice requirements, ensuring that they
uphold the IAPSC code for professionalism
and ethical conduct. For more information,
to find an IAPSC security consultant, or to
become a member of the association, visit
www.iapsc.org.*

Index

Page numbers in *italics* refer to figures. Page numbers in **bold** refer to tables.

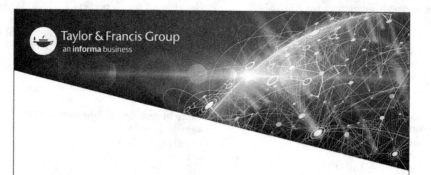

Printed in the United States
by Baker & Taylor Publisher Services